WITHDRAWN

ANNA KARENINA
AND OTHER ESSAYS

ANNA KARENINA

AND OTHER ESSAYS

By

F. R. LEAVIS

1967

CHATTO & WINDUS

LONDON

PUBLISHED BY
Chatto & Windus Ltd
40 WILLIAM IV STREET
LONDON W.C.2

★

Clarke, Irwin & Co. Ltd
TORONTO

PRINTED IN GREAT BRITAIN BY
R. & R. CLARK, LTD., EDINBURGH

To
The University of York

CONTENTS

1. Anna Karenina   *page* 9

2. The Pilgrim's Progress   33

3. Adam Bede   49

4. The Europeans   59

5. What Maisie Knew   75

6. The Shadow-Line   92

7. The Secret Sharer   111

8. Pudd'nhead Wilson   121

9. The Americanness of American Literature   138

10. The Complex Fate   152

11. Pound in his Letters   161

12. 'Lawrence Scholarship' and Lawrence   167

13. T. S. Eliot as Critic   177

14. Johnson as Critic   197

15. Towards Standards of Criticism   219

16. The Orthodoxy of Enlightenment   235

Index   243

ACKNOWLEDGMENTS

Acknowledgment is made for permission to reprint the following matter: to The New American Library for the foreword to 'Adam Bede' and the afterword to 'The Pilgrim's Progress', both in their Signet Classics editions; to the Editor of *The Sewanee Review*, published by the University of the South, Tennessee, for the essays on 'The Shadow-Line' and on ' "Lawrence Scholarship" and Lawrence'; to the American Jewish Committee for the articles on 'The Americanness of American Literature' and 'T. S. Eliot as Critic', both of which first appeared in *Commentary*; to the Editors of *Scrutiny* and to the Cambridge University Press for 'The Europeans', 'Pound in his Letters' and 'Johnson as Critic'; to Messrs. Lawrence & Wishart Ltd. for the introduction to 'Towards Standards of Criticism', originally published by Wishart & Co.; and to *The Spectator* for the article first called 'The New Orthodoxy' and reprinted here as 'The Orthodoxy of Enlightenment'.

I

ANNA KARENINA: THOUGHT AND SIGNIFICANCE IN A GREAT CREATIVE WORK

IN addressing the Cambridge University Slavonic Society I felt acutely conscious of the fact that I know no Russian. I have been assured, however, by those familiar with Tolstoy's use of the language that it would be a mistake, as a critic, to feel altogether disqualified by a dependence upon Aylmer Maude, and I have permitted myself to accept the assurance. The real formidableness of my undertaking is constituted by the magnitude of *Anna Karenina*—the greatness and the largeness; the greatness that entails largeness. There is a necessary point made in the last phrase; or not necessary, you may prefer to say, since it hardly needs making. It is the range and variety of human experience going with the depth and vividness in the rendering that one would point to and start to comment on if, having ventured (as one might) that *Anna Karenina* was the greatest of novels, one were challenged to give one's grounds for expecting assent. The triad, 'range', 'depth', and 'vividness', however, doesn't satisfy one as an intimation of the nature of the greatness; one is left looking for a way of conveying another essential emphasis, and this way doesn't immediately present itself—doesn't present itself at all if what one is looking for is a word, or a phrase, or even two or three sentences. The emphasis regards the nature of the concern for significance that characterizes this art—an art so unlike that of Henry James. The cue for this comparative reference is given by what James himself (in a letter to Hugh Walpole of 1913) said about Tolstoy:

Tolstoy and Doistoieffsky are fluid pudding, though not tasteless, because the amount of their own minds and souls in solution in the broth gives it savour and flavour, thanks to the strong, rank quality of their genius and their experience. But there are all sorts of things to be said of them, and in particular that we see how great a vice is their lack of composition and their defiance of economy and architecture.

It is 'him', of course, I'm concerned about; the 'them' and the 'their' are in any case unacceptable. The confident censure might seem astonishing, coming from so intelligent, and so intensely serious, a student of the novelist's art. When, writing in 1887, Arnold, having noted that there are 'many characters' in *Anna Karenina*, says 'too many, if we look in it for a work of art in which the action shall be vigorously one, and to that one action everything shall converge', and makes his intention plain by pronouncing that we are not to take Tolstoy's masterpiece as a work of art, but as a 'piece of life', we recognize the naïveté as inevitable in a critic of Arnold's education at that date (though *Little Dorrit*, *Great Expectations* and *Middlemarch* had appeared—as had also *Madame Bovary*, and the novels of Jane Austen). But James, who hadn't Public School Classics and Aristotle and Oxford behind him and didn't take it for an axiom that 'the crown of literature is poetry', is known for his concern to vindicate for the novelist's art its right to the fullest attention that sophisticated intelligence can devote to it. The explanation, of course, is what I pointed to in making the reference to James. The sense of the possibilities of the novel that informed his criticism was determined by his own creative preoccupations, and his conception of the art was personal and his own in a limiting way that (significantly for the criticism of his own achievement) he failed to realize: it is not without some implicit prompting from him that we are offered his collected Prefaces as 'the novelist's *vade-mecum*'. My concern in saying these obvious enough things is with the distinctive nature of Tolstoy's genius; I want to insist that the relation between art and life it exemplifies for us is the characteristic of the highest kind of creativity—a higher kind than James's. If Tolstoy gave no heed to any Jamesian canons it was not because he failed to give the most intelligent kind of attention to the demands of art. To confute James's critical censures and show what is the nature of the 'composition' that makes *Anna Karenina* superlatively a great work of art is to illustrate what D. H. Lawrence had in mind when he wrote:

The novel is a great discovery: far greater than Galileo's telescope or somebody else's wireless. The novel is the highest form of human expression so far attained.

It is a large claim, but Lawrence made it with full intention; he was not talking loosely. He was prepared to say that by the 'highest form of human expression' he meant the highest form of thought, the thought in question necessarily being, for him, thought about the nature, the meaning, and the essential problems of human life. He didn't the less, of course, think of the novel, whenever it should answer to his account, as supremely art. Thought, to come at all near truth and adequacy, must engage the whole man, and relate in a valid way—such a way, that is, as precludes and defeats the distorting effects of abstraction and selection (both inevitable)—all the diverse elements of experience.

The organization of *Anna Karenina* expresses an intense devotion of this kind to the pursuit of truth, and Lawrence might have had the book in front of him when he wrote: 'The novel is the highest form of subtle inter-relatedness that man has discovered.' It was a significant lack of responsiveness to the given devotion that enabled James to find *Anna Karenina* lacking in 'composition' and defiant of economy and architecture. His ability to use the word 'architecture' betrays the difference between the idea of 'art' that informs his own work and that implicit in Tolstoy's. A limited and clearly conceived interest determined the 'composition' and economy of a Jamesian novel. A firm plan, expressing a definitive and masterful purpose and excluding all that doesn't seem necessary in relation to this, determines the perfection that James aims at. An addiction to 'art' in this sense entails a severe limitation in regard to significance—to the nature of the significance the artist's concern for which is the principle of organization that controls his creating. James's significances are those which, in relation to each given enterprise, he can bring, he feels, into the critical consciousness for thorough analysis, discuss with himself exhaustively, and provide for in relation to firmly grasped criteria.

The relation of art to life in Tolstoy is such as to preclude this kind of narrowly provident economy. It is an immensely fuller and profounder involvement *in* life on the part of the artist, whose concern for significance in his art is the intense and focused expression of the questing after significance that characterizes him in his daily living. This, of course, amounts to saying that Tolstoy is a different kind of man from James—he is the kind of man the greatest kind of artist necessarily is. Tolstoy might very well have answered as Lawrence did when asked, not long before his death, what was the drive behind his creating: 'One writes out of one's moral sense; for the race, as it were.' 'Moral', of course, is an ambiguous word, but Lawrence was thinking of that manifestation of his own vitality of genius, the distinctive preoccupation with ultimate questions—those which concern the nature of one's deepest inner allegiances and determinations, the fundamental significances to be read in one's experience of life, the nature and conditions of 'fulfilment' (a word for what is to be sought that he finds more apt than 'happiness'). An artist of this kind will have strong didactic impulses. But it will be a certainly not less important characteristic of his to be, in the essential spirit of his art, intent on ensuring, with all its resources, that the didactic impulses shall not get out of hand.

'In a novel', writes Lawrence, 'everything is relative to everything else, if that novel is art at all. There may be didactic bits, but they aren't the novel. . . . There you have the greatness of the novel itself. It won't let you tell didactic lies and put them over.' What Tolstoy has to guard against is the intensity of his need for an 'answer'. For the concern for significance that is the principle of life in *Anna Karenina* is a deep spontaneous *lived* question, or quest. The temptation in wait for Tolstoy is to relax the tension, which, in being that of his integrity, is the vital tension of his art, by reducing the 'question' into one that *can* be answered—or, rather, one to which a seemingly satisfying answer strongly solicits him; that is, to simplify the challenge life actually is for him and deny the complexity of his total knowledge and need.

While what makes itself felt as we read *Anna Karenina* is decidedly a positive or creative nisus, it affects us as an exploratory effort towards the definition of a norm. It necessarily, then, concerns itself everywhere—or is never long felt not to be concerning itself—with the relations between men and women: love in its varieties, marriage in its varieties, the meaning of marriage. The essential mode of the book carries with it the implication that there *could* be no simple statement of a real problem, or of any 'answer' worth having. It is the very antithesis of a didactic mode. The book says in effect, 'This is life'—which is a different thing from saying as Arnold does, 'It is not a work of art, but a piece of life.' The greatness of *Anna Karenina* lies in the degree to which, along with its depth, it justifies the clear suggestion it conveys of a representative comprehensiveness. The creative writer's way of arriving at and presenting general truths about life is that which Tolstoy exemplifies with such resource, such potency, and on such a scale, and there is none to replace or rival it. Only a work of art can say with validity and force, as *Anna Karenina* does, 'This is life.'

There is of course a character in the book particularly close to Tolstoy himself—Levin; and, apart from biographical facts, we know this because Levin, we recognize, is the focus of what I have called the 'deep, spontaneous, lived question'. That, however, is not the same as saying that he *is* the author, the artist, directly present in the book; a point that can be enforced with the observation that Levin is *not* a great novelist. It is an essential difference. Taken together with the perceived intimacy of relation, it is important for the understanding of *Anna Karenina* as a great creative work, and it has its bearings (as I shall suggest) on the development of the author into the Count Leo Tolstoy who wrote *What then must we do?*, was tragically at odds with his wife, and died at Astapova railway station.

Levin, in fact, while being a great deal more besides, is the focal presence of the temptation (that essential element in the creative vitality). It is dramatized in him. Not that we think of him as a dramatized temptation—or tend to use the word at all (unless at the end of the book) in relation to him. The Constantine Levin whom we know with such intimacy is so much more than an earnest 'seeker', addicted to intense pertinacities of meditation on death, the meaning of life, and the behest (if only one could be sure what that was) of the living clear-sighted conscience. We have no difficulty in thinking of him as a Russian aristocrat, or believing that, different as he is from Vronsky and Oblonsky, he has had as such a normally 'immoral' past. It is as a matter of

B

immediately acceptable fact that we see him finding Oblonsky, when he meets him at the club, a warmly *sympathique* old friend, and joining happily in the epicure-choice of an expensive meal. He is a paternal but businesslike landlord, a modernizing farmer, a writer on agricultural economy, and a sportsman with the proper pride of a first-class shot. We almost inevitably credit him with Tolstoy's own very knowledgeable delight, which the account of the steeplechase conveys so powerfully, in the functional and vital beauty of thoroughbred horses. When in the book he first encounters Kitty it is on a winter's day at the Zoological Gardens, where he has a reputation he proceeds to justify of being the 'best skater'.

And here, of course, in this episode of the drama of his relations with Kitty, we come to what, in a brief post-Arnoldian account of *Anna Karenina* as a closely-organized whole, would figure as the essential main part that Levin plays in its significance—plays together with Kitty. Love, courtship, and marriage: it seems reasonable to say, harking back to the word 'norm' as I used it earlier, that Kitty and Levin have, for that crucial matter of the relations between men and women, a clear normative significance —that they represent, at any rate, the especially clear affirming presence of the normative spirit that informs the whole work. They certainly provide a foil to Anna and Vronsky.

When, however, we think of the way the book closes we may very well draw back from suggesting that a confident normative prescription has, in sum, been offered. The strong deep current of Levin's meditating on life, death, and the peasants moves, beyond question, towards consequences in regard to marriage that Kitty, if they should really threaten, couldn't do anything but fight. Nevertheless, the consequences lie outside *Anna Karenina;* and there is no sign that Tolstoy, the highly and subtly conscious artist, could have recognized the novel's significance as being anything but what the tragedy of Anna, implicitly commented on by the context in general and the Levin-Kitty theme in particular, conveys. Yet some inner prompting made him bring into the context, as the close of the whole organization, that quite other-than-clinching effect of Levin's later development.

It is a close in full keeping with the creative mode of the work;

with the delicate wholeness of the 'sincerity' (the inverted commas a reminder that every great creative work compels us to reconsider the meaning of that word) with which Tolstoy pursues his aim of inducing life to propose and define the 'questions'—a process that is at the same time a conveying of such 'answers' as life may yield. There is in *Anna Karenina* no suggestion either of the controlled-experiment convention that the conditions of the theatre compelled upon Shakespeare for the treatment of his theme in *Measure for Measure* (where Angelo is the victim of a frankly contrived demonstration) or of the writing-up of findings and significances that forms the close of that play. Tolstoy, great creative power in the tradition of the novel that owes so much to Shakespeare, is great enough to vindicate, by showing it marvellously realized, the conception of the novel and of its supreme advantages I have adduced from Lawrence. That conception enforces the maxim: 'Art-speech is the only speech.' And by 'speech' Lawrence means the utterance of thought—thought of the anti-mathematical order.

It no doubt seemed to James as well as Arnold an instance of a characteristically large casualness in respect of form in *Anna Karenina* that the book, though committed to the two main actions (Arnold's phrase), each of which in Tolstoyan treatment entails a generous abundance—redundance, for James—of wide-ranging specificity, should open, not with either, but with the trouble in the Oblonsky household. We, of course, see here the rightness and sure command of the great artist in terms of his own undertaking, and don't need explanations of the part played by the Oblonsky theme in relation to 'form' and significance. We aren't prompted to say that the 'normal' distinctively unideal and not happy married relations (though the marriage remains 'successful') between the goodnatured, life-loving, and irresistible Stephen Oblonsky and the wholly admirable Dolly provides a third main action. But the theme nevertheless continues, through the book, to keep us reminded of itself and of its relevance to the main action. And, unmistakably of the first importance for the significance we are to have seen, at the close, in Anna's fate, there are the married relations of Anna and Karenin, which are evoked with such pregnant economy and, for the evaluative response of our deepest moral sense, our innermost sense for what ultimately and essentially offends against life and what makes for it, such decisive power.

It will be an economy at this point, the title-theme being in question, the significance of which depends on the reader's full sense of the Tolstoyan ethos of art, to make a brief use of Arnold. And it will bring out by the way the force of Lawrence's contention that the discovery of the novel was a great advance for human thought. For Arnold was a man of distinguished intelligence, who didn't in general tend to slight the importance of literature, its place and function in life. And of the sequel to the episode of the steeplechase and of Anna's avoval to Karenin of her relations with Vronsky he writes,

Hard at first, formal, cruel, thinking only of himself, Karénine, who, as I have said, has a conscience, is touched by grace at the moment when Anna's troubles reach their height. He returns to find her with a child just born to her and Wronsky, the lover in the house and Anna apparently dying. Karénine has words of kindness and forgiveness only. The noble and victorious effort transfigures him, and all that her husband gains in the eyes of Anna, her lover Wronsky loses.

Having quoted from the painful scene at the bedside of the delirious Anna, Arnold goes on:

She seems dying, and Wronsky rushes out and shoots himself. And so, in a common novel, the story would end. Anna would die, Wronsky would commit suicide, Karénine would survive, in possession of our admiration and sympathy. But the story does not always end so in life: neither does it end so in Count Tolstoi's novel.

But not only does it not *end* so; we find ourselves exclaiming: 'But that is *not* the story!' 'Karénine has words of kindness and forgiveness only. The noble and victorious effort transfigures him' —who would divine from that the disturbing subtlety of the actual presentment? The state of feeling actually produced in us is very different from that which Arnold suggests with his 'in possession of our admiration and sympathy'. The way we take the scene, its moral and human significance for us, is conditioned by all that goes before, and this has established what Karenin is, what Anna is, and what, inexorably, the relations between them must be. We know him as, in the pejorative Laurentian sense, a purely 'social' being, ego-bound, self-important, without any spontaneity of life in him and unable to be anything but offended and made uncomfortable by spontaneity of life in others. This is conveyed to us, not by statement, but in innumerable ways: mode of speech, for instance—so rendered by Tolstoy as to give us the tone and inflection. The same subtle power has suggested the effect, even before her 'awakening' by Vronsky, on Anna.

It is the effect conveyed with something like violence when, back at Petersburg after that first fatal encounter with Vronsky, she is persuading herself that nothing has happened, that her profound sense to the contrary was an illusion, and that she has towards her husband the proper feelings of a wife:

He pressed her hand and again kissed it.

'After all, he is a good man: truthful, kind and remarkable in his own sphere', said Anna to herself when she had returned to her room, as if defending him from someone who accused him and declared it was impossible to love him. 'But why do his ears stick out so? Or has he had his hair cut?'

In the scene of Anna's delirium (Part IV, chapter XVII) this inner conflict takes on, when Karenin comes into the bedroom, a nightmare intensity, the disturbing power of which as Tolstoy evokes the scene it would take a long quotation to suggest: 'With one hand she held him, while with the other she thrust him away' —what is summarized there is a prolonged dramatic immediacy that keeps us in acute discomfort through several pages. The reader, even at the moment when Karenin seems most noble and most commands sympathy and Anna's self-abasement is deepest, can hardly falter in his certainty that revulsion from Karenin is basic and invincible in Anna.

As for the 'noble and victorious effort that transfigures him', when (as Arnold puts it), 'he is touched with grace', the effect of the episode on us, even before we know that this is the way his admirer and consoler, the Countess Ivanovna will put it, is so embarrassingly painful because it is so much more complex than such an account suggests. Karenin's inability to bear the spectacle of acute distress and suffering (especially, we have been told, in a woman) doesn't impress us as an unequivocal escape from the ego: that disconcerting fact is what, added to Vronsky's repellent and horribly convincing humiliation, makes the scene so atrociously unpleasant. And it is in place to note again that the question, 'What is sincerity?', represents for us, as we inquire into the organization and significance of *Anna Karenina*, a sense we recurrently have of the nature of the creative energy in Tolstoy's art. As for the way the later relation between the Countess Lydia Ivanovna and Karenin reflects back on Karenin's 'noble and victorious effort', that is a clear instance of the kind of significant 'relatedness' (Lawrence's word) that Arnold ignores.

We are in no doubt about how we are to take the Countess's 'spirituality' or 'pietism', and it is plain beyond all question that she establishes and confirms Karenin in his 'religious' nobleness, the refuge he finds from self-contempt, by playing on his egotism, his conceit, and his self-deceiving animus. I must add at once that, if we are disposed to come at all easily to general conclusions about the nature, according to Tolstoy, of ostensible saintly goodness— of states of being 'touched with grace'—we had better consider Madame Stahl and Varenka and the episode of Kitty's temporary 'conversion'. The discrimination between the three is firmly and finely made—done in dramatic presentation. That Madame Stahl's spirituality is bogus, a compensation for the denial of more direct and ordinarily feminine self-satisfaction, becomes quite plain. Kitty's revulsion passes an unequivocal judgment on her own fit of dedicated Christian 'goodness': she recognizes that it wasn't sincere—that it falsified the reality of herself and was something to be ashamed of. 'I cannot live but by my own heart, but you', she says to Varenka, 'live by principle.'

But Varenka, Madame Stahl's companion and *protégée*, who herself has been disappointed in love, *is* really good. Yet—yet the whole affair of the proposal that didn't come off, Koznyshev's failure to decide ('Won't bite', says the disappointed Kitty) and the relief felt by both of the mutually attracted pair as if they had escaped something, conveys a suggestion of critical reserves about both of them. What these amounted to we suspect that Tolstoy himself ('Never trust the artist, trust the tale') would not have been ready to say much about analytically. But we know well enough that we have an example of the characteristic significant organization of the book when, in the next chapter, the attitudes of Levin and his visiting half-brother, Koznyshev, towards the peasants are contrasted.

Had Constantine been asked whether he liked the peasants he would not have known what to answer. He both liked and disliked them, just as he liked and disliked all human beings.

Of Koznyshev, the intellectual, on the other hand, we are told that 'his methodical mind had formed definite views on the life of the people', and it is made plain to us that he likes the peasants on 'principle' (to use Kitty's word).

Constantine considered his brother to be a man of great intellect, noble in the highest sense of the word, and gifted with the power of working for the general welfare. But the older he grew and the more intimately he came to know his brother, the oftener the thought occurred to him that the power of working for the general welfare—a power of which he felt entirely destitute—was not a virtue but rather a lack of something, not a lack of kindly honesty and noble desires and tastes, but a lack of the power of living, of what is called heart. . . .

—'Heart' was Kitty's word.

We can't help relating the whole exploration of 'sincerity' in religion that we find in *Anna Karenina* with Levin's own religious preoccupation—I am thinking in part of the way (there is an irony in it) in which the book leaves him identifying the idea of being 'good' with peasant-like Christian belief, inspired as he is by his intimate contacts with the peasants to feel, with that tense and pertinacious tentativeness of his, that he has almost grasped a saving certitude and prescription for his own use.

But to return to the main theme: whatever the old Leo (as Lawrence calls him) would have pronounced, the book confronts us with the impossibility, the sheer impossibility, of Anna's going on living with Karenin. How pregnant, and right (we feel), her diagnosis is when she says: 'If he had never heard people talk of love, he would never have wanted that word.' We too feel directly the revulsion she feels. The fact that we know the life-history that has made him like that doesn't make the revulsion less: *tout comprendre* is not *tout pardonner*—emotionally it can't be.

Positive sympathy does indeed enter in for us, to render the full complexity of life in that marvellous way of Tolstoy's, when we suddenly have to realize that even in this repellently 'social' being the spontaneity can come to life, and something unquestionably real assert itself. There is the tenderness that takes him by surprise in his feelings towards the baby, Vronsky's child.

In that smile also Karenin thought he saw himself and his position ridiculed.

'Unfortunate child!' said the nurse, hushing the baby and continuing to walk up and down with it. Karenin sat down on a chair and with a look full of suffering and despondency watched the nurse as she paced the room. When the child was pacified and laid in her deep cot, and the nurse after smoothing the little pillow went away, Karenin rose, and stepping with difficulty on tiptoe approached the infant. For a moment he stood silent, regarding the child with the same despondent expression; but suddenly a smile, wrinkling the skin on his nose, came out on his face, and he quietly left the room.

He rang the bell in the dining-room and told the nurse to send for the doctor once more. He was vexed with his wife for not troubling about the charming baby. . . .

But even if Anna had been aware of this development in Karenin, it could hardly have tended to make living with him seem less impossible. The stark fact of impossibility—that is immediate and final and inescapable for her. No one who had been fully exposed to Tolstoy's evocation of life, to the work of his creative genius, could question it. To say that, however, is not to take D. H. Lawrence's line: 'No one in the world is anything but delighted when Vronsky gets Anna Karenina.' 'O come!'— that gives my own reaction as I read the opening sentences of Lawrence's commentary on the book. What he is recognizing, of course, is the impossibility of Karenin for Anna, and that it is in her relations with Vronsky that she has come to life. But he ignores all the tormenting complexity—the shame-feelings that Anna, inevitably, can't escape, her sense of guilt, her perception of irreconcilable contradictions, Vronsky's sense that the son (Karenin's), so dear to Anna, is a nuisance. Lawrence asks 'what about the sin?', and answers: 'Why, when you look at it, all the tragedy comes from Vronsky's and Anna's fear of society. . . . They couldn't live in the pride of their sincere passion, and spit in Mother Grundy's eye. And that, that cowardice, was the real "sin". The novel makes it obvious, and knocks all old Leo's teeth out.'

It is astonishing that so marvellously perceptive a critic as Lawrence could simplify in that way, with so distorting an effect. What the novel makes obvious is that, though they might live for a little in the 'pride of their passion', they couldn't settle down to live *on* it; it makes it plain that to live on it was in the nature of things impossible: to reduce the adverse conditions that defeated them to cowardice is to refuse to take what, with all the force of specificity and subtle truth to life, the novel actually gives. Anna, we are made to see, can't but feel (we are considering here an instance of the profound exploration of moral feeling enacted in the book) that, though Karenin is insufferable, she has done wrong. The dreadful contradiction is focused for her in Serëzha, her son. It is given in the dream of hers in which he has two fathers. Further, what would be involved in getting her husband's necessary collaboration in the obtaining of a divorce is something that, for shame (nothing to do with Mrs Grundy), she can't face. She shrinks from analysing the dreadful *impasse* that torments her, but we are made to share her state, and we know the meaning of the curious withdrawal and the knit look between the eyes with which she meets Vronsky's attempts to start a discussion of the necessary steps towards the divorce that will put everything on a decent footing ('We can't remain like this'). She doesn't want to think about it; at the upper level she can half believe she hopes, but underneath she knows that there is no issue. He, not understanding, and, moreover, impatient, underneath, of the part played in her essential life by Serëzha, inevitably senses in her an indocile force of perverse and dangerous will. This phase of paralysis they suffer, this being held up in a perversity of cross currents and undertows, is wonderfully done in the novel—done (it had to be in order to convey its significance) as something long drawn out.

Lawrence, in a letter of an appropriate date in his own life, writes that Frieda 'had carefully studied *Anna Karenina* in a sort of "How to be happy though livanted spirit" '. Whatever he may be implying as to the lesson that Frieda might have learnt, he is referring, of course, to Anna's finally going off undivorced with Vronsky, and to the absence of any cheering example of happiness so won. We don't, I have suggested with some confidence, accept Lawrence's account, implicitly given in the later-written passage on *Anna Karenina* I have quoted, of the reasons for the Russian Livanters having been decidedly, and in the end disastrously, *less* successful than he and Frieda. We can use the challenged comparison as a way of bringing out the significance of Anna's and Vronsky's case as Tolstoy's art evokes it.

Anna was not an amoral German aristocrat—that seems to me an obvious opening comment. Frieda didn't give up *her* children without some suffering (*Look! We have Come Through*), but she got over that, and attained a floating indolence of well-being as, placidly undomesticated, she accompanied Lawrence about the world (we always see *him* doing the chores). There are delicacies in the way of offering to push further our divinations from such evidence concerning Frieda as we have, but we can see that what Tolstoy makes present to us in Anna is certainly something finer. Frieda's vitality and charm, in fact, have close affinities (she being as decidedly feminine as he is masculine) with those of Stephen Oblonsky—Stiva, Anna's brother, who 'can't believe that anything is wrong when it gives him so much enjoyment'. But the vitality that makes Anna's beauty irresistible manifests itself in a distinction of spirit that it is her brother's charm to be without. She has a delicate inner pride, a quick proud sense of responsibility towards life, that puts the easy accommodations of amoral 'realism' out of the question for her.

As for Vronsky, he is altogether unlike Lawrence. There is nothing of the artist in him. We are prompted to make the point in this way by the very fact that, in Italy, he tries to persuade himself, with some success for a while, that he *is* one. If we ask why he, the aristocrat ex-Guardsman (to *be* a Guardsman being his vocation) should have cultivated that illusion, we find ourselves inquiring into the whole problem that Lawrence, with his too simple diagnosis, dismisses. Why aren't Vronsky and Anna happy in Italy? Why don't they settle down to their sense of a solved problem? They have no money troubles, and plenty of friends, and, if happiness eludes them, the explanation is *not* Mrs Grundy or Society, at any rate in the simple way Lawrence suggests. All this part of the significance of *Anna Karenina* Lawrence ignores; he refuses (for I think it *is*, at bottom, that) to see the nature of the tragedy. And this is a serious charge, for the book gives the compelling constatation of a truth about human life. The spontaneity and depth of Vronsky's and Anna's passion for one another may be admirable, but passion—love—can't itself, though going with estimable qualities in both parties, make a permanent relation. Vronsky, having given up his career and his ambition for love, *has* his love, but is very soon felt to give out (and it is marvellous how the great novelist's art conveys this) a vibration of restlessness and dissatisfaction.

Lawrence *was* an artist—superlatively one. The conditions of his life with Frieda were the reverse of uncongenial to that extraordinary, inexhaustible, and endlessly inquiring intelligence of his. It ensured that he should never feel disorientated, vaguely lost, hanging in the wind. And yet—the point can't be made briefly with the proper delicacy—it is impossible (I think) not to feel that his work reveals a loss, a certain disablement, entailed by those conditions: the life of nomadic, childless, improvised, and essentially impermanent domesticities. Could he have written *Lady Chatterley's Lover*, written it as the vehicle of that didactic earnestness, if he hadn't lost his sense of what normal human life was like? The pamphlet, *Apropos of Lady Chatterley's Lover*, with which he followed the book up, implicitly admits the criticism—makes it; for the emphasis that, writing in ostensible vindication of the notorious novel, he now (with some inconsequence, one would think) lays on marriage and the family—and the whole manifesto is immensely impressive (it's a classic, I think)—can't but be taken by the reader as coming from a profound *corrective* impulse in Lawrence.

Vronsky's discovery of *his* vocation as an artist expresses merely his need of what, now he has left the army, he hasn't—a purpose, a sense of function, a place in life, a meaning. What he takes for the artist's vocation is what Lawrence in his tales deals with so well, the vocation of 'being an artist', and the pages of *Anna Karenina* that expose the bogusness of that should have appealed to the author of *St Mawr* and *Lady Chatterley's Lover*. Vronsky is too much of a man to find the lasting satisfaction in it that Lawrence's gentlemen-pseudo-artists find, and the way in which the reality drops out of it for Vronsky is done with the insight and astringent power of a novelist who is himself a real and great artist. There are the contacts with Mikhaylov, the *un*gentlemanly and unurbane genius, whose discomfort—his embarrassment when expected to take Vronsky's vocation and its products seriously—comes painfully home to us but brings no enlightenment to Vronsky, though the experience has its effect. Vronsky can derive satisfaction from the reassuring flatteries and complacencies of his friends, but the impulse to work at his own portrait of Anna lapses after he has seen Mikhaylov's. The vocation of 'being an artist' lapses with it.

We then see Vronsky and Anna back in Russia. Vronsky is trying to find a place and meaning in life as a landowner and public-spirited local magnate. But the new vocation—its factitiousness is conveyed to us by means that brief quotation can't really suggest—is still not one that can give Vronsky what he lost when he left the army and the familiar milieu, the friends and comrades with whom he had lived in his old career.

And this is the point at which to say that *Anna Karenina*, exploring the nature of the moral sense and of sincerity, explores also, with an intimately associated subtlety, the relation between the individual *qua* locus of moral responsibility and his social context. It's all very well for Lawrence to talk of thumbing one's nose at society—that is what he says Vronsky should have done. *Anna Karenina* compels us to recognize how much less simple things are than Lawrence suggests. The book, in its preoccupation with the way—the ways—in which the individual moral sense is socially conditioned, leaves us for upshot nothing like a simple conclusion. We have in the treatment of this theme too the tentative, questing spirit. There is a good deal in the book that we can unhesitatingly take for ironic commentary on the way in which moral feeling tends to be 'social' in the pejorative sense; that is, to express not any individual's moral perception and judgment, but a social climate—to be a product of a kind of flank-rubbing. But on the other hand there is no encouragement given to think of real moral judgment (and I have in mind Tolstoy's normative concern) as that of the isolated individual. It is necessarily individual, yes; but not merely individual. That, however, is no simple conclusion—which is what *Anna Karenina*, in its range and subtlety, makes so poignantly clear to us. A study of human nature is a study of social human nature, and the psychologist, sociologist, and social historian aren't in it compared with the great novelists. Tolstoy's perception is infinitely fine and penetrating, and is inseparable from his sense of relatedness (Lawrence's term). You recall how Levin's, Vronsky's, Anna's, Oblonsky's sense of things—their sense that things are right or not right, in resonance or not with their moral feeling—changes with the shift from the familiar to the unfamiliar milieu: Moscow to Petersburg, town to country, one social world to another.

Levin feels sure of his judgment and his criteria only when he is at home on his estate, engaged in the duties and responsibilities and interests that are his real life. Vronsky, intense and serious as we know his passion for Anna to be, lapses naturally into the tone and ethic in which he has been brought up and that fit the society to which he belongs, when talking with his cousin, the Princess Betsy, at the Opera.

'And how you used to laugh at others!' continued the Princess Betsy, who took particular pleasure at following the progress of this passion. 'What has become of it all? You are caught, my dear fellow.'

'I wish for nothing better than to be caught', replied Vronsky with his calm good-natured smile. 'To tell the truth, if I complain at all, it is only of not being caught enough. I am beginning to lose hope.'

'What hope can you have?' said Betsy, offended on her friend's behalf: '*entendons nous!*' But in her eyes little sparks twinkled which said she understood very well, and just as he did, what hope he might have.

'None whatever', said Vronsky, laughing and showing his close-set teeth. 'Excuse me!' he added, taking from her hand the opera-glasses, and he set to work to scan across her bare shoulder the row of boxes opposite. 'I am afraid I am becoming ridiculous.'

He knew very well that he ran no risk of appearing ridiculous either in Betsy's eyes or in the eyes of Society people generally. He knew very well that in their eyes the rôle of the disappointed lover of a maiden or any single woman might be ridiculous; but that the rôle of a man who was pursuing a married woman, and who made it the purpose of his life at all costs to draw her into adultery, was one which had in it something beautiful and dignified, and could never be ridiculous; so it was with a proud glad smile lurking under his moustache that he put down the opera-glasses and looked at his cousin.

Anna, after the fatal meeting with Vronsky in Moscow (where she had gone on her mission of reconciliation to the Oblonskys'), returns to Petersburg:

The feeling of causeless shame she had felt during the journey, and her agitation, had quite vanished. In her accustomed condition of life she again felt firm and blameless.

She thought with wonder of her state the day before. 'What had happened? Nothing! Vronsky said some silly things, to which it will be easy to put a stop, and I said what was necessary. It is unnecessary and impossible to speak of it to my husband.' She remembered how she had once told her husband about one of his subordinates who had very nearly made her a declaration, and how Karenin had answered that every woman living in society was liable to such things, but that he had full confidence in her tact and would never disgrace himself and her by being jealous. 'So there is no need to tell him! Besides, thank Heaven, there is nothing to tell!' she said to herself.

Anyone who has read the book can, in twenty minutes, find a dozen further examples, larger and smaller, of great diversity. Not that any suggestion emerges tending to qualify personal responsibility. A normative search after the social conditions the individual needs for happiness, or fulfilment, and for the individual responsive moral sense that serves it—that is the preoccupation. Vronsky, in the country-gentleman phase, for all the impressive outward show, has found neither the vocation nor the social context that can restore his sense of purpose in life or of rightness. Anna knows this, and even if she weren't tormented by yearning for her son, it would make an established happiness with Vronsky impossible. Her response is to be jealous, and her jealousy has the inevitable effect on him: it makes him feel cramped and tethered. The terrible logic or dialectic moves, like an accelerating mechanism, to the catastrophe.

'Vengeance is mine; I will repay'—we remember Tolstoy's epigraph. And there is Karenin's own orthodox formulation, 'Our lives are bound together not by men but by God', which closes in terms that come to have meaning for Anna: 'that kind of crime brings its punishment.' All the book is a feeling out, and a feeling inwards, for an adequate sense of the nature of life and its implicit laws, to break which entails the penalty. And to say this is not to pass any naïve moralistic judgment on Anna—any simple moral judgment such as was made either by Lawrence ('sincere passion') or by the old Leo.

The significance is brought out by the contrasting Levin case-history. Does Tolstoy, or the 'tale', offer this as presenting the 'norm'? Not quite that; the case-history—the case—is not so clear or conclusive. *Anna Karenina* is a work of art, and Levin (who, of course, compels our full respect) is in it the self-distrusting, ever-exploring 'seeker'. He is after happiness—as is also (we may add here, by way of noting the characteristic play of contrast) Oblonsky—which prompts us to substitute the word 'fulfilment' when thinking of Levin. For Levin marriage is a matter of love, and love of marriage. Involved in his problems of farming, religion and relations with the peasants, he knows that (as Agatha Mikhaylovna tells him) he needs a wife, but we are in no doubt that it is love—the kind into which one falls—that in due course unites him and Kitty.

We are left with *him* as the book closes. And if, as we share his sense of what are the great problems, we seem very close to the author, we note also that Levin is content for the time being with some inconsistencies (he feels them to be) and a certain tentativeness. His sense of problems to be solved focuses on the one hand (in terms of social responsibility) on the peasants, and on the other on his own need of religious belief. Or can we say that the peasants have become, at the close of the book, something like a comprehensive focus? He is still troubled by the problem of the right relations with them. But there is now a very much strengthened tendency to associate the solution of that problem in an ominous way with the solution of what, for Levin, must surely be a very different problem—that of the good life. An ominous way?—there is a clear intimation that, as Levin broods, he finds himself identifying them: the problems seem merging into one. The solution is to live with the peasants, to be a peasant among peasants. His problem of 'belief' (associated with his intense inner response to the fact of death[1]—we don't forget the grim evocation of the dying Nicholas, his brother) he sees as to be solved by his achieving the naïve 'belief' of the peasants. And this, in a curiously simple way, he identifies with being 'good'.

My summary has, as of course any summary of theme and significance in *Anna Karenina* must have, an effect of grossness from which one shrinks. The actual creative presentment is infinitely subtle, and comes as the upshot of an immense deal of immediately relevant drama and suggestion in the foregoing mass of the book. For example, I will point to chapters XI and XII in Part III, which give us Levin's visit, while still a bachelor, to his sister's village in order to look after farming interests of hers that need attention. He suspects that the peasants are cheating her over the hay harvest, and it turns out that his suspicions are well founded. Nevertheless, that matter settled, the deceits and grudges are forgotten, and he finds himself contemplating the peasants with warm idealizing sympathy as they cart the hay. The power of the episode depends upon a kind of sustained and typically Tolstoyan poetic life such as I had very much in mind when I spoke of what Tolstoy must lose in translation. This, with some cuts, is a passage of it:

Levin had often admired that kind of life, had often admired the folk who lived it; but that day, especially after what he had seen for the first time of the relations between Vanka Parmenich and his young wife, it struck him that it depended on himself to change his wearisome, idle and artificial personal life for that pure delightful life of common toil.

The old man who had been sitting beside him had long since gone home ... Levin ... still lay on the haycock, looking, listening and thinking. The peasants who were staying in the meadow kept awake almost all the short summer night. . . . The whole long day of toil had left upon them no trace of anything but merriment.

Just before dawn all became silent. The sounds of night—the ceaseless croaking of frogs, the snorting of horses through the morning

[1] 'If you once realize that tomorrow, if not today, you will die and nothing will be left of you, everything becomes insignificant.' See the whole context, Part IV, chapter VII.

mist over the meadow—could alone be heard. Awakening to reality, Levin rose from his haycock, and glancing up at the stars, realized that the night was nearly over.

Well, then, what shall I do? How shall I do it? he asked himself, trying to find expression for what he had been thinking and the feelings he had lived through in that short night. All his ideas and feelings separated themselves into three different lines of thought. The first was, how to renounce his old life and discard his quite useless education. This renunciation would afford him pleasure and was quite easy and simple. The second was concerned with his notion of the life he now wanted to lead. He was distinctly conscious of the simplicity, purity and rightness of that life, and convinced that in it he would find satisfaction, peace and dignity, the absence of which was so painful to him. But the third thought was the question of how to make the change from his present life to that other one . . . Should he have a wife? . . . 'but I'll clear it up later. One thing is certain: this night has decided my fate. All my former dreams of a family life were nonsense— not the right thing. Everything is much simpler and better than that . . .'

'How beautiful!' he thought, looking up at a strange mother-of-pearl-coloured shell formed of fleecy clouds, in the centre of the sky just above his head. 'How lovely everything is, this lovely night! And how did the shell get formed so quickly? A little while ago when I looked at the sky all was clear, but for two white strips. My views of life have changed in the same unnoticeable way.'

Leaving the meadow, he went down the high road towards the village.

He hears wheels and bells, and a coach comes by. In it, looking out as she wakes up, he sees Kitty. 'She recognized him, and joyful surprise lit up her face.'

This is before his marriage; it is in the period of disappointed love, and the last sentence makes the dawn for him, suddenly, that of a new hope. The hope proves no vain one, and in the close of the book, when the brooding on peasant-faith as a personal solution recurs, and so insistently, the dream he had dismissed as foolish has been achieved: Kitty is his wife, and they have a family. He doesn't say now that the dream was all nonsense. The assurance of an inner peace, a firm possession to be won of the saving truth, if only he can take the decision and put it into effect, has for context the incongruous preoccupations of family life,

C

enlightened farming, his own developed interests as one of the intelligentsia, and the intellectual talk of his half-brother Kozny-shev and Katavasov about Pan-Slavism. But the suggestion on which the novel ends is that the assurance, the half-grasped faith, is henceforward to be the central reality of Levin's life.

And the cogent force of the whole great work makes it plain that the answer he threatens to commit himself to with all the force of his will is a desperately simplifying one; that is, not an answer at all—unless a rejection of life is an answer. Levin's peasant solution gets no countenance from the preceding book; quite the reverse. I will allow myself a final extract, from a passage (Part III, chapter XXX) that gives something like a summary, or paradigm, of the refutation conveyed by the novel as a whole. Agatha Mikhaylovna, Levin's old nurse, is the maternal ideal-peasant housekeeper of his bachelor establishment.

Having written for some time, Levin suddenly with particular vividness remembered Kitty, her refusal, and their last meeting. He rose and began to pace up and down the room.

'What is the use of fretting?' said Agatha Mikhaylovna. 'You should go to a watering-place now that you have got ready.'

'So I shall: I am going the day after tomorrow, Agatha Mikhaylovna, only I must finish my business.'

'Eh, what is your business? Have you not done enough for the peasants as it is! Why, they are saying, "Your master will get a reward from the Tsar for it!" And it is strange: why should you bother about the peasants?'

'I am not bothering about them: I am doing it for myself.'

Agatha Mikhaylovna knew all the details of Levin's farming plans. . . . But this time she quite misunderstood what he said.

'Of course one must think of one's soul before everything else', she remarked with a sigh. 'There was Parfen Denisich, who was no scholar at all, but may God grant everyone to die as he did!' she said, referring to a servant who had died recently: 'He received Holy Communion and Extreme Unction.'

'I am not speaking about that', he said. 'I mean that I am doing it for my own profit. My gains are bigger when the peasants work better.'

'But, whatever you do, an idler will always bungle. If he has a conscience he will work, if not, you can do nothing with him.'

'But you yourself say that Ivan looks after the cattle better now.'

'I only say', answered Agatha Mikhaylovna, evidently not speaking at random, but with strict sequence of thought, 'you must marry, that is all!'

She herself may be said to represent peasant wisdom—anti-intellectual sanity, and profundity of intuitive insight and judgment. Her view of the peasants has incomparably more authority than Levin's. The disconcerting felicity of her 'you must marry, that is all' has for context something like a comprehensive insight into Levin's complexities of preoccupation—the passage makes that plain enough. 'Of course, one must think of one's soul before anything else.'—Of course, and Parfen's end was edifying; but when one says that, how much is said, peasant-life and reality being the question? She knows that any peasant would, with complete conviction, prescribe as she does—realizing with her what responsibilities, not to be shed, marriage would entail upon Levin. In so far as she glimpses Levin's religious-social ideas as they relate to the peasants, she knows that the peasants themselves would deride them. And it is impossible to believe that Tolstoy in writing this chapter had any sense of dissociation from *her* knowledge—that it wasn't for him at the same time his own. But Levin, married to the admirable Kitty, now the mother of his child, is shown once more cultivating a resolution that denies such knowledge—or defies it.

We may tell ourselves that he is merely a character in the book, and that the book makes its implicit comment on Levin. The significance of the book is what is conveyed by the whole, and the suggestion of the whole doesn't in the least encourage us to think of Levin as anything but ill-judging, ill-inspired, and in for disillusionment. With the advantage of hindsight, however, we can see that the breakdown of Tolstoy into the old Leo is here portended.

The later Tolstoy—a significant consistency, if you like—refused to see anything impressive in *Anna Karenina*. 'What difficulty is there', he said, 'in writing how an officer fell in love with a married woman? There is no difficulty in it, and, above all, there is no good in it.' But we, most of us, have to recognize a higher authority in the art, the creative power, of *Anna Karenina* than in the wisdom of the sage and prophet. The later Tolstoy—the prophetic and tragic Tolstoy—insisted on a simple answer.

Anna Karenina one of the great European novels?—it is, surely, *the* European novel. The completeness with which Tolstoy, with his genius, was a Russian of his time made him an incomparably representative European, and made the book into which his whole experience, his most comprehensive 'relatedness', went what it is for us: the great novel of modern—of our—civilization. The backwardness of Russia meant that the transcendent genius experienced to the full, taking their significances with personal intensity, the changes that have produced our modern world. In a country in which serfdom has been recently abolished, the characters of *Anna Karenina* travel as a matter of course by railway between the two capitals. The patriarchal landowner participates in a cosmopolitan culture, and, using French and English in intercourse with members of his own class, is intellectually nourished on the contemporary literature and thought of the West. Anna herself, having had at the outset of the book the shock of the fatal accident that marks her arrival at Moscow, ends her life under the iron wheels. The apparition of the little peasant with the sack who horrifies her, and is so oddly associated with the wheels and the rails, acts on our imagination as a pregnant symbol and a sinister augury (he is seen, too, later in a nightmare by Vronsky).[1] The disharmonies, contrasts, and contradictions are challenging in a way that makes the optimisms of Progress impossible for Tolstoy—as the inability of Levin, the earnest and public-spirited, to see a duty in Zemstvo-attendance very characteristically intimates. *Anna Karenina*, in its human centrality, gives us modern man; Tolstoy's essential problems, moral and spiritual, are ours.

[1] See Part IV, chapter III. And see also Part III, chapter IV.

II

THE PILGRIM'S PROGRESS [1]

IT is possible to read *The Pilgrim's Progress* without any thought of its theological intention. I myself can testify to that. When I read it in childhood, as everyone did (at least we assumed so and there seemed to be plenty of evidence for the assumption), I had not heard of Calvin or of Predestination, Imputed Righteousness, and Justification by Faith, and even if they had been explained to me I should not have seen any point in trying to relate what I could grasp of those doctrines to the book that was so stirring a presence in our imaginative life. I am not for a moment suggesting that the theological significance had not counted immensely in its becoming an established popular classic among English-speaking people. What I am emphasizing is that *The Pilgrim's Progress* was written by a highly gifted, imaginative writer and has the vitality and significance of major art.

This is an emphasis that one finds in place when reading that valuable scholarly book *John Bunyan, Mechanick Preacher*, by William York Tindall. Professor Tindall's theme is that Bunyan was one of a host of preaching tinkers, cobblers, blacksmiths, wheelwrights, tradesmen of all kinds, and field workers—all humble uneducated persons. *John Bunyan, Mechanick Preacher* is a valuable book because Tindall documents his theme so thoroughly, and thus brings out the representative quality of the life and conditions behind Bunyan's art. He provokes us, at the same time, to insist on the distinction of the art—to insist that there *is* art, and art of an impressiveness that makes Bunyan for us that rare thing, a creative genius. For Professor Tindall's treatment of the facts he presents has the effect of telling us that Bunyan was *merely* one of an ignorant and fanatical preaching host. But there was only *one* Bunyan, we reply. There were other gifted Puritan

[1] Written as an 'afterword' to the Signet Classics edition of *The Pilgrim's Progress* (New American Library, 1964).

'mechanick' preachers whose talent appears in their writings, but *The Pilgrim's Progress* stands alone; there is no rival Puritan classic in the field of creative literature.

Having said this, I wonder whether it is altogether felicitous to call *The Pilgrim's Progress* a 'Puritan classic'. Certainly it isn't in the least what 'puritanical' today suggests. Nor does it in the world and ethos it evokes remind us at all closely of Hawthorne's *The Scarlet Letter*. What I meant was that it is a classic produced by English Puritanism of the seventeenth century. And in saying this I come back to the emphasis on representativeness: *The Pilgrim's Progress* has a representative significance such as is found only in the work of a great creative writer. As I have testified out of my own experience, it can be read—and having been so read, leave a profound and lasting impression—as a dramatic and classically compelling tale innocent of theological intentions, an imaginative work that holds us by what it is in its impact as an intensely evoked particular history.

Recognizing in later life, however, that it is something more than a children's classic, and thinking about the nature of its power, one sees that the theological intentions unmistakably demand—from anyone interested in the art—a recognition different in tone and less simple in implicit judgment than is exemplified by Professor Tindall's commentary. His tone is an ironic dryness. He assumes that the embattled and quarrelsome certitudes of sectarian Calvinistic theology can, by the modern reader, be seen only as bigotry, fanaticism, and ignorance. But if one is interested in the art, one tells oneself that the religious ethos of *The Pilgrim's Progress* isn't fairly suggested by an account of Bunyan's theology as a Particular Open-Communion Baptist, even though religious ethos and theology can hardly be altogether separated. Bunyan himself, one recognizes as an essential and very germane truth, would have greeted with astonishment the distinction just implied. But although (finding, too, the associated bigotry repellent) one may be unable to regard the doctrine with any sense of attraction or enlightenment, it is hardly possible to admire *The Pilgrim's Progress* as a creative work without being moved by its religious quality and seeing that this inheres in the power of the art. And to take stock of this complexity of perception and recognition that one finds in oneself is to acquire a more lively sense of a representative significance in John Bunyan.

The tone of Tindall's commentary, as I have intimated, carries a reductive judgment on the world—or the culture (for the term, we shall see, is appropriate)—to which Bunyan belonged. The force of the adjective 'puritanical', as currently used, doesn't tend to advert us to the need for a fuller and juster sense of that word. But to ponder the vitality and depth of Bunyan's art is to see in *The Pilgrim's Progress* an incontrovertible document of seventeenth-century Puritanism—a representative product the clear human significance of which refutes the too-simple judgments and preconceptions in a most salutary way. And in throwing a revelatory light on seventeenth-century Puritanism, *The Pilgrim's Progress* at the same time gives us an insight into that past of our civilization which is not in time very remote, but that, if we really think of it, we have to think of as a civilization of the past—as not ours, but the civilization that produced Shakespeare.

John Bunyan was born in 1628, near the market town of Bedford. Bedford lies thirty miles to the west along the road that runs a hundred yards from where I write. Fifteen miles northward from here (from Cambridge, that is) lies Huntingdon, county town of the shire where Cromwell farmed. Puritanism was not confined to any part of England; it was pervasive and had many centres, but this eastern region was one where it was notably strong. The Civil War broke out in 1642, and there can be little doubt, though the particular facts of his service are not on record, that when in 1644 Bunyan was enlisted, it was in the Parliamentary army. It seems that he saw no fighting—there was none in the neighbourhood of Newport Pagnell where he was stationed. But this was not garrison duty in a country at peace; among his fellow soldiers there will have been those whose memories of action were both vivid and matter-of-fact and who could communicate to the boy a strong sense of belonging to a fraternity from the members of which, in the natural order of things, the mustering of courage and address for the hazards of armed hand-to-hand encounter would be required. The presence of this adolescent experience in the preacher-allegorist is to be

seen in *The Pilgrim's Progress*, where for the most part the terms
of the allegory, in which arms and the use of them play a prominent part, obviously belong, in their convincing reality, to the
texture of the artist's daily life.

Bunyan the Puritan allegorist *was* an artist; however incongruous a word for him it may seem, it is worth insisting on as
a way both of challenging recognition for the nature of great art
and of making the point that he might have had his spiritual
intensity and steadfastness without having the creative writer's
gift that makes him a great name in the history of prose fiction;
he might, that is, have had as intense, painful, and undeviating a
concern for the certitude of personal salvation. I touch here on a
delicate matter for thought, one that cannot be ignored in considering the time-honoured status of *The Pilgrim's Progress*, though
I think it would be crass to suppose one can formulate neatly
definitive conclusions as the upshot. In shifting, in the sentence
before the last, from my first phrase to 'an intense, painful, and
undeviating concern for the certitude of personal salvation', I
point to something essential in Bunyan that pulls most modern
readers up when they become acutely aware of it, for it reminds
them that Bunyan's intensity was indeed that of a seventeenth-
century Puritan. For Professor Tindall it seems to be at the best
something for a pitying smile, being a manifestation of ignorance,
bigotry, and fanatical conceit. And actually, though I have meant
to be taken as suggesting that Bunyan may properly be seen as
representative of seventeenth-century Puritanism, he belonged to
a minority even among seventeenth-century Puritans. As W.
Hale White says in his *John Bunyan*:

His awful doubts and fears were not shared by others, not even by
'the people of God'. 'They would pity me and would tell me of the
Promises.' The 'people of God' at Bedford believed in their Calvinism,
but they sat in their shops and quietly went about their business un-
troubled by their creed.

The way in which Bunyan was, as the voluminous body of
his writings manifests, troubled by his creed (and he insisted
indefatigably, and with moving conviction, that the people of
God cannot but be so moved) is given in what Hale White recalls
to us of Samuel Johnson:

It is strange . . . that Johnson resembled Bunyan. His spectres haunted Johnson, and the *History of My Melancholy*, which he once thought of writing but never dared to write, would undoubtedly have reminded us of another history by the author of *The Pilgrim's Progress* which he loved so well. 'You seem, sir,' said Mrs. Adams to Johnson, 'to forget the merits of our Redeemer.' 'Madam,' he replied, 'I do not forget the merits of my Redeemer; but my Redeemer has said that He will set some on His right hand and some on His left.' 'He was in gloomy agitation', adds Boswell, 'and said I'll have no more on't.'

Johnson the High Church Tory was not a Calvinist; we think with sympathetic horror of his suffering in this way, and see it as something to be thought of as coming under the head of pathology. But Bunyan *was* a Calvinist; that in him which leads Hale White to make the comparison with Johnson was something entailed on Bunyan by his taking his creed with the intensity of full belief. How could an imagination possessed by such a creed create a humane classic, for Bunyan's 'puritan classic' *is* that. He, of course, with that paradoxical security registered in the way in which the pilgrim, having escaped from the Slough of Despond, has still Doubting Castle, Giant Despair, and so many hazards of the same significance in front of him, had—as Johnson had not —the assurance of being one of the Elect. But it is hard to think of that relation to the sectarian exclusiveness of his polemical and damnation-dispensing theology as conducive to a generous creative power.

Yet the creative power is beyond question there in *The Pilgrim's Progress*. It is so compelling there that, through reading after reading, one remains virtually unconscious of the particular theology—remains so even when one could, if challenged, offer a fair account of the detailed doctrinal significances of the allegory in which the intention of this is given. Here and there, perhaps, one retains a faint sense of knowing some reason for entering a kind of protest—as, for instance, when, remembering that glimpse through the opened door where 'they also thought that they heard a rumbling noise, as of fire, and a cry of some tormented, and that they smelt the scent of brimstone', we read at the close of the First Part how at the King's command the two Shining Ones, Christian's and Faithful's conductors, dealt with

Ignorance—on whose particular allegorical significance in terms of Restoration controversy Talon,[1] in his standard work, throws an interesting light:

Then they took him up, and carried him through the air, to the door that I saw in the side of the hill, and put him in there. Then I saw that there was a way to hell, even from the gates of heaven, as well as from the City of Destruction.

But the clear if paradoxical truth is that one's sense of a religious depth in the book prevails with such potency that particular theological intentions to be elicited from the allegory don't get much recognition for what they doctrinally are, or, if noticed and judged to be incongruous with one's basic response, don't really tell. That is, in considering *The Pilgrim's Progress*, we have to recognize that we do very much need the two words 'theological' and 'religious'. Bunyan's religion, like his art, comes from the whole man. And the man, we can't help telling ourselves as we reflect on the nature of the power of his masterpieces, belonged to a community and to a culture, a culture that certainly could not be divined from the theology. The next step—one that follows necessarily in a critical appreciation of *The Pilgrim's Progress*—is to recognize the force of the obvious truth that seventeenth-century Puritanism considered in the context of English life from which in the concrete it was inseparable looks very different from an abstracted Puritanism, in our sense of which an account of its theological characteristics predominates. In fact, what is apt to predominate is the Calvinistic ethos as Dickens, the incomparable recorder of Victorian civilization, evokes it for us. We have it in Mrs Clennam of *Little Dorrit*—morose, repressive, anti-human, the enemy of happiness, childhood, art, and life. But the Puritanism of Bunyan's England is not to be identified with this. It is worth recalling that Cromwell, the arch-Roundhead, wore long hair and delighted in music. But the sufficient evidence is there in *The Pilgrim's Progress* itself, from which it is plain that the 'people of God' did not in their revulsion against Vanity Fair think it necessary to ban from their lives the humane arts and graces. The place of music, dancing, and the social pleasures of the table in the

[1] Henri A. Talon, *John Bunyan: The Man and His Works*, 1951.

Second Part, where a whole party make their pilgrimage together, is especially significant. And the Delectable Mountains are not a symbol that we can think of as belonging to Mrs Clennam's imaginative life.

But I must return briefly to Bunyan's personal history. The youth we left under arms at Newport Pagnell was not, to go by his own account, devout, and certainly not a Puritan; that is why, the record not being specific, some nineteenth-century biographers felt at liberty to conjecture that he might have been in the King's army. He was soon back at Bedford, and there, having married at about the age of twenty, he was 'converted' by the Bedford minister, John Gifford (ex-major of the King's army), and in 1653 baptized. Since Gifford had been a royalist officer, we can accept as fact the account of him as having been before his conversion a reckless profligate. But confessions to such an effect, as Professor Tindall's book brings out, were common form among converts, and without imputing any insincerity to Bunyan we can believe that the wickedness he avowed as having characterized his un-regenerate days was less lurid than the profligacy of a blackguard royalist major. The account he himself gives of it seems to make it nothing worse than swearing and bell-ringing (the church bells being in question) and not having obeyed or even listened to the call to become a 'pilgrim'. He now began his career of preaching, which may be said to have been, in one form and another, the main occupation of his life.

His addiction to it was compulsive; it led to his spending a large part of his life in prison. That fate closed down on him in 1660, the first year of the Restoration, when monarchy in the person of Charles II came back to England. Charles had under-taken in the Declaration of Breda that the Nonconformists—the Protestant rebels to the authority of the Anglican church—should be left their freedom of worship, but the promise was not kept and Bunyan was one of the first victims. The Clarendon code of penal laws, together with his obduracy, ensured that he should be an inmate of Bedford jail from 1660 to 1672. He was im-prisoned again for some while in 1686, and, dying in 1688, the year of the Revolution, he didn't live to enjoy the established toleration inaugurated then.

Froude's suggestion that Bunyan's imprisonment wasn't for the most part very rigorous, so that we may think of him as slipping out from time to time to preach in the neighbourhood, is not now regarded as well founded. Parted from wife and children, for whose welfare he suffered painful anxiety, he was confined in what was indeed a 'den'—a breeding-place of jail-fever. There was no chimney in it, and we have to think of him as sleeping in straw. Yet in prison as out he was a preacher—a preacher and a shepherd of souls in that given Puritan tradition. Opportunities for the exercise of his vocation were not lacking in prison, and he took them assiduously. Moreover, he wrote immensely, and his themes, as we can see from the great body of his writings, were those of his preaching, and always the same. They were those of his spiritual autobiography, Grace Abounding to the Chief of Sinners, and those yielded by a summary of the theological significance of The Pilgrim's Progress—those of the Puritan sectarian's intensely fostered Calvinistic preoccupations: the terrifying realization of one's total depravity, conversion and joyful hope, infinitely subtle promptings of the devil, recurrent despair, the paradoxical struggle for faith, the difficulty of keeping the narrow doctrinal way, the assurance of Election and of salvation by Imputed Righteousness—over and again. How could this fanatical treadmill-concentration issue in or be compatible with a generous humane art—a creative presentment of human life that counts for so much (and not the less essentially because not measurable) in the subsequent history of major art achieved in prose fiction? If we think of the uglier characteristics of sectarian controversy, it has to be recorded that Bunyan can't be acquitted of these. His earliest published book was a brutally bigoted polemic against the Quakers.

Yet The Pilgrim's Progress was, unquestionably, the work of the preacher—his most successful and popular work; and the more we know of his other writings the more emphatically can we say that, if unique, it was no sport. The best way of approaching the considerations that throw light on the paradox is to read G. R. Owst's Preaching in Mediaeval England and Literature and Pulpit in Mediaeval England. Owst shows, with an abundant particularity of illustration, that Bunyan as a popular preacher and homiletic writer was in a tradition that went back beyond the Reformation, in unbroken continuity, deep into the Middle Ages. I see an economy in quoting at this point a couple of sentences that, appealing to Owst's testimony, I have written elsewhere.[1] 'If one observes that this tradition owes its vitality to a popular culture, it must be only to add that the place of religion in the culture is obvious enough. The same people that created the English language for Shakespeare's use speaks in Bunyan, though it is now a people that knows its Authorized Version.' Bunyan, that is, had behind him—or rather, had around him and in him— that pervasive and potent continuity, a living culture; it was the air he breathed, the spiritual food (doctrinal Puritanism being only an element in it) that nourished him, the more-than-personal sensibility that as a writer he was. 'One writes', D. H. Lawrence late in his life replied to a questioner, 'out of one's moral sense', going on immediately to give 'moral' an intense special force by adding 'for the race, as it were'. Bunyan the creative writer wrote out of a 'moral sense' that represented what was finest in that traditional culture. He used with a free idiomatic range and vividness in preaching (the tradition he preached in ensured that) the language he spoke with jailers and fellow prisoners, with wife and children and friends at home. A language is more than such phrases as 'means of expression' or 'instrument of communication' suggest; it is a vehicle of collective wisdom and basic assumptions, a currency of criteria and valuations collaboratively determined; itself it entails on the user a large measure of accepting participation in the culture of which it is the active living presence.

The vigour of Bunyan's prose is more than a matter of an earthy raciness that consorts happily with biblical turns and resonances. And the way in which the creative writer's art transcends the intention belonging to the allegory is illustrated here:

Christian. Pray, who are your kindred there, if a man may be so bold?

By-Ends. Almost the whole town; and in particular my Lord Turnabout, my Lord Timeserver, my Lord Fair-speech (from whose

[1] 'Bunyan Through Modern Eyes', in *The Common Pursuit* (London: Chatto & Windus, 1952; New York: New York University Press, reissued 1964).

ancestors the Town first took its name), also Mr Smoothman, Mr Facing-both-ways, Mr Anything, and the Parson of our parish, Mr Two-tongues, was my mother's own brother by father's side; and to tell you the truth, I am become a gentleman of good quality; yet my grandfather was but a waterman, looking one way and rowing another; and I got most of my estate by the same occupation.

Christian. Are you a married man?

By-Ends. Yes, and my wife is a very virtuous woman, the daughter of a virtuous woman; she was my Lady Feigning's daughter, therefore she came of a very honourable family, and is arrived at such a pitch of breeding that she knows how to carry it to all, even to prince and peasant. 'Tis true we somewhat differ in religion from those of the stricter sort, yet but in two small points: First, we never strive against wind and tide; secondly, we are always most zealous when religion goes in his silver slippers; we love much to walk with him in the street, if the sun shines, and the people applaud him.

Professor Tindall comments:

To Bunyan the name By-ends connoted ends other than that of salvation by imputed righteousness. . . . By-ends is the product of the resentment against the Anglicans of an enthusiastic evangelist and despised mechanick. . . . Bunyan's fortunate discovery that through these controlled debates between his hero and these caricatured projections of his actual enemies he could experience the pleasures of combat without the complications of reality invests *Pilgrim's Progress* with the character of a controversial Utopia.

The first sentence of this commentary states an unquestioned fact. One's return comment is that one can respond to the characteristic power of that passage of Bunyan, and respond in a critically admiring way, without reminding oneself of the fact, even though one knows it, and that when one does remind oneself of it there is little difference to register in one's response or one's appreciation. As for what follows, one can only reply that while the doctrinal preoccupation, which naturally tended to be associated with a polemical habit, without doubt sharpened Bunyan's observation of character and gave vivacity to his analysis, what strikes one is the rendered observation, its life and truth and depth. And so far from suspecting Bunyan of trying to create for himself, with small-minded bigotry, an unreal 'controversial Utopia', one is possessed by the strong sense one has of an actual reality evoked. The art, one sees, belongs to a popular culture. The names and the racy turns of speech are one with the general style, and the style, concentrating the life of popular idiom, is the expression of cultural habit. What we have is something more than an idiomatic raciness of speech, expressing a naïve gusto of malicious observation: it is an art of social living, with, where the valuation of character is concerned, a fund of experience to draw on and shrewd criteria.

Lively characterization, of course, constitutes a major strength of *The Pilgrim's Progress*. Along with By-ends, everyone remembers Worldly Wiseman and Talkative and Pliable. But the spirit and quality of Bunyan's art in this respect are not adequately suggested in terms of the characters in the book that are observed satirically; there is no lack in his characterization of sympathetic perception and rendering or of warm human feeling. One would know confidently from *The Pilgrim's Progress* that he was a tender husband and father, a steadfast friend, and a man, authoritative in his human insight and his integrity, whom a close neighbourhood of the devout would naturally choose for their pastor—as the Bedford 'people of God' chose Bunyan in 1672, the year of his release from jail. The tradition in which he preached and wrote, together with the culture to which it and he himself belonged, ensured that the qualities and traits glanced at should be strongly present in his imaginative work.

The above considerations do something to explain how it is that even when we tell ourselves from point to point what the allegorical intention is, no consciousness of the allegory in terms of such a gloss as Professor Tindall gives us impedes or alters our fuller response—the inevitable response (we feel) to Bunyan's art; and how it is that we should find ourselves taking a religious significance that is not identical with the theological but transcends it. I confess for myself that the occasions when the doctrinal habit associated with the allegory has to be taken note of for an unsympathetic response are those when I am merely bored a little, rather than balking at something repellently unacceptable offered for acquiescence. I am thinking of those recurrent quasi-dramatic disquisitions and those dialogues in the pastoral mode: I won't pretend that I return with any eagerness to such things as the conducted and lectured viewing of 'emblems' and tableaux in the house of the Interpreter.

To attempt to say anything positive about the religious quality of *The Pilgrim's Progress* is a delicate matter. One's awareness of a religious significance as distinguished from a theological intention is challenged by that opening to the First Part:

As I walked through the wilderness of this world, I lighted on a certain place, where there was a den . . . and as I slept, I dreamed a dream. I dreamed, and behold, I saw a man clothed with rags standing in a certain place, with his face from his own house, a book in his hand, and a great burden upon his back. I looked, and saw him open the book, and read therein; and as he read, he wept and trembled; and not being able longer to contain, he brake out with a lamentable cry, saying, 'What shall I do?'

The den, we know, is Bedford jail. The dream convention doesn't in the least tend to diminish the intense reality with which the world of external facts belonging with Bunyan's spiritual autobiography is presented. To consider its use is to recognize the way in which the personal intensity gets, in the creative presentment, while being for that none the less intense, a necessary impersonalization. This effect is hardly separable from the sense we have of there being, in the order of reality in which this history is enacted, a dimension over and above those of the common-sense world. The events follow one another in a time succession, but now and then, taking it quite naturally, we are referred to a different, or 'normal', reality of time—that left behind by Christian in the City of Destruction, or by the other pilgrims in whatever this-worldly place they came from. I am thinking of the way in which a pilgrim, being overtaken by— or even overtaking—another from the same place, will, on inquiring about family or acquaintance, be given an account of what has happened there since his departure. It is plain in these cases that the two ostensibly parallel passages of time cannot be reconciled as belonging to the same real world, and yet we feel no need to object or question.

Of course, the word 'convention' that I used above can be

invoked as a sufficient explanation: we accept the dream convention and are not troubled by these anomalies. But 'convention' is a word, and more can be said by way of recognizing that quality of *The Pilgrim's Progress* to which we are attuned by the opening paragraph, where 'dream' carries no suggestion of relaxation or unreality. There is something irresistible and unanswerable about the steadfastness of inner life (Bunyan's own steadfastness, something so profoundly and essentially disinterested as to make one flinch from talking about it in terms of fanaticism or a 'concern for personal salvation') that carries the pilgrims through defeats, lapses, disasters, and felicities. This, we recognize, thinking of Tom Brangwen in the first chapter of Lawrence's *The Rainbow*, is the effective 'knowing we do not belong to ourselves';[1] and we recognize, though theologies may have become unacceptable or odious and we may feel that we have nothing left that Bunyan could have called 'faith' or 'belief', a change-defying validity. The close to the Second Part, where the pilgrims one by one cross the river, remains, even when we have told ourselves that the timbre or tone of exaltation belongs to Bunyan's world and not to ours, immensely impressive.

Though closing with this supreme exaltation, the Second Part, in which Christiana and her children, along with a whole party, go on the pilgrimage, is more novel-like than the First Part; that is, it suggests more readily that Defoe could have found in it something congenial to the prompting of his own talent (as it was to be found on so large a scale in Bunyan's *The Life and Death of Mr Badman*). Nevertheless, it is astonishing to reflect that Defoe, already nearing manhood, was to be Bunyan's successor as the great popular writer and bestseller. The Second Part of *The Pilgrim's Progress* (the First having come out in 1678) came out in 1684. The Revolution of 1688, the year of Bunyan's death, marks the unequivocal triumph of the new civilization, of which we see Defoe as a formidable representative. He was educated at a Dissenting Academy, and French writers about English literature describe him as '*puritain*'. But there is nothing either theological or what we readily call spiritual in Defoe's Nonconformity. He is

[1] 'But during the long February nights with the ewes in labour, looking out from the shelter into the flashing stars, he knew he did not belong to himself.'

D

Robinson Crusoe, *terre-à-terre*, commonsensical, infinitely re-
sourceful—an invincibly sane man of *this* world, an adventurer,
but not conceivably a pilgrim.

When I say 'man of this world' and 'invincibly sane' I am,
while paying tribute to positive qualities, at the same time intimating limitations: we cannot pass from Bunyan to Defoe without a sense of loss. 'Our excellent and indispensable eighteenth
century' (Matthew Arnold's phrase) was notably *not* characterized
by something that is strongly present in the great creative periods.
Of course, Dissenter though he was, Defoe's decent human feeling
had no touch of that morose distrust and rejection of life that we
associate with Calvinism—the Calvinism of *The Scarlet Letter* and
of Dickens's Mrs Clennam. But then, in spite of the doctrine of
Total Depravity to which as a theological expositor Bunyan
subscribed, the attitude towards life and the world he expresses,
out of the whole man, in his art, is as we have seen, no more
life-rejecting than Defoe's. True, life and the world to his sense
are much more dangerous than to Defoe's, for all the shipwreck
and the cannibals of *Robinson Crusoe*; for Bunyan bottomless
sloughs and dreadful abysses menace the pilgrim, mountains
seem about to fall on him, and not to be a pilgrim is to be certainly
and eternally damned. But the hazards and menaces are the
negative accompaniments of something positive that is not there
in Defoe's world: the concern, intense and profound, for what,
talking loosely, as we *have* to talk (for no precision is possible),
we speak of as the 'meaning of life'. Such a concern, felt as the
question 'What for—what ultimately for?' is implicitly asked in
all the greatest art, from which we get, not what we are likely to
call an 'answer', but the communication of a felt significance;
something that confirms our sense of life as more than a mere
linear succession of days, a matter of time as measured by the
clock—'tomorrow and tomorrow and tomorrow. . . .'

Bunyan's theological *statement* of the significance he wishes to
enforce is abstract; but the sense of significance that actually
possessed him couldn't be stated, it could only be communicated
by creative means. It might be objected that Bunyan identifies
the significance of life with a belief in a real life that is to come
after death, and that therefore *The Pilgrim's Progress* cannot, for

readers who do not share that belief, have the kind of virtue I have attributed to it. But these things are not as simple as that. However naïvely Bunyan, as pastor, might have talked of the eternal life as the reward that comes after death to the Christian who has persevered through the pains and trials of his earthly pilgrimage, the sense of the eternal conveyed by *The Pilgrim's Progress* and coming from the whole man ('trust the tale', as Lawrence said, not the writer) is no mere matter of a life going on and on for ever that starts after death. It is a sense of a dimension felt in the earthly life—in what for us *is* life, making this something that transcends the time succession, transience and evanescence and gives significance.

Such a sense is conveyed with great potency by *The Pilgrim's Progress*. There it is, an unquestionable reality for us, a vitalizing reminder of human nature, human potentiality, and human need, and remaining that for us even though we may find wholly un-profitable the theology with which Bunyan accompanies it, and, moreover, may tell ourselves that so confident and exalting a sense of significance could not have been achieved in our time and our civilization. One of the things we learn from frequenting the great works of creative art is that where life is strong in any culture, the 'questions' ask themselves insistently, and the 'answers' change from age to age, but in some way that challenges our thought; the profound sincerity of past 'answers' will invest them for our contemplation with a kind of persisting validity. And what is 'validity'? To that challenge there is no simple reply— which is very far from saying that it won't repay endless consid-eration: the nature and the life of the human world (that which Sir Charles Snow is so blank about when he exalts the 'scientific edifice of the physical world' as the 'most beautiful and wonderful collective work of the mind of man')[1] are in question.

The play of 'significance' goes in *The Pilgrim's Progress* with the homely day-to-day reality in the evoking of life that convinces us of Defoe's indebtedness to Bunyan. At this level itself (so far as it can be separated for consideration) one may reasonably judge Bunyan superior to Defoe as a pioneer of the novel. His 'realism'

[1] A contention I discuss in *Two Cultures? The Significance of C. P. Snow* (London: Chatto & Windus, 1962; New York: Pantheon, 1963).

comes from deeper down; his dialogue, in its homely rightness, is much more subtle and penetrating in its power of characterization and has an immensely wider range of tones. As for 'homely', that word in its bearing on Bunyan's art must not be allowed to suggest limitations. As I have already remarked, against the penetrating vividness and economy of his satiric portrayals is to be set the tender potency of his sympathetic evocation of day-to-day life. This is especially so in Part Two. The theme is pilgrimage, but the distinctive note is that of a family party, and the rendering yields abundant matter that might have been invoked in illustration by the historian John Richard Green for the enforcement of his once well-known contention: the home, as we think of it now, was the creation of the puritan.

I cannot allow myself to come to an end without insisting once more that 'puritan' must not be taken to suggest a stern or morose austerity, or, in the preoccupation with Grace, any indifference to the graces of life. Bunyan's 'homely' spirituality entails no contempt for the good things of this world. Our satisfaction in the thought of the children enjoying their bread well spread with honey is patently assumed, and the pleasures of the table, socially enjoyed, play an essential part in the culture that is incidentally revealed for our contemplation. So do music and dancing: this puritanism assumes that art is necessary to life. There is some reason for supposing that Bunyan, in prison, made himself both a violin and a flute, and certainly his Christiana plays the viol, his Mercy plays the lute, and his Prudence accompanies on the spinet her own singing. 'Wonderful! Music in the house, music in the heart, and music also in Heaven'—the exclamation suggests aptly that actual 'unpuritanical' sense of earthly life in relation to the eternal which informs *The Pilgrim's Progress*. This is the religious feeling, the unquestioned spirituality, that the creative work conveys, even though an account of Bunyan's allegorical intention in terms of the theological doctrines (with Total Depravity as the basic note) would convey something very different.

III

ADAM BEDE [1]

IN *Adam Bede* we can see George Eliot becoming a novelist—learning, that is, in the course of writing her first real novel, how a novel might be achieved. To put it in this way is to recognize that *Adam Bede* is not perfect, and that it is a very different thing from the almost contemporary French classic, Flaubert's *Madame Bovary*. But George Eliot was a greater creative power than Flaubert, and, in relation to any adequate conception of art (a word for which, significantly, we don't find ourselves using a capital letter when talking of her), a greater artist. She was in fact a novelist of the greatest kind. Though she started her novelist's career so late (at close on forty), she had all the gifts and a peculiarly rich and varied store of experience for her creative vitality to draw on. Her late first novel, a classic in itself, opened the way to a long, productive, and continually renewed development, so that her greatest work was produced at the close.

In *Adam Bede* we can see the promise of the things to come, and see also an illuminating case of one of the major original artists learning from predecessors. For George Eliot is widely and deeply rooted in literature of the past as well as decisively influential on major novelists succeeding her—e.g. James, Hardy, and Lawrence. She is at the centre of the creative achievements of the English language in the phase of its history to which we still belong, and incites to pregnant reflections on vital continuity in art: we see that there is indeed an English literature—something more than an assemblage of individual masterpieces or separate authors.

She began her career as a writer of fiction with the tales that compose *Scenes of Clerical Life*. The material for these was reminiscence of her young days. The more ambitious enterprise

---

[1] Written as a foreword to the Signet Classics edition of *Adam Bede* (New American Library, 1961).

is announced to Blackwood in a letter of 1st September, 1857 (see J. W. Cross's *Life*):

I have a subject in my mind which will not come under the limitations of the title 'Clerical Life' and I am inclined to take a large canvas for it and write a novel.

She had meant to do another clerical type, Mr Irwine, the cultivated gentleman-parson—representative of a higher worldly wisdom and a refined and genial human dignity rather than of any challenging spirituality. The traces of this beginning are to be seen in *Adam Bede* in the attention claimed for Mr Irwine over and above what, in relation to his function in the novel, is strictly necessary. The idea of making the advance and writing a novel presented itself to George Eliot in terms of the possibility of bringing together in the one work a variety of other materials from her store of memories. Especially she wanted to use the memories she had cherished of her Methodist aunt, including the story of the confession got from the condemned girl-mother in prison. This entailed the seduction, and that brought in the Hall Farm and Mrs Poyser, and gave George Eliot the freedom of the rustic world of her youth.

She had material enough, but she knew that it takes more than material to make a novel. Several years later, referring in a letter to Carlyle's memoirs, she wrote:

What a memory and what an experience for a novelist! But somehow experience and finished faculty rarely go together. Dearly beloved Scott had the greatest combination of experience and faculty—yet even he never made the most of his treasures, at least in his mode of presentation.

George Eliot here pays her tribute to the master from whom she herself had learnt to be a novelist, and at the same time records her realization that one of the main things she had learnt in starting with him as the exemplar was that his 'mode of presentation' was not, after all, really adequate to the novelist she was meant to be. But who else was there? Thackeray, with his particular, very limited field, his clubman's wisdom, and what his critics in his own time called his lack of ideas, was of no use to her. Dickens's genius had little direct bearing on what she, with her interests, needed to find out how to do. But with the author of *The Heart of Midlothian* she had very deep affinities. His treatment of the remembered past, the strong imaginative piety that gives life and depth to his evocations, was wholly congenial to her. She too, in using her memories, places her action at a time she can only, in her childhood, have heard talked about. She herself was born in 1819, but the events of *Adam Bede* belong to the end of the previous century. She doesn't need to go in for 'historical re-construction': her memories of England before the railway age *are* memories, but they have this peculiar atmospheric depth. The encouragement of Scott's example helped her too in her use of dialect. This she felt to be essential to her purpose, but she had to insist against strong opposition (Lytton, for instance, tried to persuade her to eliminate it), and the precedent of Scott was obviously a strength to her.

A manifestation of his influence that suggests, rather, the serious limits of his use to her is seen in the opening of the book. That stranger who reins in his horse and observes, for our benefit, what passes on the village green, is a 'mode of presentation' from Scott: he has no part in the novel except to put in the same kind of appearance at the close.

George Eliot's own distinctive bent and quality of interest might in any case have been counted on to make that familiar Victorian convention, the seduction theme, something notably more than mere convention. One might have thought that this would have been done mainly through the intensity of her interest in Dinah, for the sake of whose part in the prison scene the story of the seduction was in the first place conceived. But actually, though the figure of the charming Methodist, moving with impressive quietness through the book, is memorably enough evoked, it clearly turned out that she could be made to yield only a very limited return to any treatment she invited from the developing great novelist. George Eliot's distinctive interest focused rather on Arthur Donnithorne, and the inner drama of conscience in *him*. It is deeply characteristic of George Eliot: it is the theme, psychological and moral, that is to be developed in the study of Tito Melema in *Romola*, of Bulstrode in *Middlemarch*, and of Gwendolen in *Daniel Deronda*.

Yet, characteristic as the bent of interest is, even here one can see her indebted, at least for stimulus and suggestion (of kinds that matter immensely to an artist engaged in self-discovery as George Eliot was), to a great predecessor. This time it was not the genial Scott, but the novelist of Puritan New England. George Eliot had read *The Scarlet Letter* when it came out, and (what doesn't surprise us) expressed a great admiration for Hawthorne. The idea that Hawthorne's influence can be discovered in *Adam Bede* was prompted, as it came to me, by the name Hetty. Once one thinks of Hester Prynne, the effect of the suggestion has its compelling significance, even if one is at first inclined to dismiss the echo as mere chance. The treatment of the agonized conscience in Arthur Donnithorne convinces one before long that in the treatment of the seduction theme *The Scarlet Letter* has told significantly. This real affinity (for all the differences of temperament and art between the two authors) brings home to one, in fact, that the association of the names was more than a chance clue. One notes, further, that Hawthorne's male sinner is also Arthur —Arthur Dimmesdale for George Eliot's Arthur Donnithorne.

We have here, unmistakably, a case of that profound kind of influence of which the artist in whom it works is unaware. It is of the same order as that influence of George Eliot herself on Henry James which I noted some years ago in discussing *The Portrait of a Lady*.[1] The influence of Hawthorne on George Eliot was not so important for her as hers was for James, yet one would be rash to judge it a minor matter, of marginal interest. For a writer in George Eliot's position, with no obvious model to start from, a congenial hint that goes home deeply as a creative impulsion or reinforcement may have a disproportionate momentousness. And we have observed that Arthur Donnithorne opened for George Eliot a series of intensely characteristic studies: Hawthorne's influence, then, was at the centre and deep down. Since Hawthorne himself, we know, was a major influence on James, the three novelists together offer a suggestive illustration of the intimate creative relations that may exist between artists of widely different genius.

[1] See *The Great Tradition*, Chapter III, i (London: Chatto & Windus, 1948; New York: New York University Press, reissued 1963).

When we ask what influences told decisively in George Eliot's formation, helping her to become the distinctive major novelist she is for us, one to which we have to give an important place is not from the literature of her own language: it is Greek Tragedy. Notoriously she was an awe-inspiring intellectual, immensely learned and well-read. What has to be insisted on is that there must be no opposing of the intellectual in her to the novelist. The intellectual, the finely trained intelligence, and the knowledge entered naturally and vitally into the work of the creative writer who could win a general warm applause by evoking the humours of Mrs Poyser's kitchen. She was inward with Greek Tragedy, but there is nothing assertively intellectual about the manifestations in *Adam Bede* (or elsewhere) of her interest in it. She responded above all to the Aeschylus of the *Oresteia*, the effect of which, in being moral and religious, was for her intensely imaginative, and expressed itself in her sensibility. We feel it in *Adam Bede* in her treatment of the themes of guilt and retribution. And we have here again our introduction to something characteristic of George Eliot's treatment of life that appears in more mature forms in her later work. In the consummately done Transome drama of *Felix Holt*, for instance, we have unmistakably, in modern terms, a tragedy of Hubris and Nemesis. And in the tragic irony of Gwendolen Harleth's fate in *Daniel Deronda* we feel again the congenial, assimilated influence of the Greek.

In *Adam Bede* we can, again and again, put our finger on it locally in the way in which we are given the irony of Arthur's good resolutions, and in his anticipations of a happy life as the virtuous and well-beloved young squire. And we note that when, with the intention (doomed to defeat) of making a clean breast of his temptation in order to be fortified in resisting it, he comes in to breakfast at the rectory, Mr Irwine has open at his elbow on the table 'the first volume of the Foulis Aeschylus, which Arthur knew well by sight', and Mr Irwine enlarges to him on the theory of Nemesis.

The George Eliot who found Aeschylus so congenial might be said to be the George Eliot who admired *Rasselas*—the influence of which can be seen in *Adam Bede*. But there would be more point in referring in this connexion to Shakespeare. Shakespeare

was a great living fact behind the English novelists of the nineteenth century; he can be felt, in different ways, as a vital informing power in their work, and George Eliot was no exception.
Her ability to absorb Aeschylus so naturally into her own art is
inseparable from this basic and pervasive presence of Shakespeare.
His name being mentioned, however, most people probably
would first point to the affinity as being manifest in her rendering
of English rustic life. And one needn't be concerned to deny that
Shakespeare must count for a great deal there.

But what one thinks of is the original, characteristic genius
of George Eliot working on her experience and observation.
Memory, with its emotional accompaniments, recalling over the
long gap of time, can be recognized as telling essentially in the
effect. But the effect is the product of a creative writer's art;
George Eliot is fully and consciously a novelist. She insisted, for
instance, that Mrs Poyser was *not* her own mother, even though
suggested by her. In the same way she insisted that the proverbial
trenchancies and pregnancies that characterize Mrs Poyser's
speech were not actual rustic currency recorded, or actual remembered utterances. We readily believe her, since it is impossible
that she should have set down from memory the rustic dialogue
that figures so abundantly in her pages; and the racy vitality of
that is clearly not a different thing from Mrs Poyser's vivid
analogical fertility. George Eliot had grown up in a community
in which that traditional art of speech flourished—the popular,
generally cultivated art of speech that made the English language
that made Shakespeare possible. As a novelist, dramatizing rustic
characters, she could do their utterance creatively.

In Adam Bede himself we have another influence that tells a
great deal in this book, as elsewhere in George Eliot—that of
Wordsworth. Adam, we know, though again not a portrait, was
inspired by memories of her father. In the presentment of his
simple strength and integrity there is an element of idealization,
and the spirit of this is Wordsworthian; we think of Michael.
Adam all the same—there is of course, no paradox about this—
consorts naturally with the other characters, convincing products
as these are of creative memory in the novelist whose genius made
her an incomparable social historian. It is indeed Adam who

occasions one of her finest passages of direct reflection on the nature of pre-industrial civilization, the closing paragraph of chapter XIX, giving George Eliot's account of Adam's representativeness:

He was not an average man. Yet such men as he are reared here and there in every generation of our peasant artisans—with an inheritance of affections nurtured by a simple family life of common need and common industry, and an inheritance of faculties trained in skilful courageous labour. . . .

—And so to the end of the chapter.

But the historical value of *Adam Bede* doesn't lie mainly in such general records of observation, intelligent as George Eliot's always are. It lies in her novelist's creation of a past England—of a culture that has vanished with the triumph of industrialism. The England preserved for us in George Eliot's art, the England of before the railway, was locally rooted and, to an extent very remote from our experience, locally self-sufficient. This we all know in a theoretical kind of way, but *Adam Bede* brings home to us what it meant in actual living—the feel and texture of daily life. There is a sense in which, paradoxically, the inhabitants of that so provincial England live in a larger world than their successors. The neighbouring shires have a most unquestionable reality; their hills can be seen, and everyone knows someone who has been there recently. But places twenty miles away are remote and known to be different—in speech, habit, and rural economy. Traffic passes along the roads through the length and breadth of England, the remoter parts are positively known to be there, and imagination has a good deal to play upon.

It might have been thought that life so rooted and spatially limited would be humanly starved—deadeningly monotonous and brutalized by poverty of essential civilization. But George Eliot makes us realize how very far the actuality was from being so. The Poysers, after the disgrace of Hetty's trial, are desolated at the thought of having to move into a strange country twenty and odd miles away and be buried in a strange churchyard ('We should leave our roots behind us, I doubt, and niver thrive again', says old Mr Poyser). But everything in this book brings home to us that this local fixation doesn't mean mere clodlike dullness of human culture, or any vital poverty; that, in fact, rootedness has very decidedly its advantages. Old Lisbeth Bede's determination that her husband's body shall lie under the white thorn in the churchyard ('on account of a dream as she had') where she herself will, in due course, be buried too, illustrates the way in which, for the inhabitants, all the familiar particularities of the village and the environment become invested with particular values and form part of a human significance.

In that rooted community, too, not only is the typical workman master of a craft, practising a skill and serving a function that bring the man a sense of his meaning something in life; George Eliot shows us a world in which people possess and practise arts of living, the creative products of generations. For us, the one there is perhaps most point in insisting on is the art of speech. Not having the radio, television, newspapers, or literacy, they have speech, which *is*, George Eliot makes it impossible not to recognize, a creative art and an art of living. And she makes us realize the essential debt that literature and intellectual culture owe to it.

The gifts and qualities she shows here are not merely sympathetic observation and insight and retentive piety; she is supremely intelligent, and we can see that the intelligence that serves her so well as a novelist is informed by wide knowledge and trained. She had been a distinguished intellectual long before she became a novelist and the novelist benefited. We see it, this intelligence of the supremely qualified *novelist* in what, for want of a less rebarbative word, we may call her sociology—an impressive aspect of her strength in *Adam Bede* as in her other novels. We have it, for instance, here:

. . . the picture we are apt to make of Methodism in our imagination is not an amphitheatre of green hills, or the deep shade of broad-leaved sycamores, where a crowd of rough men and weary-hearted women drank in a faith which was a rudimentary culture, which linked their thoughts with the past, lifted their imagination above the sordid details of their own narrow lives, and suffused their souls with the sense of a pitying, loving, infinite Presence, sweet as summer to the houseless needy. It is too possible that to some of my readers Methodism may mean nothing more than low-pitched gables up dingy streets, sleek grocers, sponging preachers, and hypocritical jargon—elements which are regarded as an exhaustive analysis of Methodism in many fashionable quarters. That would be a pity, for I cannot pretend that Seth and Dinah were anything else than Methodists—not, indeed, of that modern type which reads quarterly reviews and attends in chapels with pillared porticoes, but of a very old-fashioned kind. They believed in present miracles, in instantaneous conversions, in revelations by dreams and visions. ...

As sociologist and social historian she is scrupulously precise. We see this in old Lisbeth who, belonging to an earlier generation than her sons, belongs also to an earlier world. The society in which she was formed was even more locally confined than that of the book. This is apparent in her speech—the dialect as she uses it is much less modified by contact with common educated English, and she is quite illiterate. Moreover, her superstitiousness is significant. She represents that pagan England which persisted through so many centuries of Christianity. But we are not *told about* her; she is presented in action and precise detailed living.

So with George Eliot's psychological insight, and her powers of rendering it. It is in the first place a native intelligence which cannot be distinguished from imaginative sympathy, but in such characteristic passages as this we can see the strength she derived from her intellectual culture:

Was there a motive at work under this strange reluctance of Arthur's which had a sort of backstairs influence, not admitted to himself? Our mental business is carried on much in the same way as the business of the State: a great deal of hard work is done by agents who are not acknowledged. In a piece of machinery too, I believe there is often a small unnoticeable wheel which has a great deal to do with the motion of the large obvious ones.

The novelist who wrote that was not in need of instruction from modern psychologists. It points forward to *Felix Holt*, *Middlemarch*, and *Daniel Deronda*. What is extraordinary is that the author of these intellectual novels of educated and sophisticated life (and the corresponding comprehensive 'sociology' is all there) should have been also the author of *Silas Marner*, that classic (Wordsworthian *and* Shakespearian) of the basic human simplicities in a traditional rural community of the days of the pack-horse.

The later novel immediately in view for us as we read *Adam Bede*, annunciatory as this is of George Eliot's later works in general, is *The Mill on the Floss*. The Poysers and their circle become the Dodsons and the tribe of kindred. We no longer feel there, as we do in *Adam Bede*, that the rural drama and its setting are seen from the metropolitan point of view. The idealizing and softening elements are gone. There is an immediacy of the author's own intimate experience—the living reality of a child's vision and reaction—in the presentment. At the same time the informing intelligence strikes one as anthropological rather than as being inclined to indulgent piety. But the cognizance taken of society in the book as a whole is less inclusive than in *Adam Bede*.

IV

THE EUROPEANS[1]

I HAVE recorded elsewhere the conviction that *The Europeans* is a masterpiece—one that, like *Hard Times*, has gone without recognition because of its virtues as a work of art: it is wholly and intensely significant, and the accepted ideas about 'the novel' induce blindness towards such virtues. *The Europeans* is 'slight'— that seems to have been the general verdict (William James's concurrence in which the author took especially hard). And it is true that Henry James's touch in what must be admitted to be a short novel is light, and that the mode belongs decidedly to comedy. But that is not to say that a light touch cannot be sure or comedy profound, or that a serious burden cannot be conveyed in two hundred pages. The liveliness, which ought surely to have been found attractive, lends itself to illustration, but the stress must fall on the closeness with which the interest is organized: I have called *The Europeans* a 'moral fable' because a serious intention expresses itself in so firm and clear an economy of organization, and the representative significance of every element in the book is so insistent.

What we have, in fact, is a comparative inquiry, enacted in dramatic and poetic terms, into the criteria of civilization, and the possibilities—a kind of inquiry that issues out of a radical bent of preoccupation engendered in James by his peculiar life and history. He is peculiarly qualified to give us the interplay of different traditions, and, his being a profoundly serious mind, the upshot of the interplay as he presents it transcends the vindication of one side against the other, or the mere setting forth of the for and against on both sides in a comedy of implicit mutual criticism. The informing spirit of the drama is positive and constructive: James is unmistakably feeling towards an ideal possibility that is neither Europe nor America.

[1] Reprinted from *Scrutiny*, December 1947.

At the opening of the book it might appear that New England was to be the subject as well as the scene—unsophisticated and provincial New England presented through the surprised eyes of the visiting European cousins, whose experience of a riper world was to provide a critical irony, sometimes more and sometimes less indulgent. But it becomes immediately apparent that the criticism is not going to preclude a good deal of strongly positive appreciation. It becomes further apparent, in due course, that we have to make a radical distinction between the two Europeans—that they stand for different things: they have, in their symbolic capacities, different—even conflicting—values.

Felix, who of the pair, is in speech and attitude, very much the less critical and the more appreciative of New England, actually constitutes, by his dramatic and poetic part in the fable, by far the more damaging criticism. The note of his report, when he comes back to his sister in the hotel at Boston from his visit, 'among the meadows and woods', to the home of the Wentworths ('he had found that the big unguarded door stood open with the trustfulness of the golden age'), is enchantment:

'Is it handsome—is it elegant?' asked the Baroness. Felix looked at her a moment, smiling. 'It's very clean! No splendours, no gilding, no troops of servants; rather straight-backed chairs. But you might eat off the floors, and you can sit down on the stairs.'

'That must be a privilege. And the inhabitants are straight-backed too, of course.'

'My dear sister!' cried Felix, 'the inhabitants are charming.'

'In what style?'

'In a style of their own. How shall I describe it? It's primitive; it's patriarchal; it's the *ton* of the golden age.'

'And have they nothing golden but their *ton*? Are there no symptoms of wealth?'

'I should say there was wealth without symptoms. A plain homely way of life; nothing for show, and very little for—what shall I call it?—for the senses; but a great *aisance*, and a lot of money, out of sight, that comes forward very quietly for subscriptions to institutions, for repairing tenements, for paying doctor's bills; perhaps even for portioning daughters.'

But, pressed by Eugenia, Felix has to admit that the inhabitants are not gay:

'They are sober; they are even severe. They are of a pensive cast; they take things hard. I think there is something the matter with them; they have some melancholy memory or some depressing expectation. It's not the epicurean temperament.'

It is Gertrude, the younger daughter, who, as her case becomes plain to us, turns this perception of Felix's into a strong criticism of the Puritan ethos. She is 'restless', she is difficult and unsettled— that, in the family, is her recognized character; and there is an agreement to assume that she will marry Mr Brand, who, earnest young Unitarian minister and professional representative of the cult of duty and responsibility, 'understands' her and will be a steadying influence. On the bright spring morning on which Felix calls and finds her alone to receive him in the Wentworth home, she has with characteristic 'oddity' first sent her sister Charlotte off, puzzled, to church without her, and then declined to follow with Mr Brand, who has called expressly to take her. Putting down a volume of *The Arabian Nights*, she goes to the door, and beholds, as it seems to her, 'the Prince Camaralzaman standing before her'. She gives Felix, with a glass of wine, the slice of cake that Charlotte had indicated as a proper refreshment to be offered to Mr Brand. The *tête-à-tête* with Felix contrasts amusingly and significantly with those in which, earlier in the same chapter, Mr Brand and, before that, Charlotte was the other party.

The advent of Felix is decisive. Gertrude (who 'had never seen a play in her life') now knows beyond question that she will never marry Mr Brand; and she can henceforth be fully explicit, at any rate with herself, in associating her refusal of the family prescription for her restlessness with her rejection of the Wentworth moral habit. 'Why do they try and make me feel guilty?' she asks. And, her 'difficult temperament' being in question:

'Why do you call it difficult? It might have been easy, if you had allowed it. You wouldn't let me be natural. I don't know what you wanted to make of me. Mr Brand was the worst.'

Charlotte at last took hold of her sister. She laid her two hands upon Gertrude's arm. 'He cares so much for you,' she almost whispered.

Gertrude looked at her an instant; then kissed her. 'No, he does not,' she said.

E

Felix Young's quite unbellicose triumph is complete. He not only marries Gertrude and takes her off with him out of the moral climate where she can never thrive. His presence acts as a general solvent of the constrictions and self-deceptions that go with the too habitually braced and anxious conscience. Charlotte is made to feel that, if she constantly watches Mr Brand, it isn't purely out of concern for his success with Gertrude, and Mr Brand to feel that it wouldn't be unpleasant to him, or unsuitable, if Charlotte really were (as Felix suggests she is) interested in him on her own account. Owing, in fact, to Felix, Charlotte and Mr Brand find their happiness in one another.

There is no mystery about Felix Young's representative value: it is given in his name. He stands for the opposite of the puritanic temperament and attitude to life. One must hasten to add that, if his face 'was not at all serious, yet it inspired the liveliest confidence', and rightly; for the happy nature that he expresses with such irresistible spontaneity is also good. 'He was so bright and handsome and talkative that it was impossible not to think well of him; and yet it seemed as if there was something almost impudent, almost vicious—or as if there ought to be—in a young man being at once so joyous and so positive.' This is Mr Wentworth's point of view. As he registers, Felix, for all his happy vivacity, is no lightweight; he is in fact morally irresistible: 'It is to be observed that while Felix was not at all a serious young man there was somehow more of him—he had more weight and volume and resonance—than a number of young men who were distinctly serious.'—Not being afraid or distrustful of life, and being at the same time very intelligent, he has profited by a wide and varied experience: he is mature in valuation, and in understanding of human nature.

I have said that his representative value is plain. That is, there can be no doubt about the qualities he stands for. But there may be some question about the sense in which he may be said to represent Europe. What he bodies forth is an ideal possibility cherished in James's imagination. If, as he says, he is a Bohemian, he is without the Bohemian vices. He shows that there may be a person of radical responsibility who has at the same time all the virtues of the artistic temperament (for that is what his being an artist means—'The world', he says, 'will never hear of me'). 'It is beside the matter to say that he had a good conscience; for the best conscience is a sort of self-reproach, and this young man's brilliantly healthy nature spent itself in objective good intentions which were ignorant of any test save exactness in hitting their mark.'

In justification for making him a European James would no doubt have urged that an American without an experience of Europe couldn't have conceived the possibility. Felix implies a background in which it is not extravagantly original to postulate, and practise, an art of living—implies a mature civilization and a sophisticated social culture. He doesn't, any more than his sister, 'think of life as a discipline'; he is like her, not only disposed to enjoy, but qualified for refinement in enjoying, having cultivated the art. The contrast with the New England ethos is complete:

This was not Mr Wentworth's way of treating any human occurrence. The sudden irruption into the well-ordered consciousness of the Wentworths of an element not allowed for in its scheme of usual obligations, required a readjustment of that sense of responsibility which constituted its principal furniture. To consider an event, crudely and badly, in the light of the pleasure it might bring them, was an intellectual exercise with which Felix Young's American cousins were almost wholly unacquainted, and which they scarcely supposed to be largely pursued in any section of human society. The arrival of Felix and his sister was a satisfaction, but it was a singularly joyless and inelastic satisfaction. It was an extension of duty, of the exercise of the more recondite virtues . . .

The opportunities of comedy presented by the contrast in ethos are decidedly in James's line. He takes them with a master's hand. If one is to instance from so great a wealth, there is the conversation (Chapter VII) between Felix and Mr Wentworth who, without having given a positive consent—having, in fact, expressed nothing but embarrassed unwillingness—finds himself sitting for his portrait. The talk turns upon the Wentworth son:

'Clifford's situation is no laughing matter', said Mr Wentworth. 'It is very peculiar, as I suppose you have guessed.'
'Ah, you mean his love-affair with his cousin?'

Mr Wentworth stared, blushing a little. 'I mean his absence from college. He has been suspended. We have decided not to speak of it unless we are asked.'

'Suspended?' Felix repeated.

'He has been requested by the Harvard authorities to absent himself for six months. Meanwhile he is studying with Mr Brand. We think Mr Brand will help him; at least we hope so.'

'What befell him at college?' Felix asked. 'He was too fond of pleasure? Mr Brand certainly will not teach him any of those secrets!'

'He was too fond of something of which he should not have been fond. I suppose it is considered a pleasure.'

Felix gave his light laugh. 'My dear uncle, is there any doubt about its being a pleasure? *C'est de son âge*, as they say in France.'

'I should have said rather it was a vice of later life—of disappointed old age.'

Felix glanced at his uncle with lifted eyebrows, and then, 'Of what are you speaking?' he demanded, smiling.

'Of the situation in which Clifford was found.'

'Ah, he was found—he was caught?'

'Necessarily, he was caught. He couldn't walk; he staggered.'

'Oh', said Felix, 'he drinks! I rather suspected that, from something I observed the first day I came here. I quite agree with you that it is a low taste. It is not a vice for a gentleman. He ought to give up up.'

Felix prescribes the influence of a clever and charming woman, and indicates Eugenia:

'With Clifford', the young man pursued, 'Eugenia will simply be enough of a coquette to be a little ironical. That's what he needs. So you recommend him to be nice with her, you know. The suggestion will come best from you.'

'Do I understand', asked the old man, 'that I am to suggest to my son to make a—a profession of—of affection to Madame Münster?'

'Yes, yes—a profession!' cried Felix sympathetically.

'But, as I understand it, Madame Münster is a married woman.'

'Ah', said Felix, smiling, 'of course she can't marry him. But she will do what she can.'

Mr Wentworth sat for some time with his eyes on the floor; at last he got up. 'I don't think', he said, 'that I can undertake to recommend to my son any such course.' And without meeting Felix's surprised glance he broke off his sitting, which was not resumed for a fortnight.

The comedy involves, it will be seen, the difference of manners and social conventions as well as of radical ethos—Felix *is* a European. But his sister Eugenia, Baroness Münster, morganatic wife of the younger brother of the reigning prince of Silberstadt-Schreckenstein, is much more positively and representatively Europe. Her name and titles proclaim plainly enough what she stands for: a hierarchical order, and a social system at once feudal and sophisticated, involving the conventions of 'birth', status and precedence, and associating rank and title with power and material advantage. There is a suggestion of a weight of history lying oppressively on an undemocratic present.

The Baroness might be expected to find a lack of sophistication and of form in the social life of New England, and she does. This makes her tribute the more significant. The girls, she admits, are perfect ladies; 'it was impossible to be more of a lady than Charlotte Wentworth, in spite of her little village air'—though ' "as for thinking them the best company in the world", said the Baroness, "that is another thing . . ." ' In the strength of the first impression, before she has had time to be bored, she pays, embodiment of worldliness that she is, an even more significant tribute:

There were tears in her eyes. The luminous interior, the gentle tranquil people, the simple, serious life—the sense of these things pressed upon her with an overmastering force, and she felt herself yielding to one of the most genuine emotions she had ever known. 'I should like to stay here', she said. 'Pray take me in.'

And she recognizes, appreciatively, that the unworldliness of the Wentworths ('the Wentworth household seemed to her very perfect of its kind—wonderfully peaceful and unspotted; pervaded by a sort of dove-coloured freshness that had all the quietude and benevolence of what she deemed to be Quakerism') is founded upon a degree of material abundance for which, in certain matters of detail, one might have looked in vain at the little court of Silberstadt-Schreckenstein. But the most significant tribute of all is the magnitude of her defeat as she feels it—for that is her part in the fable: to suffer, in contrast with her brother, defeat, complete and unambiguous.

She has come to America with a view to making a good marriage (her morganatic status in Silberstadt-Schreckenstein being both unsatisfactory and terminable). She finds someone eminently eligible in a cousin of the Wentworths, Robert Acton, 'the man of the world of the family'. He is, by her standards too, a man of the world, and he has 'quintupled a fortune already considerable'. We are told, significantly, that 'his national consciousness has been complicated by a residence in foreign lands', and that he 'yet disliked to hear Americans abused'. He has a consciousness, then, that is central to the fable, and his valuations have a peculiar authority. He is strongly attracted by the Baroness: 'He was in love with her now', we are in due course told, '. . . and the only question with him was whether he could trust her.'

His final judgment is adverse, and its significance for us is defined with the greatest delicacy and precision. Being Robert Acton's, it is not a New England judgment, and for that reason has its force as an endorsement of New England. There is nothing narrow, provincial, or inexperienced about Acton's morality; he still goes on admiring and being attracted after the point at which he can say: 'She is a woman who will lie.' What he admires are the qualities Gertrude also, we are significantly told, admires her for. They are the qualities of the refined social civilization of which she is the representative. Those qualities involve, essentially, a very different code from that voiced with appropriate simplicity by Charlotte: 'There can surely be no good reason for telling an untruth.' For the Baroness things cannot be as simple as that. 'There were several ways of understanding her', we are told—the occasion being something she has said to her brother, concerning which she herself is 'wondering in what manner he really understood her': 'there was what she said, and there was what she meant, and there was something between the two that was neither.' The essential difference between the codes is brought out dramatically when she is detected in an inveracity that is for her simply a piece of normal social behaviour—something she does easily and naturally with a grace that constitutes her charm.

The Baroness turned her smile toward him, and she instantly felt she had been observed to be fibbing. She had struck a false note. But who were these people to whom such fibbing was not pleasing? If they were annoyed, the Baroness was equally so.

Significantly, it is Robert Acton whom she sees to be judging her here. The fib concerns him and his mother: 'He has talked to me immensely of you.' Where they touch his mother he finds such insincerities indeed displeasing—and the fib is a peculiarly inappropriate one, though the inappropriateness isn't apparent to the Baroness's kind of percipience. Much later in the drama 'he felt a downright need to tell her that he admired her and that she struck him as a very superior woman.' He reflects that 'she had conformed to the angular conditions of New England life, and she had had the tact and pluck to carry it off.'

The 'angularity' predicated here is angularity by the Baroness's criteria—criteria partly endorsed, no doubt, by Robert, 'the man of the world of the family'. But something that is unequivocally to be judged as 'angularity' by us gets a good deal of salience in the fable. We have it in the extreme form of provincial crudity in the scene (chapter XI) leading up immediately to that of the Baroness's final discomfiture: it is enacted by the two gentlemen who have driven over from Boston in a buggy.

One of them, indeed, said nothing to her; he only sat and watched, with intense gravity, and leaned forward solemnly, presenting his ear (a very large one), as if he were deaf, whenever she dropped an observation. He had evidently been impressed with the idea of her misfortunes and reverses; he never smiled. His companion adopted a lighter, easier style; sat as near as possible to Madame Münster; attempted to draw her out, and proposed every few moments a new topic of conversation.

We have it too, in the same scene, in Clifford Wentworth's exhibition of himself as decidedly not a finished man of the world. The effect is to emphasize the significance of the Baroness's defeat: in spite of the attendant 'angularity', better the New England on which she has failed so utterly to impose herself than the Europe she represents—an upshot endorsed, in his mature decision, by Robert Acton, a qualified judge along the whole scale of values.

But this head of 'angularity' must not be dismissed so simply; it covers some important discriminations that are delicately established for us. We can concur easily in the Baroness's verdict that 'Clifford, really, was crude'. But the 'pretty manners' she is proposing to teach him when she passes it engage her whole European code. And we must keep that positive code well in sight even when James himself may reasonably be taken to be making, dramatically, a critical note about the lack of form and of forms in this American social life. Here we have the Baroness's first appearance at the Wentworths':

> They were all standing round his sister, as if they were expecting her to acquit herself of the exhibition of some peculiar faculty, some brilliant talent. Their attitude seemed to imply that she was a kind of conversational mountebank, attired, intellectually, in gauze and spangles. This attitude gave a certain ironical force to Madame Münster's next words. 'Now this is your circle', she said to her uncle. 'This is your *salon*. These are your regular habitués, eh? I am so glad to see you all together.'
>
> 'Oh', said Mr Wentworth, 'they are always dropping in and out. You must do the same.'

This, we may feel, is unmistakably a point scored against 'angularity'. Yet it is significant that the criticism (if we are to take it as such) associates very intimately with that made by the Baroness herself, when she says to Acton: 'in this country, you know, the relations of young people are so extraordinary that one is quite at sea. They are not engaged when you would quite say they ought to be.' And this, we feel, is not something we have to take as simply a point scored against New England. To set against the Baroness's criticism we have the appreciative notes with which her brother, registering the same social characteristics, takes stock of the recognition that 'he had never before found himself in contact so unrestricted with young unmarried ladies':

> He had known, fortunately, many virtuous gentlewomen, but, it now appeared to him that in his relations with them (especially when they were unmarried), he had been looking at pictures under glass. He perceived at present what a nuisance the glass had been—how it perverted and interfered, how it caught the reflexion of other objects and kept you walking from side to side.

It is here that we have to consider Robert's sister, Lizzie Acton, and her value in the scheme of the fable. The Baroness marks her at the introductory meeting with the family as 'very much more [than the Wentworth daughters] what we have been accustomed to think of as the American type'. And we are told later that the Baroness 'disliked this little American girl'. 'Lizzie struck her as positive and explicit almost to pertness; and the idea of combining the apparent incongruities of a taste for housework and the wearing of fresh, Parisian-looking dresses suggested the possession of a dangerous energy.' Such a 'little girl', even if extremely pretty, should have been insignificant, but somehow Lizzie unmistakably isn't. It avails the Baroness nothing to reflect that American girls have no manners; she has to pay Lizzie the tribute of dislike and a strong sense of irritation. The ground is, 'not an aspiration on the girl's part to rivalry, but a kind of laughing, childishly mocking indifference to the results of comparison'. This is what the Baroness cannot forgive. It insinuates doubt into the 'feeling of almost illimitable power' given her by 'the sense . . . that the good people about her had, as regards her remarkable self, no standard of comparison at all'. And in fact it is to be the irony of her defeat that she should have to see this as a matter of the helplessness of her advantages in the face of people who, having 'no standard', fail to recognize them:

If she could have done something at the moment, on the spot, she would have stepped upon a European steamer and turned her back, with a kind of rapture, upon that profoundly mortifying failure, her visit to her American relations. It is not exactly apparent why she should have termed this enterprise a failure, inasmuch as she had been treated with the highest distinction for which allowance had been made in American institutions. Her irritation came, at bottom, from the sense, which, always present, had suddenly grown acute, that the social soil on this big, vague continent was somehow not adapted for growing those plants whose fragrance she especially inclined to inhale, and by which she liked to see herself surrounded—a species of vegetation for which she carried a collection of seedlings, as we may say, in her pocket. She found her chief happiness in the sense of exerting a certain power and making a certain impression and now she felt the annoyance of a rather wearied swimmer who, on nearing shore to land, finds a smooth straight wall of rock when he had counted upon a clean firm beach. Her power, in the American air, seemed to have lost its prehensile attributes; the smooth wall of rock was insurmountable.

That is the account Madame Münster gives herself. But it is not for nothing that her sense of utter defeat, at the bitterest moment, should be focused upon Lizzie Acton, who, for us, represents something quite other than any mere lack, limitation, or barrenness in America. In the scene of Madame Münster's final discomfiture, when she already knows that Robert Acton has decided against her, the cruellest blow comes when she is told, to her utter surprise, that Clifford is to marry Lizzie—Clifford whom, acting on the principle that 'a prudent archer has always a second bowstring', she had been, with confident and complacent unawareness, favouring with her charm. This disconcerting shock is what the formlessness of New England manners had been preparing for her.

'Formlessness', quite clearly, is not to be our own summing-up. Lizzie Acton belongs to this society, and there is a good deal else about it too that, reflecting on our response to James's art, we find ourselves recognizing for positive valuation. The 'formlessness' beyond question comprises some angularity, but, in sum, it affects us as an admirable naturalness. We see that James largely approves of the social order that enables young men and girls to mix with such innocent freedom—for it *is*, for all its informality, an order, embodying a number of positive values: he associates freedom with a habit of sincerity and mutual respect in personal relations though he notes also a timidly helpless lack of responsibility towards the young on the part of the senior world.

But perhaps it would be better not to refer, in this way, to James himself. When we elicit judgments and valuations from the fable—which is perfectly dramatic and perfectly a work of art—we don't think of them as coming from the author. It is a drawback of the present kind of commentary that it tends in some ways to slight this quality of art, this creative perfection; it doesn't suggest the concrete richness and self-sufficiency of the drama, or the poetic subtlety of the means by which the discriminations are established. No instancing can convey the variety and flexibility of these means; one illustration must suffice to suggest the delicacy and precision that characterize them everywhere. The Wentworths, after the Baroness's introductory call, are discussing how she is to be accommodated:

'She will be very comfortable here', said Charlotte, with something of a housewife's pride. 'She can have the large north-east room. And the French bedstead', Charlotte added, with a constant sense of the lady's foreignness.

'She will not like it', said Gertrude, 'not even if you pin little tidies all over the chairs.'

'Why not, dear?' asked Charlotte, perceiving a touch of irony here, but not resenting it.

Gertrude had left her chair; she was walking about the room; her stiff dress, which she had put on in honour of the Baroness, made a sound upon the carpet. 'I don't know', she replied. 'She will want something more—more private.'

'If she wants to be private she can stay in her room', Lizzie Acton remarked.

Gertrude paused in her walk, looking at her. 'That would not be pleasant', she answered. 'She wants privacy and pleasure together.'

Robert Acton began to laugh again. 'My dear cousin, what a picture!'

Charlotte had fixed her serious eyes upon her sister; she wondered whence she had suddenly derived these strange notions. Mr Wentworth also observed his younger daughter.

'I don't know what her manner of life may have been', he said; 'but she certainly never can have enjoyed a more refined and salubrious home.'

Gertrude stood there looking at them all. 'She is the wife of a Prince', she said.

'We are all princes here', said Mr Wentworth; 'and I don't know of any palace in this neighbourhood that is to let.'

What we have to notice here is how the attitude towards Mr Wentworth shifts as we pass from his first observation to his retort, and in shifting makes one of James's essential discriminations. Both utterances have a distinctively American note. The earlier one illustrates James's debt to the Dickens of *Martin Chuzzlewit*. When a wooden house 'eighty years old' is thus exalted we can't mistake the intention; we know that we are to feel an ironical amusement at a characteristic American complacency characteristically expressed, and that the nicely chosen adjectives, 'refined' and 'salubrious', register a critical irony induced in the observer by certain elements of the native ethos, the speaker being unironically solemn. But the retort is quite another matter: it exemplifies a characteristic American humour that reminds us of Mark Twain—the critical irony has changed direction. We perceive that Mr Wentworth at this point has his creator's backing and, opposed as he is here to the Baroness, stands for an American democracy that James offers with conviction (his art tells us—and it is that alone we are reporting on) as an American superiority. James's right to count on a responsiveness that will qualify the reader to take such signals duly has been established by the sensitive precision, the closeness of organization combined with flexibility, of the art everywhere.

The 'democracy' that James endorses gets its definition in the whole dramatic poem. He may be said to be engaged in defining it when he is dealing, in the ways discussed above, with the aspects of New England society that strike the Baroness as provincial crudity and formlessness; for what he approves of in the manners and social habits of the Wentworths and Actons clearly belongs to the spirit of 'We are all princes here'. With this spirit he would like to associate (and the association is effected by his art) the Wentworth virtues of sincerity and moral refinement—virtues ideally, his art implies, separable from the restrictive aspects of Puritanism. And he also values very highly, among the qualities that go with the Puritan heritage, that steady underlying seriousness which is defined by contrast when the Baroness, in her last interview with Mrs Acton, shrinks from the matter-of-factness with which that old gentlewoman refers to her own imminent end ('The Baroness hated to be reminded of death'). This seriousness, it is implied, has its essential part in the ethos of the ideal civilization.

The respects in which, for all its indispensable virtues, James finds New England lacking are suggested by the symbolic parlour into which Felix, calling for the first time, is led by Gertrude: it is 'a high, clean, rather empty-looking room'. (Imagery of this poetic kind, arising with inevitable naturalness in the presentment of the drama, plays a great part in the definition of theme and attitude.) The Baroness, accommodated by Mr Wentworth with a smaller house across the way for her own occupation, tries to relieve the emptiness—'the little white house was pitifully bare'—

by disposing shawls and other draperies (she 'had brought with her to the New World a copious provision of costumes') over the chairs and sofas and mantel-shelves and by hanging curtains: the symbolism needs no explaining. But even the Baroness herself, as she gets ready to depart, sees them as vulgar irrelevancies: '*Bonté divine*, what rubbish! I feel like a strolling actress; these are my properties.'

It is not the Baroness, but her brother Felix, who represents the important things for lack of which James's New England has to figure as 'rather empty-looking'. And this is the point at which to complete with a corrective addition the account given earlier of his significance as an artist. It is true that he is not a Roderick Hudson; he is not Creative Genius—he stands for an attitude towards life and for the un-Puritanic 'Bohemian' virtues. But he stands too for a conception of art and of its function in a civilized community—that function of which the Wentworths (Gertrude had never seen a play) are so sadly unaware. *The Europeans*, in fact, is closely related in theme and pre-occupation to the novel called after Roderick Hudson—James's first, which is less essentially a study of creative genius than its title implies.

What this account of *The Europeans* hasn't suggested is the extraordinarily dramatic quality of the book. I use the word 'dramatic' here in its most obvious sense: *The Europeans* could be very readily adapted for performance. The dialogue—and the action never departs far from dialogue—is all admirable 'theatre', and the whole is done in scenes and situations that seem asking to be staged. The whole, too, in its astonishing economy, is managed with the art of a master dramatist. That culminating twelfth chapter, in which the various constituents of the comedy of personal relations are brought together in a *dénouement*, rivals the admired and comparable things of Shakespeare and Molière.

In the theatre, of course, a large part of the subtler and essential imagery and symbolism by means of which the profounder pre-occupations are engaged would be lost. All the same, much of the symbolism is obvious enough in its naturalness and felicity. To the instances already mentioned I will add that of the three houses: the Wentworths', the Actons', and that occupied by the Baroness, each expressing its occupants. The Baroness's is embllished with her 'curtains, cushions and gimcracks', and has the studio improvised by Felix attached. The Actons' differs from the Wentworths' in being just such a one as the Baroness would have liked to possess: it is the appropriate dwelling of a cultivated and wealthy man who knows the larger world and who—a point for the reader's appreciation if not for the Baroness's—has yet decided to remain an American.

Rich as *The Europeans* is in symbolic and poetic interest, deep and close as is its organization as fable and dramatic poem, it can still be read straightforwardly as novel of manners and social comedy. This may help to explain why its distinction has escaped notice. Jane Austen's novels are known as novels of manners, and, high as her conventional reputation stands, the qualities that make her a great artist have commonly been ignored. Her name comes up naturally and properly here. For in *The Europeans* it is pretty clearly from Jane Austen that James descends; what he offers is a development in the line of *Emma* and *Persuasion*.

V

WHAT MAISIE KNEW[1]

I AGREE with Mr Bewley in setting a very high value on *What Maisie Knew*, the work, of those he discusses, in which I am most interested. Nevertheless I find myself protesting vehemently against his treatment of it. In fact the *What Maisie Knew* he offers us is not the *What Maisie Knew* I admire, and I am convinced that it is not James's. The parallel that Mr Bewley proposes with *The Turn of the Screw* seems to me wholly invalid, and in the course of making it out he falsifies, I think, both his terms.

I am not myself much interested in the famous thriller, and such attention as I now give it is wholly incidental to the defence of *What Maisie Knew*. Not that I don't think *The Turn of the Screw* a success in its way. It achieves perfectly what James aimed at. It is a triumph, conceived in a spirit that Poe might have applauded, of calculating contrivance, and I cannot see why so much heavy weather should have been made of interpreting it as notoriously has been—even if James hadn't told us so plainly in the Preface the nature of the aim and the calculation.

For Mr Bewley, of the two tales, *The Turn of the Screw* might almost seem to be the major concern. It is in the interest of his version of that story that he makes out the version of *What Maisie Knew* against which I protest.

The whole meaning of *The Turn of the Screw* revolves around the question of whether the children are innocent or have been corrupted. But without resorting to evidence from another novel, *What Maisie Knew*, the question seems to me unanswerable. Appearance and reality have been separated in *The Turn of the Screw* to just this appalling extent. It is almost impossible to bring the problem of evil to a particular or significant focus because of this separation.

[1] Reprinted from *Scrutiny*, Summer 1950. Mr Bewley invited me to elaborate certain dissentient remarks of mine on his essay, later included— with this 'Disagreement'—in his book *The Complex Fate* (London: Chatto & Windus, 1952).

Unless at the level of the play on the nerves of a Christmas ghost-story, I find nothing appalling about *The Turn of the Screw*, though on the other hand, I can't doubt that James means us to believe the children corrupted. The 'ambiguity' that Mr Bewley examines as 'a destructive foray into the grounds for moral judgment'—as demanding 'that kind of attention which a work of art ought not to require'—is created, it seems to me, by Mr Bewley himself, and I find the ingenuity of the creating, the way in which he arrives at his 'evoked' demons, with the odd elusive status he attributes to them, astonishingly perverse. The actual inferiority of *The Turn of the Screw* is a less interesting affair than that which we are asked to contemplate.

If it is 'impossible to bring the problem of evil to a particular or significant focus' in *The Turn of the Screw*, that is because, in that story, 'evil' had no particular significance for James. When he tells us, in the Preface, that Peter Quint and Miss Jessel are not 'ghosts' at all, that is not by way of making it possible for us to believe (which is Mr Bewley's suggestion) that the bodily valet and governess might very well have been quite unsinister. He has already told us that 'this perfectly ... irresponsible little fiction is a piece of ingenuity pure and simple, of cold artistic calculation, an *amusette* to catch those not easily caught', and he is explaining how his *ad hoc* inventions, Peter Quint and Miss Jessel, have the function of producing a given kind of effect:

> They would be agents, in fact: there would be laid on them the dire duty of causing the situation to reek with the air of Evil.

The nature of his interest here in Evil he makes perfectly plain:

> Portentous evil—how was I to save that, as an intention on the part of my demon-spirits, from the drop, the comparative vulgarity, inevitably attending throughout the whole range of possible brief illustration, the offered example, the imputed vice, the cited act, the limited deplorable presentable instance? To bring the bad dead back to life for a second round of badness is to warrant them as indeed prodigious, and to become hence as shy of specifications as of waiting anti-climax.

Peter Quint, then, and Miss Jessel are the consistently bad

ghosts of bad persons—James is explicit about it (if that were necessary). Again:

What, in the last analysis, had I to give the sense of? Of their being, the haunting pair, capable, as the phrase is, of everything—that is, of exerting, in respect to the children, the very worst action small victims so conditioned might be conceived as subject to.

But though James would seem to leave us in no doubt as to the status he intends for the 'haunting pair' as actors in the drama, and agents of portentous evil, he nevertheless doesn't care what we conceive the evil to be, so long as we feel the situation to 'reek with the air' of it. He has no particular vision or felt significance pressing for definition. His idea is to trick us into generating for ourselves the dire 'significance' that—where these things are in question—we find most congenial:

Only make the reader's general vision of evil intense enough, I said to myself—and that already is a charming job—and his own imagination, his own sympathy (with the children) and horror (of their false friends) will supply him quite sufficiently with all the particulars. Make him *think* the evil, make him think it for himself, and you are released from weak specifications.

Mr Bewley, with so many other readers, justifies James's reckoning. And yet James, I am sure, would have been surprised at the perversity that focuses the evil, not in the 'haunting pair', but in the governess. And Mr Bewley, we know, has not been alone in doing that. For this perversity (may I say?) I see no real excuse; but for an explanation why it should have been possible we can invoke, I think, the quality that makes *The Turn of the Screw* so limited in interest—the story has no ponderable significance; it is a mere thriller: 'my values', says James, 'are positively all blanks save so far as an excited horror, a promoted pity, a created expertness . . . proceed to read into them more or less fantastic figures'. A non-significant thriller, done, nevertheless, with the subtlety of the great master, will naturally tend to escape recognition for what it is, and to get its subtlety accepted by some admirers of James as being of another order—the servant, that is, of some intended significance: hence ingenuities of interpretation and the discovery of radical ambiguities.

F

All the same I am very much surprised that Mr Bewley should be still able to think Mr Edmund Wilson's interpretation worth invoking in support. For when the 'unfortunate emphasis on the reality of the ghosts' has been dealt with, what is left? Since, as critics have pointed out—e.g. A. J. A. Waldock and (see *Partisan Review* for February 1949) Oliver Evans—Mrs Grose, the house-keeper, recognizes the dead valet in the highly specific description of the sinister intruder given by the governess, who had never before heard of Peter Quint, it is hard so see why Mr Bewley should go on explaining the apparitions as somehow 'evoked' by the governess in consequence of her alleged infatuation with her master. Or rather, one can see that his 'evoked', and the corresponding odd status attributed to the 'demons', represents Mr Bewley's attempt to accept, at the same time, both Edmund Wilson's theory and the conclusive criticism of it. But I have to insist that Mr Bewley himself has invented that equivocal status, and the kind of ambiguity or trickery with which he credits James.

From Edmund Wilson he takes over too that remarkable mis-representation of the 'authority' that James, in the Preface, tells us he has given the governess. It hadn't occurred to James that he might be taken to be encouraging a view of the governess that credits her with a capacity for mesmeric moral bullying. All he means (as Oliver Evans points out) is that he has invested her with authority for the reader, who will know that he is to trust her implicitly.

But the refutation of Mr Bewley's reading of *The Turn of the Screw* doesn't depend on anything that James *tells* us. We need only, without distorting preconceptions, read the story itself. Mr Bewley will not mind my saying that his *parti pris* finds major support in an ignorance of English possibilities that he shares with Mr Wilson. Elaborating his case against the governess he says:

One can study his method at its absolutely representative level in Chapter II, in which she receives the letter from Miles's headmaster, saying that the boy is dismissed from his school. Neither the governess nor ourselves ever know the facts of the case, and there is no reason for magnifying the incident into an incriminating episode. Mr Edmund Wilson has rightly remarked in his essay, *The Ambiguity of Henry*

James, that the governess 'colours' the dismissal 'on no evidence at all, with a significance somehow sinister'.

But James, by the time he wrote the story, was Englishman enough to know that no English headmaster would have dared to expel a boy—and a boy belonging to a family of a distinguished 'County' standing—without being prepared to substantiate against him as grave a charge as the governess divines from the letter.

With no evidence to go on except an extremely ambiguous letter, and with a great deal to contradict her, the governess is yet able in an incredibly short space to present Miles as, in all probability, vicious. . . .

The evidence of the letter, for an English reader, must tell very heavily indeed; and as for the 'great deal that contradicts' it, there we have James's theme under the aspect that answers to Mr Bewley's general formula: the conflict between appearance and reality. The children look so angelically good, but their very 'innocence', in its sustained imperturbability, is a measure of their corruption. That is the peculiar horror (the thrill focused in the brave governess's agonized sense of isolation and helplessness) that James intends as the note of *The Turn of the Screw*.

We have the note sharply enough defined in the scene in which Miles deliberately—it is unmistakable—turns on his 'innocence' with special intensity and holds the governess entranced while he performs on the piano, with the result that she forgets to keep watch on Flora, who is thus enabled to slip away and keep an assignation with the female 'demon', Miss Jessel. The 'innocent' charm of the boy is really poised and sinister calculation, the antithesis of child-like: that is what unquestionably (it seems to me) we are meant to feel. As for Flora's depravity, the housekeeper (will Mr Bewley argue that she is bullied into it?) bears fully explicit testimony to that in her talk with the governess after the scene by the lake.

The attempt to establish a parallel doesn't, then, generate light: I hope I have said enough about *The Turn of the Screw* to enforce that judgment. But it is the consequences, or concomitants, of that attempt for *What Maisie Knew* that I care about. That Mr Bewley should stultify (as I see it) James's intention by preserving the innocence of Miles and Flora doesn't trouble me much, so little being at stake; but when he projects Evil into *What Maisie Knew* I brace myself for a stern repelling action. For with 'portentous evil' (to use James's own phrase) James is not at all concerned in that masterpiece. With squalor, yes; but that is another matter. The tone and mode of *What Maisie Knew*—this is what one has to insist on—are those of an extraordinarily high-spirited comedy. The comedy doesn't exclude pathos, that is true; but the pathos bears no relation to that of *The Turn of the Screw*. It is no more the pathos of innocence assailed or surrounded by *evil* than the distinctive pathos of the early part of *David Copperfield* is that.

This comparison has point, for the idea, the treatment—and how do we distinguish from theme here?—of *What Maisie Knew* would pretty obviously not have been conceived by James if he hadn't read *David Copperfield*. It was in Dickens that he found the tip that taught him how he might deal, in this kind of comedy, with his moral and emotional intensities—those to which he was moved by his glimpses of late Victorian Society. It is not too much to say that he had at times been horrified by these glimpses: there is a letter of the 'eighties in which, shocked by a peculiarly repellent scandal of the day, he prophesies for Great Britain an equivalent (it would appear) of the French Revolution. The note of moral horror is to be found in *A London Life* (1888), where the horror is registered in the innocent consciousness of Laura, the nubile American girl who has to watch the career of her married sister, the Society beauty, in the fastest London *beau monde*, a career resembling Maisie's mamma's. But over against Laura is her friend, old Lady Davenant, who, far from registering moral horror, takes a Regency attitude towards the scandals. James's own attitude has enough of her in it to produce the witty and satirical treatment in which *A London Life* relates closely to *What Maisie Knew*. He suggests, however, in the story, a third attitude besides Laura's and Lady Davenant's. We have it when Laura asks herself:

Was she wrong after all—was she cruel by being too rigid? ... It was not the first time the just measure seemed to slip from her hands as she became conscious of possible, or rather of very actual differences of standard and usage. On this occasion Geordie and Ferdie asserted themselves, by the mere force of lying asleep upstairs in their little cribs, as on the whole the just measure.

This hint is developed in *What Maisie Knew*; the hint that the criterion of judgment must be the consequences for the children. Instead of developing it in *A London Life* he takes the opportunity for satiric humour offered by the pair of hearty and insensitive cubs, who are obviously going, not to suffer, but to belong happily and whole-heartedly to their class and kind.

The next story to consider when we are inquiring into the genesis of *What Maisie Knew* is *The Pupil* (1891), which James reprinted for the Collected Edition in the same volume as *Maisie* and with which he associated it in the Preface in an account that bears out my case. There is a clear relation between Laura's role of critical innocence in a world of moral squalor and the joint roles of the pupil, Morgan Moreen, and his unfortunate exploited tutor, Pemberton. Moreover Morgan, the precociously intelligent and incorruptibly nice child, develops a potentiality of pathos that one perhaps hardly registers as such in the brace of hearty, healthy young cubs in *A London Life*. But in *The Pupil* we no longer have the note of horror; the squalor the story deals in is not a kind to evoke any sense of 'portentous evil', and it is not sexual. Except for not paying their bills the Moreens are intensely respectable. In fact—it should be plain once the suggestion has been made—they are the Micawbers translated higher in the social scale and given a cosmopolitan setting; seen, also, too fully for what they are to be presented with a warmly sympathetic humour. James has unmistakably found his inspiration in Dickens.

When we come to *What Maisie Knew* we see that the hint now has been taken from David himself; David—'only Brooks of Sheffield'—puzzling over the banter of Mr Murdstone's friends, and David the Micawbers' lodger, the small child deprived of parents and committed to a paradoxical kind of adulthood among adults—small child and man-of-the-world:

I never can understand whether my precocious self-dependence confused Mrs Micawber in reference to my age, or whether she was so full of the subject that she would have talked about it to the very twins if there had been no one else to communicate with. . . .

So prompted, James achieves a remarkable economy, which brings at the same time a rich gain in positive values. In Maisie we may say we have Laura, the innocent girl of *A London Life*, but this time bringing to the part the innocence of actual childhood. Morgan, the 'pupil', with his precociously developed moral perception and his sensitive integrity, has come in between, contributing obvious elements to the conception of Maisie, in whom, moreover, we have once again the pathos. And James, looking back on *The Pupil* in the light of his new conception, has seen that he doesn't need Pemberton, the tutor, or any equivalent adult observer and commentator.

The whole is presented through Maisie—through her developing awareness and understanding. The thing might seem to be impossibly difficult, and it is done with almost incredible perfection.

It was to be the fate of this patient little girl to see much more than she at first understood, but also even at first to understand much more than any little girl however patient, had perhaps ever understood before. . . . She was taken into the confidence of passions on which she fixed just the stare she might have had for images bounding across the wall in the slide of a magic-lantern. Her little world was phantasmagoric—strange shadows dancing on a sheet. It was as if the whole performance had been given for her—a mite of a half-scared infant in a great dim theatre.

The performance as apprehended by the child, with her growing powers, in her phantasmagoric little world, and fitted more and more with meanings, is evoked with astonishing vividness and economy:

By the time she had grown sharper, as the gentlemen who had criticized her calves used to say, she found in her mind a collection of images and echoes to which meanings were attachable—images and echoes kept for her in the childish dusk, the dim closet, the high drawers, like games she wasn't yet big enough to play. The great strain meanwhile was that of carrying by the right end the things her father said about her mother—things mostly, indeed, that Moddle, on a glimpse of them, as if they had been complicated toys or difficult books, took out of her hands and put away in the closet. A wonderful assortment of objects of this kind she was to discover there later, all tumbled up too with the things, shuffled into the same receptacle, that her mother had said about her father.

The things that Maisie hears and sees are much of the order of those which horrified Laura in *A London Life*, but *What Maisie Knew*, in tone, is even more removed from that earliest of the three stories than *The Pupil* is. Inspired by the hint from Dickens, this un-Dickensian genius has found a way of treating without the note of horror matter from which it might seem to be inseparable so long as there was to be no sacrifice of moral intensity. And that *What Maisie Knew* is a happy example of marked moral intensity no admirer will question. But to suggest as Mr Bewley does in making his comparison that *What Maisie Knew* like *The Turn of the Screw* deals with evil is to convey an utterly false impression. It deals with moral squalor; with ugly conduct that from some approaches might very well be brought under 'depravity'; but this last term suggests a vibration that is absent from *What Maisie Knew*. Though sexual misconduct, adultery, figures so centrally, it has clearly evoked as such no noticeable moral thrill in James—no marked interest for itself, in fact; though a creative writer's moral preoccupation could hardly be more intent and penetrating than James's is here. What we are given is comedy; where adulterous relations are concerned, the comedy of 'history repeating itself':

. . . an upright scarlet plume, as to the ownership of which Maisie was instantly eager. 'Who is she?—who is she?'

But Mrs Beale for a moment only looked after them. 'The liar—the liar!'

Maisie considered. 'Because he's not—where one thought?' That was also, a month ago in Kensington Gardens, where her mother had not been. 'Perhaps he has come back', she said.

'He never went—the hound!'

That, according to Sir Claude, had been also what her mother had not done, and Maisie could only have a sense of something that in a maturer mind would be called the way history repeats itself.

'Who *is* she?' she asked again.

In its central aspect it is the comedy of a child's innocence; a comedy that, while being so high-spirited, is at the same time, and essentially, a rendering of the pathos of Maisie's situation:

> She therefore recognized the hour that in troubled glimpses she had long foreseen, the hour when—the phrase for it came back to her from Mrs Beale—with two fathers, two mothers and two homes, six protections in all, she shouldn't know 'wherever' to go.

There is no tendency to the sentimental in this pathos. Perhaps the distinctive quality of it as, in its astringent purity and strength, the extraordinarily subtle methods of James's comedy disengage it from the given situation, is better suggested by the following passage, which, with its 'bread and butter', has an obvious symbolic force:

> The next moment, however, he laughed gaily enough. 'My dear lady, you exaggerate tremendously *my* poor needs.' Mrs Wix had once mentioned to her young friend that when Sir Claude called her his dear lady he could do anything with her; and Maisie felt a certain anxiety to see what he would do now. Well, he only addressed her a remark of which the child herself was aware of feeling the force. 'Your plan appeals to me immensely; but of course—don't you see?— I shall have to consider the position I put myself in by leaving my wife.'
>
> 'You'll also have to remember', Mrs Wix replied, 'that if you don't look out your wife won't give you time to consider. Her ladyship will leave *you*.'
>
> 'Ah my good friend, I do look out!' the young man returned while Maisie helped herself afresh to bread and butter. 'Of course if that happens I shall have somehow to turn round; but I hope with all my heart it won't. I beg your pardon,' he continued to his stepdaughter, 'for appearing to discuss that sort of possibility under your sharp little nose. But the fact is I *forget* half the time that Ida's your sainted mother.'
>
> 'So do I!' said Maisie, her mouth full of bread and butter and to put him more in the right.
>
> Her protectress, at this, was upon her again. 'The little desolate precious pet!'

The strength of the pathos, as of the comedy in which it finds its felicitous definition, is the strength of the affirmation of positive values that it conveys. We have it here, the affirmation; the normative concern with a concept of an essential human goodness: ' "So do I!" said Maisie, her mouth full of bread and butter and to put him more in the right.'—The comedy of that 'So do I!' is a far subtler thing than the isolated passage might suggest. Our response, as we read the passage in its context, is neither her 'protectress's' (Mrs Wix), nor the antithesis, which would be a snigger, but something more complex.

Maisie is good. She represents a positive concept of goodness, though we have no difficulty in taking her as an actual individual little girl. Mr Bewley, of course, is far from wishing to dispute this proposition. Nevertheless I have to protest against the misrepresentation involved in his attempt at assimilating Maisie to the children of *The Turn of the Screw*: it is to me a more striking illustration of the power of a wrong-headed preconception to distort than this presentment (utterly baseless, I think) of the governess as a neurotically cunning moral bully who insinuates ideas into the mind of the unsuspecting housekeeper. He writes:

... we find that the essence of Miles's offence consists in his having lied to Mrs Grose, the housekeeper at Bly, concerning his familiarity with Peter Quint. And it is obvious that his reason for doing so is to shield Quint's and Miss Jessel's assignations from the prying curiosity of the other servants. This fact, when the governess learns of it from Mrs Grose, is interpreted by her in the blackest possible colours for little Miles. But we must remember that this 'sin' is precisely the one of which Maisie has been guilty. Surrounded by adulterous lovers, Maisie has never failed to lie for them when necessary—to lie valiantly, scrupulously, innocently.

But on what evidence does Mr Bewley assert so roundly that Maisie lies, and lies 'for' the 'adulterous lovers'? That we are to think of Miles and Flora as practising deliberate cunning, deceit, and doing so in collusion with the depraved haunting couple, I do not see how we can doubt, if we take without *parti pris* what James gives us. But it seems to me that on the evidence of the text Maisie wholly deserves the tribute that Sir Claude pays her: 'I know when people lie—and that's what I've loved in you, that you never do.' And this is the worst that she can bring against herself: 'There had been times when she had had to make the best of the impression that she was deceitful; yet she had never

concealed anything bigger than a thought.' 'For Maisie moreover', we have been told, 'concealment had never necessarily
seemed deception; she had grown up among things as to which
her foremost knowledge was that she was never to ask about
them.'

Maisie doesn't lie. And that Mr Bewley can suggest that the
'pacific art of stupidity' she does practise amounts to lying, and
that she practises it in the interest of adulterous lovers, merely
shows how disastrously infelicitous are the generalizing preoccupations that can attempt to parallel *What Maisie Knew* with
The Turn of the Screw as dealing in evil, horror, and sexual depravity. This sufficiently explicit key passage occurs early in
What Maisie Knew (it opens the second paragraph of chapter II):

The theory of her stupidity, eventually embraced by her parents,
corresponded with a great deal in her small still life: the complete vision,
private but final, of the strange office she filled. It was literally a moral
revolution accomplished in the depths of her nature. The stiff dolls on
the dusky shelves began to move their legs and arms; old forms and
phases began to have a sense that frightened her. She had a new feeling,
the feeling of danger, on which a new remedy rose to meet it, the idea
of an inner self or, in other words, concealment. She puzzled out with
imperfect signs, but with a prodigious spirit, that she had been a centre
of hatred and a messenger of insult, and that everything was bad
because she had been employed to make it so. Her parted lips locked
themselves with the determination to be employed no longer.

She acts with more and more subtlety on 'her little instinct of
keeping the peace'. We have the comedy and also 'the small
strange pathos on the child's part of an innocence so saturated
with knowledge and so directed to diplomacy'. But the 'little
instinct of keeping the peace' is more than that; it is the agent of
of a positive judgment that develops as we watch it more and
more discrimination. Hatred, malice, desire to wound or humiliate
or make uncomfortable—these are what Maisie resolves she will
not lend herself to. And we see this kind of discrimination, as it
becomes more experienced, becoming a surer and surer judgment
of personality. There are poignant conflicts when judgment
cannot square with established loyalties and pieties, but, though
these conflicts promote the growth that brings greater subtlety,

judgment never loses: that is Maisie's moral genius, which it is an extraordinary proof of James's genius to make us accept so unhesitatingly.

She exercises her 'art of stupidity' against her beloved Sir Claude, after the encounter with Ida and the Captain in Kensington Gardens. She does so, partly because 'His conversation with her mother had clearly drawn blood, and the child's old horror came back to her, begetting the instant moral contraction of the days when her parents had looked to her to feed their love of battle'; but also because she had seen the Captain to be a kind, loyal and innocent soul (whatever conventional morality might have to say about him).

These judgments, personal and real as they are, represent the only morality she can conceive, as comes out in the comedy, with its characteristic pathos, of her parting exchange with the Captain:

'Goodbye.' Maisie kept his hand long enough to add, 'I like you too'. And then supremely: 'You *do* love her?'

'My dear child—!' The Captain wanted words.

'Then don't do it only for just a little.'

'A little?'

'Like all the others.'

'All the others?'—he stood staring.

She pulled away her hand. 'Do it always!'

This particular effect gets its completion in the farewell scene with Ida at Folkestone, when Maisie is moved to 'horror', 'the first flare of anger that had ever yet lighted her face for a foe', by her mother's reception of a reference to the Captain (' "I thought you liked him."—"Him!—the biggest cad in London!" ').

The education we see Maisie undergoing is exemplified in the change of her attitude towards her old governess—that one who marries her father. In nothing does James's art, on reflection, astonish us more than in his power of giving us in so short a space (*What Maisie Knew* is only a *nouvelle*) Maisie growing up from little more than an infant to almost an adult. Miss Overmore's beauty and elegance had charmed her little pupil. Maisie continues to be under the spell, but we watch her, as she develops, becoming more and more critical, and more and more conscious of being critical, of the personality behind the beauty and the elegance. Finally, in the close of the book, the erstwhile governess being now Mrs Beale and Sir Claude's mistress, Maisie pronounces definitively against her—at the moment when Mrs Beale lays herself out to play a fully maternal role.

Mrs Wix has neither beauty nor elegance; in fact, in a Dickensian way (she fairly obviously derives from Dickensian inspiration) she is positively ugly. She represents good nature, affectionateness and maternal feelings, these virtues being altogether unrecommended by external advantages. On first acquaintance Maisie suffers a revulsion, and the significance of its being so quickly and finally overcome is emphasized by the episode of Mrs Cuddon. Maisie sees that Mrs Cuddon is kind; she divines an essential, if obscure, resemblance to the Captain. But the poor lady's ugliness is too much for the child, who repels her advances, and shudders away with a wounding obviousness.

The virtues, then, that Mrs Wix represents are solid and strongly self-recommendatory, and she represents too (unlike Mrs Cuddon, who is keeping Maisie's papa) respectability—as Mr Bewley notes. He notes it, but nevertheless he makes an attack on her respectability that is perhaps the oddest of the perversities (so they seem to me) of his treatment of *What Maisie Knew*.

Elderly, ugly, fantastic as she is, Mrs Wix falls in love with Sir Claude. The fact isn't insisted on, and it might even be possible to interpret in non-erotic terms her passionate avowal to Maisie that she 'adores' Sir Claude, although I doubt it.

And Mr Bewley talks of Mrs Wix's 'erotic infatuation'. But I venture that he finds no difficulty about interpreting in non-erotic terms Maisie's passionate avowal that she 'adores' Sir Claude—as she clearly does. It should surely be plain enough (even if we hadn't James's note to that effect) that Mrs Wix's and Maisie's 'adorations' are of the same order. Girl and woman, it is true, are both females, and Sir Claude is an attractive man, and 'erotic' in these days is a term of extensive and uncertain application. But it is surely a very odd term to apply to poor Mrs Wix's state, and the context given it by Mr Bewley adds to the emphasis with which it must be rejected.

The atmosphere of 'horror' in Maisie is one of its solid achievements, more substantial and enduring than the 'horror' of *The Turn of the Screw*, and these touches in Mrs Wix, however they are to be interpreted in other respects, add their own contribution to that atmosphere.

I, as I have said, detect no atmosphere of 'horror' in *What Maisie Knew* and I see Mrs Wix's adoration of Sir Claude sufficiently defined in such a passage as this:

He laughed back at Mrs Beale; he looked at such moments quite as Mrs Wix, in the long stories she told her pupil, always described the lovers of her distressed beauties—'the perfect gentleman and strikingly handsome'.

Sir Claude, in short, is the *beau idéal* of her romantic day-dreams, and her feeling about him is as much, and as little, 'erotic' as Maisie's, if more positively a matter of comedy—since, after all, a childish 'adoration' in her is less in place than in a child. I concede to Mr Bewley, without embarrassment, that perhaps Maisie as well as Mrs Wix is jealous of Mrs Beale.

An element of jealousy may contribute to Maisie's decision to go back to England with Mrs Wix. But I have to insist that sex, in this story, is only marginal to James's preoccupation; he shows, here, no moral feeling at all that is directed upon sex as such. The absence of such feeling is an essential condition of the kind of poignant comedy in which, in this story, his genius manifests itself. Think, for instance, of the way in which, in the closing act at Boulogne, it is conveyed to us that Sir Claude has spent the night with Mrs Beale. Preparing, in the morning, to go out for breakfast with Maisie, Sir Claude looks for his stick.

'A moment—my stick.'
But there appeared to be no stick. 'No matter, I left it—oh!' He remembered with an odd drop and came out.
'You left it in London?' she asked as they went downstairs.
'Yes—in London: fancy!'

It is in Mrs Beale's room. There is no hint here of any moral intensity directed upon sexual misconduct (the context makes that plain), or of enough interest in it as such to lead to moral judgment about it at all. The moral sense that James defines and conveys in this story is that focused in Maisie, of whom, Mr Bewley will agree, it is not paradoxical to say that, though her attitude towards Sir Claude is feminine right enough, she remains to the end uninterested in, and uncognizant of, sex. Her discriminations and judgments regard the qualities of personality and the capacities for sensitive personal relations revealed by her adults as they perform the evolutions that are so largely set off by the spring of which she remains unaware. The 'moral sense' that Maisie can't produce for Mrs Wix's satisfaction is the one that, in the world of *What Maisie Knew*, doesn't matter. The satire that plays upon it appeals for its positives to the sense defined in Maisie herself.

To come back to the drama at Boulogne: Maisie sees that Sir Claude is lying and that he is ashamed of his relations with Mrs Beale. Though she may not put it to herself so, she has divined that for Mrs Beale she figures as a mere convenience. And at this point I may remark that Mr Bewley's account of *What Maisie Knew* as a struggle for the possession of Maisie badly misrepresents the case. Maisie, for the parties with a 'claim' to her, is a burden to be shifted, or a means (if retained for a limited period) of annoying the other, or a possible convenience. In the final act at Boulogne she is for Mrs Beale a mere convenience; and we need not suspect Sir Claude, for all his playful description of himself as a born nurse, of being moved by any overbearing maternal, or paternal, passion. He is kind, he has a sense of decency and a conscience, and he likes Maisie; but he clearly has doubts about the convenience her presence in a *ménage à trois* would in sum be, as well as about the decency. The only party who may be supposed really to want Maisie is Mrs Wix, as Maisie has sufficiently ascertained—to note which fact is to complete the explanation why, when it has become plain that kindness and sense of decency will not avail to separate Sir Claude from Mrs Beale in order that he may perform his assumed duty by his stepchild, she opts for Mrs Wix.

The reason that Mr Bewley gives for that choice—it would surely have to be thought of as James's reason rather than Maisie's —is that (it being 'Maisie's mission in life to educate her elders') 'of the people struggling for possession of Maisie in the concluding chapter only poor Mrs Wix remains amenable to education'.

This suggestion seems to me to be jarringly out of resonance with the whole distinctive tone and spirit of the tale, which, for all its preoccupation with triumphant goodness, is so convincing in its realism. I see no reason at all for supposing that Mrs Wix's ' "moral sense" is capable of being educated into fineness'. She will go on in her honest muddled conventionality; affectionately admiring Maisie's 'goodness' on the one hand, and knowing, on the other, that nothing matters more than a 'moral sense' in her own sense. And perhaps—may we not reflect?—it is as well that Maisie, after the childhood that has provided us with James's comedy, should enter adolescence under that kind of respectable tutelage.

VI

THE SHADOW-LINE[1]

SOMETHING under twenty years ago I made a study of Conrad;
by which I mean that I read through his works with close
attention, and pondered and compared and (where I felt the
challenge) re-read, until I arrived at a clear understanding with
myself as to what, as they impressed me, his distinction and his
greatness were, and in what places they were most notably to be
found. Since, with some misgiving, I accepted the invitation to
address this society I have done a great deal of re-reading: I have
re-read all those things of Conrad's which I most admire and a
number of those which I admire less, and have confirmed with a
recalling glance here and there my sense that some things may be
left hereafter un-read. The upshot that I have to report, in fact, is
that my judgment of Conrad has not materially changed, and in
saying this I indicate the nature of the misgiving to which I
referred a moment ago: what I should still wish to say about
Conrad is (as I thought likely) what I said in a critique that has
long been accessible in print. Of course, I am not suggesting that
I exhausted the subject, or my interest in it, in what I have written
and published, but it seems to me that on an occasion like that
which brings us together tonight what one should try to say about
the great writer whose memory we are honouring are the central
and essential things.

While I was reflecting on the problem of getting these things
said without incurring the embarrassment of hearing myself too
obviously engaged in summarizing and re-phrasing what I had
said before, I picked up the November number of *The London
Magazine*, which billed on its cover a symposium called 'Joseph
Conrad To-day'. There, if I found no fresh light on Conrad, I

[1] Given as the Robert Spence Watson Lecture to the Literary and Philoso-
phical Society, Newcastle-upon-Tyne, December 1957, and first printed in the
Sewanee Review, April-June 1958, under the title 'Joseph Conrad'.

did at any rate find some stimulus; stimulus resulting in a confirmed sense, where my own disquisition was concerned, that
after all there might be fresh emphases, and point in offering
them.

In Mr John Wain's contribution indeed, I found the challenge
to say something I certainly shouldn't otherwise have said; it
would have seemed to me too obvious. I read this:

> In attracting an artist as big as Conrad, we, the English, had a stroke
> of luck. But of course it was more than luck. We had, in those days,
> the reputation of being a good audience, intelligent and serious enough
> to deserve the best that a great author could do. Have we still got that
> reputation? Would a modern Conrad still make that choice?

The alleged 'choice' was the choice to write in English rather
than French. But to anyone really contemplating the nature of
Conrad's greatness it must be plain that 'choice' in the sense
imputed cannot have played any such part—it must have been
plain even if Conrad himself had not assured us that there was no
choice in any sense. His self-committal to English was actually
as inevitable as if he had been born to the language—with which
he had, in fact, been acquainted, as with the literature (his father
translated Shakespeare), from boyhood. 'I had read the whole of
Shakespeare by 1880,' he once said. And in *A Personal Record* he
wrote:

> The impression of my having exercised a choice between the two
> languages, French and English, both foreign to me, has got abroad
> somehow. That impression is erroneous. . . . I have a strange and over-
> powering feeling that [English] has always been an inherent part of
> myself. English was for me neither a matter of choice nor adoption.
> The merest idea of choice had never entered my head. And as to adop-
> tion—well, yes, there was adoption; but it was I who was adopted by
> the genius of the language, which, directly I came out of the stam-
> mering stage, made me its own so completely that its very idioms, I
> truly believe, had a direct action on my temperament and fashioned
> my character.

Again, he wrote to Hugh Walpole:

> When I wrote the first words of *Almayer's Folly*, I had been already
> for years and years *thinking* in English. . . . And there are also other

G

considerations; such as the sheer appeal of the language, my quickly awakened love for its prose cadences, a subtle and unforeseen accord of my emotional nature with its genius. . . . You may take it from me that if I had not known English I wouldn't have written a line for print, in my life.

What, without the provocation supplied by Mr John Wain, would have seemed to me (as I said) too obvious to say is that, for all the unidiomatic touches and the suggestions of French (every page yields them), Conrad's English, as we read his supreme things, compels us to recognize it as that of a highly individual master, who has done his creative thinking and feeling—explored most inwardly the experience moving him to creation—in that language. It is impossible, for instance, to think of *The Shadow-Line* as translated from the French; it is equally impossible to think of it as translated into French without loss. The point I am making is that, as a writer, he had to English the relation we think of as that of the distinguished poet. He used it to bring to definition an intensely personal sense of life, and did this with a responsiveness to the finer potentialities of the language so vital and delicate that he stands among those writers whom (if we do them justice) we see as pre-eminently its maintainers.

You are decidedly not, then, giving proof of a perceptive response to the genius while you are capable of proposing a Conrad who should have been persuaded to enlist as a glory of English literature by the kind of calculation that Mr Wain imputes. That Conrad counted on becoming a great English writer, so rewarding the country for providing him with an intelligent public, seems to me improbable: gifted as he was, and strong as was his impelling vocation, he had neither the transcendent genius of D. H. Lawrence, nor the just and admirable confidence that went with it. I see him rather as devoting himself resolutely, but with misgivings, to the painful task of becoming a creative writer at all. And if we, the English, *had* in those days the reputation of being a good audience, intelligent and serious enough to deserve the best that a great author could do, we wholly and lamentably failed to justify it in respect of Conrad.

I take over Mr. Wain's 'we' because I think that we ought, with whatever apparent irrationality, to feel a disturbing sense of personal responsibility for the suffering and frustration inflicted, by neglect and unintelligence, on great writers in the past. I won't argue this conviction; the point of it seems to me plain enough. Well, Conrad, having given up the sea, was certainly committed to earning a living by his pen. He had a family to maintain and children to educate. It must be conceded that he did actually contrive to earn a living, but it was with the greatest difficulty: grind and worry were the constant conditions of his life. Yet by 1915 he had produced *Nostromo, Under Western Eyes, The Secret Agent, Chance,* and *Victory*—five major novels that we now see to be classics of English literature, besides *Typhoon* and *The Shadow-Line,* tales of novel length which, along with a number of the many shorter ones he had written, are among the finest expressions of his genius. In the years after the war he had general recognition as a living master, but living, all the same, was not made easier for him: the need for unrelaxing toil continued to drive him mercilessly, and I believe it is true to say that he died of overwork.

And we cannot flatter ourselves, 'we, the English', that he had had at any rate the consoling sense of being intelligently appreciated by a small public representing enlightened critical opinion. His fate in this respect was like Henry James's; neither of those two geniuses could at the end of his life tell himself hopefully that the critical battle had begun—that the essential things had been clearly said or were becoming commonplaces among an *élite,* so that intelligent recognition of the nature of his achievement could be counted on to prevail in due course. Conrad had very good reason for protesting against the way in which he was placed and known as a writer about the sea. *Nostromo* could pass for a story of adventure, an exciting romance of treasure and revolution in a South American republic, and nothing more. I don't think we should have had such an account of Conrad's great novel from Conrad's publisher in 1917 (I have one in front of me) if there had been any current recognition at all of the nature of its greatness. Virginia Woolf and E. M. Forster didn't pass just that kind of reductive judgment; but neither did they say about *Nostromo,* or the Conrad it represents, anything more positively intelligent. I adduce Mrs Woolf and Mr Forster because, as everyone knows, they were at the centre of the original Bloomsbury, a Bloomsbury that emerged from the war of 1914 the hardly questioned centre of the literary world—the conscious controlling centre of taste, enlightenment, and higher fashion. Mrs Woolf's sense of Conrad is to be found in the obituary article that is reprinted in *The Common Reader*, and of which we have the upshot here:

Therefore, though we shall make expeditions into the later books and bring back wonderful trophies, large tracts of them will remain by most of us untrodden. It is the earlier books—*Youth, Lord Jim, Typhoon, The Nigger of the Narcissus*—that we shall re-read in their entirety.

How much of Conrad had Mrs Woolf ever read? one can't help wondering. I myself should include *Typhoon* among his finest things, but I can't believe that a critic who puts it in that company for such a summing up really perceives its distinction. From the article by Forster that is reprinted in *Abinger Harvest* I will recall a paragraph that I quoted once in writing about Conrad:

What is so elusive about him is that he is always promising to make some great philosophic statement about the universe, and then refraining with a gruff disclaimer. . . . Is there not also a central obscurity, something noble, heroic, beautiful, inspiring half-a-dozen great books, but obscure, obscure?

And Mr Forster suggests:

that the secret casket of his genius contains a vapour rather than a jewel; and that we needn't try to write him down philosophically, because there is, in this direction, nothing to write. No creed, in fact. Only opinions, and the right to throw them overboard when the facts make them seem absurd. Opinions held under the semblance of eternity, girt with the sea, crowned with stars, and therefore easily mistaken for a creed.

I call attention again to this passage because, while I think that, in its context (from which it gets nothing like sufficient qualification), it illustrates impressively my theme of the moment, the lack of intelligent recognition suffered by Conrad to the end, I also think that one could find in his *œuvre* places that might seem to justify Forster. It points, in fact, to the truth that there are discriminations to be made; there are things of Conrad that one doesn't re-read as often as others, things in respect of which one makes distinctions between what is strong in them and what is weak, and things that one doesn't re-read at all. And it prompts me immediately to a distinction regarding Forster's own intention in that paragraph—a distinction between what may seem to be excusable in it and what must certainly be rejected:

we needn't try to write him down philosophically, because there is, in this direction, nothing to write. No creed, in fact. Only opinions, and the right to throw them overboard . . .

The whole paragraph gives 'philosophic statement about the universe' a kind of force that checks one's readiness to take up the challenge. One remembers certain prose of Conrad's. And does one in any case want 'to write him down philosophically'? Yet the passage clearly covers more ground than *can* be conceded— if Conrad is really a great writer (and Forster, involving himself, surely, in a contradiction, speaks of 'half-a-dozen great books'). Is it true that Conrad brought to his art from his experience of life and his pondering of that experience nothing more impressive in the way of basic attitude, nothing more like wisdom or pro- fundity or a great writer's insight than what is dismissible as 'only opinions'—opinions that can be dropped 'when facts make them look absurd'? I think I may fairly say, obviously not. But the questions raised by such a challenge may be profitably borne in mind.

Opinions held under the semblance of eternity, girt with the sea, crowned with stars, and therefore easily mistaken for a creed.

The immediate provocation behind such a sentence can be seen, perhaps, in some part of the prose of a tale specified by Mrs Woolf as among Conrad's best things: *Youth*. I am thinking of the account of the end of the burning *Judaea*, a passage antholo- gized by Q in the *Oxford Book of English Prose*. And it is true that Conrad does lend himself a good deal to the purposes of the anthologist.

I might, by way of duly placing the suggestion that his genius is fairly represented by his most anthologizable prose, or by the kind of noble impressiveness against which Forster directs his irony, turn to *Typhoon*. The impressiveness of that tale—beyond question, it seems to me, an impressiveness of great art—doesn't depend in the least upon the suggestion of a profound 'philosophic statement about the universe' or upon exaltations of poetic prose. It evokes with astonishing force the violence of the typhoon; nothing more remarkable in that kind has ever been done. But the essential point to make about the tale is that it is the work of a great *novelist*—a writer, that is, whose interest is centred in his human theme, and the point of whose conception depends upon the felicity and convincingness with which his individual human actors are made present to us. The tale certainly has its sublimity; yet the opening is by a master of comedy, and the art predominant there (it is in some ways suggestive of Dickens) has its essential role all the way through.

I might, I say, turn to *Typhoon*. I don't, however, because of something else I came on in that number of *The London Magazine*. In the symposium, 'Joseph Conrad To-day', there is an article by Mr Tom Hopkinson. Mr Hopkinson says, among other things, this:

One word comes before long to haunt the mind of any persistent reader of Conrad's stories—the word 'melodrama'. Why does he do it? What has he got against ordinary life? What is the purpose of all these feuds, assassinations, revolutionary plottings, these fearful disasters and betrayals—against which, it seems, only the stolid application to duty of the totally unimaginative can hope to hold 'ground'?

I shall have to leave the charge conveyed in that word 'melodrama' to be dealt with incidentally and by implication. What concerns me immediately is that closing suggestion, with its implied account of Conrad's 'creed' or 'philosophy'—for it clearly does convey an account of something more profound and stable than opinions; something that a responsive reader must feel to be implicit in the structure of values and significances communicated by Conrad's art. One doesn't, then, go to *Typhoon* if faced with enforcing one's judgment that the account is inadequate and the suggestion unjust: Captain Mac-Whirr was probably in Mr Hopkinson's mind when he formulated his suggestion. That hero (and he *is* for us a hero) is certainly stolid and unimaginative; it is hard, indeed, to disengage unimaginativeness in him from sheer unintelligence. Out of unimaginativeness (shall we say?) Captain MacWhirr steams straight into the centre of the typhoon, dismissing with contempt the 'storm-strategy' that would have taken him round it. The same 'unimaginativeness' in its positive aspects—for by an inevitability of art we are made to see it as a matter of positive qualities and capacities—takes the *Nan-Shan* triumphantly through the typhoon, and enables a handful of ordinary men to impose order on a frantic mob of coolies.

Well, it is true that the ship, the ship's company, and the tradition of the Merchant Service figure largely and significantly in Conrad's work—play an important part in the expression of his distinctive sense of human possibilities. But is it true that those possibilities as he sees and presents them are as limited as Mr Hopkinson suggests? Mr Hopkinson is more explicit than I have yet indicated. He says: 'Just as to Thomas Hobbes the civil contract is the one thing which prevents man sliding into anarchy, so to Conrad—it seems—the accepted codes and standards of behaviour are man's sole protection against bloody ruin and abandonment. Rarely indeed do we get even a glimpse (as in *The Return*) of a man trying to live by a gleam of inner truth rather than by accepted standards.' The intention is plain; it is to make the Merchant Service as represented by the *Nan-Shan* Conrad's symbol for civilized living and for the necessary conditions of the best that can be conceived as successful human life, and to suggest that anything subtler, more finely and fully human, more alive than Captain MacWhirr is irreconcilable with the symbolic Merchant Service.

Summing up, Mr Hopkinson charges Conrad with an over-simplification of man's problems in the world.

When I read this account of Conrad I thought of *The Shadow-Line*. It is central to his genius, and it might have been written to facilitate the refutation of such an account. Having made this last suggestion I withdraw it—or withdraw that way of making the point: *The Shadow-Line* is clearly something Conrad *had* to write. It comes out of experience that was intimately and urgently personal; when we read it we can't doubt that. It isn't, like *Typhoon*, by an *observer*; Conrad writes as a direct and full participant in the experience he records. *The Shadow-Line* also is a tale of novel-length—it fills a volume by itself anyway; and it too evokes a testing crisis of the seafaring life. But the young Captain, far from being an unimaginative extrovert, manifestly gives us something very close to Conrad himself, which—since the Captain tells the tale as a personal memory—is a condition of the exquisitely sensitive crispness of the prose; prose that, with all its poetic resourcefulness and its finish, keeps closely in touch with speech. One tends to think of *The Shadow-Line* as a poem, so intense is its imaginative power; but then one tells oneself again that the genius is that of a great *novelist*. The distinctive gifts that make us say this are thus manifested in the young Captain's presentment of the actors in his drama—the vividness of his evocation of them and the nature of his interest in them and of his insight into them. The interest and the insight affect us as truly belonging—belonging beyond question—to this actual young Captain, who is also most certainly a seaman and a Master Mariner. That is, *The Shadow-Line* gives us the whole and wholly-engaged Joseph Conrad—seaman by vocation, but such a seaman as could be at the same time a potential novelist by vocation too. I make this point so insistently in order to ensure proper recognition for the significance of the tale—or drama (one thinks of it as a drama because the presentment has so vivid an immediacy). For when I said that *The Shadow-Line* is central to Conrad's genius I was thinking of it as having a representative fullness of significance such as I wouldn't attribute to *Typhoon*. It is the fullness of personal engagement on Conrad's part and the accompanying fullness (which means also depth) of significance that I am insisting on.

The ship and the command are, for the young Captain, a symbol and a test: the experience in the Gulf of Siam is an ordeal, a kind of *rite de passage*; these things are plain, and indeed, explicit. But the maturity with which he emerges from the ordeal is an immensely more subtle matter than anything suggested by the idea of Master Mariner, by proof now worthy of the Red Ensign and its traditions. For the novelist recalling and recreating the experience the maturity in question is that of the whole man he was himself, conscious of complex potentialities and subtle demands on life. And whatever we conclude to be, as positive significance, the upshot of the ordeal, an 'oversimplification of man's problems in the world' may fairly be said to be just that against which the tale, of its very essence, is directed.

'Man' is represented in *The Shadow-Line*, not by a Captain MacWhirr, but by a being of the finest consciousness and the highest powers of imaginative realization—by, in fact, the potential author of *Nostromo*. Why does the young chief mate (as he is to begin with) throw up his berth? Not from ambition—the natural and proper ambition of a good seaman: that is made very plain. And the 'youth' to which we are referred by way of explanation is evoked to notably different effect from that of the 'youth' celebrated in the tale of that name (a tale much overrated, I think). Let me remind you of the exquisite opening of *The Shadow-Line*.

Only the young have such moments. I don't mean the very young. No. The very young have, properly speaking, no moments. It is the privilege of early youth to live in advance of its days in all the beautiful continuity of hope which knows no pauses and no introspection.

One closes behind one the little gate of mere boyishness—and enters an enchanted garden. Its very shades glow with promise. Every turn of the path has its seduction. And it isn't because it is an undiscovered country. One knows well enough that all mankind had streamed that way. It is the charm of universal experience from which one expects an uncommon or personal sensation—a bit of one's own.

One goes on recognising the landmarks of the predecessors, excited, amused, taking the hard luck and the good luck together—the kicks and the halfpence, as the saying is—the picturesque common lot that holds so many possibilities for the deserving or perhaps for the lucky. Yes. One goes on. And the time, too, goes on—till one perceives ahead a shadow-line warning one that the region of early youth, too, must be left behind.

This is the period of life in which such moments of which I have spoken are likely to come. What moments? Why, the moments of boredom, of weariness, of dissatisfaction. Rash moments. I mean moments when the still young are inclined to commit rash actions, such as getting married suddenly or else throwing up a job for no reason.

Is the moral of the tale that one must achieve a maturity for which the 'boredom' of the jaded, adult, settled-down routine of life must be accepted as inevitable once the 'shadow-line' has been passed and left behind; that one must learn to do without the sense of the intensity of existence characteristic of youth? Nothing so simple, I think. In fact, I don't think the tale is a simple enough kind of thing to have what can be called a 'moral', or the ordeal a simple enough kind of thing to have an easily summarizable outcome or significance. What one *can* do is to point to some of the major elements, themes, and insistences that work together in the delicate complexity of the total effect; the tale, as I suppose I've by now virtually said, being a kind of dramatic poem that communicates a meaning such as couldn't have been communicated in any other way.

A refusal to accept the loss of the 'intensity of existence', to acquiesce in 'life-emptiness'—the young mate's throwing up his berth is certainly that. Those phrases and their equivalents recur in the drama, and we note with what facts and events and symbols they seem to form special relations; in what musical development (so to speak) they play a part. That the young man's experience is to be representative—that is beautifully intimated in that opening passage. 'One knows well enough that all mankind had streamed that way.' But 'representative' is an equivocal word: this representative of 'man's' life in the world is to be such in the way only a very exceptional man can be; exceptionally conscious, exceptionally capable of experience, an exceptionally fine and adequate focus of human potentiality: we can't for a moment think of him as a less limited—however much less limited—Captain MacWhirr. Only a very exceptional man would have thrown up in that way a peculiarly comfortable berth under a peculiarly appreciative Captain. What is brought home to us in that prelusive episode at the Officers' Home, when he shows himself so comically unable to see what Captain Giles is putting under his nose, the significance (that is) of the shifty steward's irregular behaviour, is his state of something in the nature of concentration—concentration turned inwards and away from thoughts of ambition or the possibility of a command. He is possessed, in fact, by a state like that of Lawrence's characters when they find themselves faced with the question: What for? Has life, has *my* life, no more meaning to it than is promised by

a continued succession of days like those in which I have passed
out of youth, beyond the shadow-line? Can I conceivably be fulfilled in a mere *career*—days passing as they pass now, with the
prospect of professional advancement to make up for what is lost
and gone? Is *that* the meaning of life—*my* life? Is *that* living?
Questions such as these suggest the young Captain's state—a
state that is potently communicated to us. Of course, when in so
miraculous a way the command comes to him—and it is wonderful how we are made to feel the miraculousness, for him, against
that accepted day-to-day ordinariness of everything for other
people which has been evoked as a background to the ordeal—
when the command comes to him he is filled with exaltation.

A sudden passion of anxious impatience rushed through my veins
and gave me such a sense of the intensity of existence as I have never
felt before or since. I discovered how much of a seaman I was—in
heart, in mind, and, as it were physically—a man exclusively of sea
and ships; the sea the only world that counted, and the ships the test,
of manliness, of temperament, of courage and fidelity—and of love.

But we know better than to see anything final in this. It gives
us, so to speak, a piece of thematic material, and we know that we
have to watch what happens to it as the dramatic poem develops.
   There's no time for anything like a full analysis of *The Shadow-
Line* as a dramatic poem—and no need for it either. And in fact
all I should in any case wish to attempt would be a little pointing
to the kind of way in which it makes us read it when we become
aware of the nature of its concern with significance. Well, in
reading the passage I've just quoted we note that *this* kind of
ideal representation of the good seaman's vocational ethos—to
take it to begin with as just that—transcends what is given us in
Captain MacWhirr. One is inclined to say that it has another
dimension. And this way of putting it gathers courage and confidence when we come to the young Captain's first glimpse of his
ship (he is on the bridge of the steamer in which he is a passenger):

He laid his hand on my shoulder and gave me a slight turn, pointing
with his other arm at the same time.
   'There! That's your ship, Captain,' he said.
   I felt a thump in my breast—only one, as if my heart had then ceased

to beat. There were ten or more ships moored along the bank, and the one he meant was partly hidden from sight by her next astern. He said: 'We'll drift abreast her in a moment.'

What was his tone? Mocking? Threatening? Or only indifferent? I could not tell. I suspected some malice in this unexpected manifestation of interest.

He left me, and I leaned over the rail of the bridge looking over the side. I dared not raise my eyes. Yet it had to be done—and, indeed, I could not have helped myself. I believe I trembled.

But directly my eyes had rested on my ship all my fear vanished. It went off swiftly, like a bad dream. Only that a dream leaves no shame behind it, and that I felt a momentary shame at my unworthy suspicions.

Yes, there she was. Her hull, her rigging filled my eye with a great content. That feeling of life-emptiness which had made me so restless for the last few months lost its bitter plausibility, its evil influence, dissolved into a flow of joyous emotion.

At the first glance I saw that she was a high-class vessel, a harmonious creature in the lines of her fine body, in the proportioned tallness of her spars. Whatever her age and her history, she had preserved the stamp of her origin. She was one of those craft that, in virtue of their design and complete finish, will never look old. Amongst her companions moored to the bank, and all bigger than herself, she looked like a creature of high breed—an Arab steed in a string of cart-horses.

A voice behind me said in a nasty equivocal tone: 'I hope you are satisfied with her, Captain.' I did not even turn my head. It was the master of the steamer, and whatever he thought of her, I knew that, like some rare women, she was one of those creatures whose mere existence is enough to awaken an unselfish delight. One feels that it is good to be in the world in which she has her being.

We have transcended then any mere vocational ethos, any mere professional spirit of the good seaman, the ideal Master Mariner, as such. What is evoked for us is a need unknown to the Captain MacWhirrs; a need that is an urgent and inescapable fact in life, insistent on recognition as that, in full consciousness, only for the relatively exceptional—those who, in being exceptional, are qualified to be taken as representative. You know the question that gives the significance to the 'melodrama' (as the critic puts it) of *Nostromo*, the 'revolutionary plottings, the hazards, the suspenses': What do men live by and for? It is a question that is enacted in that book by half a dozen very diverse main actors. The writer who explores it there so methodically (so giving the book its shape), and in whose work it is everywhere an urgent presence, clearly himself knew it as a profound personal pre-occupation in its most radical and testing modes. For him, Master Mariner though he was, and devoted admirer of the tradition to which he belonged, the congenial and successful career in itself could not be all he asked of life—all that life must represent to be duly significant. He recognized a need that is figured in the effect on him, as he gives it, of his first sight of the ship: ' . . . she was one of those creatures whose mere existence is enough to awaken an unselfish delight. One feels that it is good to be in the world in which she has her being.'

Of course, in suggestion I simplify, if only for the moment, in making the point in this way. The passage doesn't stand by itself in Conrad's text. It is part of a complex process of evocation, intimation, and what I will call poetic definition, by which the idea and the sense of a world or realm of values—is that the right word? not really, but I use it for brevity—are conveyed; values on which the significance of life depends. Immediately, we see, in the young Captain's narrative the note we are considering blends into that of the professional seaman's specific exaltation, the delight of the first Command:

Half-an-hour later, putting my foot on her deck for the first time, I received the feeling of deep physical satisfaction. Nothing could equal the fullness of that moment, the ideal completeness of that emotional experience which had to come to me without the preliminary toil and disenchantments of an obscure career.

We now have to observe what happens to him as a seaman, to his *sense* of himself as a seaman and a Master Mariner, to his sense of his vocation as offering fulfilment of life and an answer to questions. I am thinking of that wonderful scene in the cabin, which he has entered for the first time:

I sat down in the arm-chair at the head of the table—the captain's chair, with a small tell-tale compass swung above it—a mute reminder of unremitting vigilance.

A succession of men had sat in that chair. I became aware of that thought suddenly, vividly, as though each had left a little of himself between the four walls of these ornate bulkheads; as if a sort of composite soul, the soul of command, had whispered suddenly to mine of long days at sea and of anxious moments.

'You, too!' it seemed to say, 'you too, shall taste of that peace and that unrest in a searching intimacy with your own self—obscure as we were and as supreme in the face of all the seas, in an immensity that receives no impress, preserves no memories, and keeps no reckoning of lives.'

Deep within the tarnished ormolu frame, in the hot half-light sifted through the awning, I saw my own face propped between my hands. And I stared back at myself with the perfect detachment of distance, rather with curiosity than with any other feeling, except of some sympathy for this latest representative of what for all intents and purposes was a dynasty; continuous not in blood, indeed, but in its experience, in its training, in its conception of duty, and in the blessed simplicity of its traditional point of view on life.

It struck me that this quietly staring man whom I was watching, both as if he were myself and somebody else, was not exactly a lonely figure. He had his place in a line of men whom he did not know, of whom he had never heard; but who were fashioned by the same influences, whose souls in relation to their humble life's work had no secrets for him.

This is a passage that might seem to invite quotation by a critic offering such an account of Conrad as I referred to earlier. True, this Master Mariner is less *borné* than Captain MacWhirr, whom one can hardly think of as committed to a 'searching intimacy with his own self'. Still, the self might seem, here in this passage, to be a simple one, fully in accord with that 'dynastic' conception of duty and the 'blessed simplicity of its traditional point of view'. If it could reasonably be argued that we have *here* Conrad's ethic or philosophy or normative doctrine, then he might not unreasonably be charged with an 'oversimplification of man's problems in the world'. Actually, of course, those who have read *The Shadow-Line* know that the passage very soon takes on in retrospect a profoundly ironical significance. Even the 'blessed simplicity' of the 'conception of duty' incumbent on a good ship's captain gets a disconcerting commentary when poor Mr Burns, the red-moustached second officer, desperately stricken with fever and in hospital ashore, pleads, as seaman to seaman, not to be left behind. The young Captain's simple duty as mere functional captain—duty towards ship and crew and owners—is quite plain; it is not to listen; as the humane and sympathetic doctor virtually tells him. But the Captain nevertheless yields, and takes Mr Burns aboard as the ship is leaving; his sense of decency, his sense of what is possible between seaman and seaman, his profoundest moral sense, compels him. (And let me remark, parenthetically, that this theme of the complexity of the moral situation in which a captain may find himself gets a study to itself in the short story called *The Secret Sharer*—which does not, I think, at all require the kind of psychological gloss hinted at in the conventional way, by a symposiast in *The London Magazine*.)

But of course in referring to irony what I was mainly thinking of was the revelation made by Mr Burns of the conduct of the late Captain. *This* was the young Captain's predecessor in the dynasty; 'continuous not in blood, indeed, but in its experience, in its training, in its conception of duty, and in the blessed simplicity of its traditional point of view'. The revelation of such evil and anti-seamanlike perversity prevailing where, in the young Captain's phrase, there should have been a 'sort of composite soul of command' is in itself calculated to shake him to the foundations. But there is more to it than that:

I asked quietly:
'Where did he die?'
'In this saloon. Just where you are sitting now', answered Mr Burns.
I repressed a silly impulse to jump up. . . .

Death, confrontation with the inescapable fact of death—this has its place in the ordeal. Death not as a mere idea or cogent proposition, but as a brute fact that has the clearest personal and practical relation to one's own prospect. 'That man had been in all essentials but his age', says the young Captain, 'just such another man as I myself.' And it isn't merely that he is now dead; what, we can see, so profoundly disturbs the young Captain is the evidence of the old man's attitude in the face of death, once the nearness admitted of no disguising. It was one of desperate, bitter, defiant, utterly unaccepting protest: this old seaman, 'just

such another man as I myself', who had had the ideal career, ending in this cabin, hadn't found at the supreme test that *this* life
had given him fulfilment; very much the contrary. That is what
the indecent treason of his last days means. The starkness of the
fact is brought home to us, by the poetic and dramatic resources
of Conrad's art, with great potency. Not only did he mean to take
the ship down with him. He, the grizzled old Captain of sixty-
five, took up in his defiance, the young Captain tells us sardonic-
ally, the roles of 'lover and artist'. 'Artist?'—the old man had
spent his last days playing his violin, which he threw, just before
the end, into the sea. The symbolism of the violin (art) and the
final, defiant, demonstrative, unseamanlike devotion to it, are plain
enough. We have here something that relates, in its ironic way,
to all those touches, those elements, in the tale in which we feel
that dimension of life to which belong the things 'whose mere
existence' (in the words of the young Captain when he first sees
his ship) 'is enough to awaken an unselfish delight'; the values
that transcend professional vocation as such, or ambition.

I won't push particular examination of the symbolism of *The
Shadow-Line* further. You may say, if you like, that the outcome
of the ordeal is the emergence of the young Captain confirmed
and fortified in his vocation; proved fit and unflawed, the good
seaman and Master Mariner, after exposure to the ultimate
spiritual strains as well as the others. And that is part of the truth.
You may take stock of the various ways, more and less subtle,
in which he has gained in maturity, and finish with Captain
Giles's concluding point:

And there's another thing; a man should stand up to his bad luck,
to his mistakes, to his conscience, and all that sort of thing. Why—
what else would you have to fight against?

You may say that the moral is given in the final 'There's no
rest for me till she's out in the Indian Ocean and not much of it
even then'—an adult acceptance of life as on the whole a matter
of glamourless routine doggedly taken ('Yes, that's what it
amounts to', Captain Giles confirms, as one Master Mariner to
another). I won't dispute it. The point I have to make is that the
significance of the kind of creative work ('dramatic poem', I

have called it) we have in *The Shadow-Line* is such that it can't be represented by any moral. I have spoken of 'symbolism': I have not meant to suggest that *The Shadow-Line* is symbolic in such a way as to admit of a neat and definitive interpretation.

It is a profound work, and complex in its profundity. Conrad himself (if he could be supposed capable of attempting it!) couldn't have provided an adequate summing up of its significance. If one perceives (as one surely must) that it is significant in the way of the greatest art, one knows that taking and pondering the significance must be a matter, first of sensitive response, then of a delicate balancing of one suggestion or intimation against another until the whole, in one's sense of it, has settled into the right inclusive poise. And it seems to me plain that the significance of *The Shadow-Line* entails far more than the emergence from an ordeal of a young Captain who, sharing the same wisdom and maturity, can speak as Master Mariner to Master Mariner with Captain Giles.

Living back through the tale one has to testify that the intimation, the kind of resonance, the effect of transcendence, represented in the first place by the young Captain's reaction to the beauty of the ship plays a very important part in it. Let me just remind you of the effect made on the Captain (and on us) by the crew, so strangely at once so ordinary and so admirable: 'The wastage of ill-health seemed to idealize the general character of the features, bringing out the unsuspected nobility of some, the strength of others. . . .' This kind of effect is developed in subtle ways through the ordeal. It is more potent in the atmosphere than the suggestion of evil associated with the old dead Captain. One remembers such things as this:

The shadows swayed away from me without a word. Those men were ghosts of themselves, and their weight on a rope could be no more than the weight of a bunch of ghosts. Indeed, if ever a sail was hauled up by sheer spiritual strength it must have been that sail. . . .

But above all it is in Ransome that the effect, the suggestion, is focused; Ransome, the intelligent, handsome, ideal good seaman, who carries in his breast the menace of his damaged heart. We are told of him: 'It was a pleasure to look at him. The man positively had grace.'

H

'Grace' in Ransome, is more than a physical quality. And I would remind you that it is on that parting with Ransome that the tale ends, and exhort you to attend very closely to the particulars of the parting. Ransome, who has behaved with recklessly selfless devotion throughout the ordeal, now fiercely demands his discharge: 'I have a right.' He wants, and wants with a fierce intensity, to live. And he, the exquisitely-mannered ('the man positively had grace'), doesn't at first notice the Captain's hand held out for the parting hand-shake. But I must send you to that close of the tale.

And what I have aimed to do in sum is to send you to the whole marvellous work, *The Shadow-Line*. I have made no show of offering anything like a close interpretation or a full commentary. But perhaps I have said enough to suggest how completely *The Shadow-Line* disposes of the criticism that Conrad over-simplifies the human problem, is subject to 'school-boy limitations', and takes little interest in the man who 'tries to live by a gleam of inner truth rather than by accepted standards'. For, I repeat, *The Shadow-Line* is central to Conrad's genius. And, apart from such crude injustices as I have just referred to, I think it is still true that his greatness as an artist has not had due recognition for what it really is. *The Shadow-Line*, of course, is what we tend to call a 'tale' rather than a novel; it is not a large work. *Silas Marner*, which we call a 'fable', is not a large work either, but doesn't therefore rank as a minor one in George Eliot's œuvre—though perhaps it doesn't always get the recognition it deserves. I myself, in fact, must confess not to have suggested, in writing about George Eliot, how major it really is, of the place it should be recognized to hold as central to her genius. I don't think I did justice to *The Shadow-Line* either, in writing, in the same book, on Conrad. *The Shadow-Line*, then, let me now venture, is Conrad's *Silas Marner*—by which, of course, I must not be taken to posit any close likeness between the two works.

VII

THE SECRET SHARER

THE SECRET SHARER, one of the three tales that make up *'Twixt Land and Sea*, is only a tale; it undertakes much less than *The Shadow-Line* does. It is a very fine thing, a work of genius, but a lesser thing in terms of significance; I can without unfairness use it as a foil to bring out the full complexity and depth that make *The Shadow-Line* a major work. Of that full significance *The Secret Sharer* specializes in one element—that which would make it an apt document for confuting the commentators who offer us Captain MacWhirr of *Typhoon* as representative of Conrad's answer to life and of his symbolic use of the ship and the Merchant Service. The young captain of *The Secret Sharer* faces in a protracted way the moral problem faced by the young captain of *The Shadow-Line* when appealed to by the sick mate, Mr Burns, not to leave him behind in hospital. His duty as a ship's master is not to listen; not to burden further the overburdened crew with another sick and helpless man. But the young captain finds himself compelled by a finer ethic, finds himself as a seaman so compelled, not to leave Mr Burns behind. As seaman to seaman he can't. That is only one element in *The Shadow-Line*. The equivalent is the main theme of *The Secret Sharer*.

The young captain of *The Secret Sharer* is, in fact, the young captain of *The Shadow-Line*, and the ship is the same; it too is becalmed at the head of the Gulf of Siam, and the captain has just taken up his first command. You might suppose here, for instance, that you were reading *The Shadow-Line*:

Here and there gleams as of a few scattered pieces of silver marked the windings of the great river; and on the nearest of them, just within the bar, the tug steaming right into the land became lost to my sight, hull and funnel and masts, as though the impassive earth had swallowed her up without an effort, without a tremor. My eye followed the light cloud of her smoke, now here, now there, above the plain, according to the devious curves of the stream, but always fainter and further away, till I lost it at last behind the mitre-shaped hill of the great Pagoda. And then I was left alone with my ship, anchored at the head of the Gulf of Siam.

—Again alone, not only as a ship's captain in the nature of his function must be, but because he is a stranger to the ship and the crew is strange to him. And he remains alone, becoming more terribly so, for he doesn't find himself fighting against a sinister spell of dead calm and fever as in *The Shadow-Line*, the adversity made both endurable and more poignant by the devotion of the stricken crew, on whom adversity and suffering have a sublimating effect, so that they seem ideal seamen in a unity of perfect devotion to a duty that takes on a decidedly spiritual value. There is no Ransome in *The Secret Sharer*.

If I say, then, that the ship and the occasion are the same as those of *The Shadow-Line*, I go on at once to add correctively that long before the end of *The Secret Sharer* what possesses us is an immense unlikeness. And that two such different crystallizations of profound and intense experience should, in the imaginative processes of his art, have found themselves associated by Conrad with what we can't doubt to be a specific actual memory out of his life—something crucial that actually happened to him—is a matter of great interest. Further reflexion on it, however, isn't in place for my present purpose; instead, without prolonging the break, I will continue the quotation I started:

She floated at the starting-point of a long journey, very still in an immense stillness, the shadows of her spars flung far to the eastward by the setting sun. At that moment I was alone on her decks. There was not a sound in her—and around us nothing moved, nothing lived, not a canoe on the water, not a bird in the air, not a cloud in the sky. In this breathless pause at the threshold of a long passage we seemed to be measuring our fitness for a long and arduous enterprise, the appointed task of both our existences to be carried out, far from all human eyes, with only sky and sea for spectators and for judges.

There must have been glare in the air to interfere with one's sight, because it was only just before the sun left us that my roaming eyes made out beyond the highest ridge of the principal islet of the group something which did away with the solemnity of perfect solitude. The tide of darkness flowed on swiftly; and with tropical suddenness a swarm of stars came out above the shadowy earth, and I lingered yet, my hand resting lightly on my ship's rail as if on the shoulder of a trusted friend.

He decides to take the first watch himself, and dismisses the men and the officers to their bunks. He is now happily and serenely alone, unaware that the prolonged and agonizing ordeal, so different from that of *The Shadow-Line*, is about to begin.

Everybody at the after end of the ship was sleeping profoundly. I came out again on the quarter-deck, agreeably at ease in my sleeping suit on that warm breathless night, barefooted, a glowing cigar in my teeth, and, going forward, I was met by the profound silence of the fore-end of the ship. Only as I passed the door of the forecastle I heard a deep, quiet, trustful sigh of some sleeper inside. And suddenly I rejoiced in the great security of the sea as compared with the unrest of the land, in my choice of that untempted life presenting no disquieting problems, invested with an elementary moral beauty by the absolute straightforwardness of its appeal and by the singleness of its purpose.

There you have the irony—an irony directed against Mr Tom Hopkinson, you might say; against that reductive account of the symbolic value for Conrad of the ship, the sea, and the Merchant Service. 'Singleness of purpose'—'singleness' turns out to be peculiarly a telling word. For what so terribly complicates life for the young captain, and makes moral responsibility for him, as ship's master and supremely a seaman, an unsupported individual defiance of code and law and precedent and all decision by the book is the sudden appearance of the double. Passing aft along the deck he notices that a rope ladder has been left hanging over the side. He steps up, gives it a light tug, and gets a surprise in the form of a sudden jerk to himself. He looks over the rail and sees a headless body, with a hand on the bottom rung.

The body is headless, it turns out, because the head, in the tropical night, lies within the opaque shadow of the ship's side. The intensity of perception and surprise conveyed sets off the calm unexcited matter-of-factness (itself intensity) of what follows: in the first place the man's manner of speech (for a whispered exchange follows first), but then the whole stealthy un-rule-booked proceedings.

'I suppose your captain's turned in?'

'I'm sure he isn't', I said.

. . . .

'Look here, my man. Could you call him out quietly?'

I thought the time had come to declare myself.

'*I* am the captain.'

The inquirer explains that he has killed a man, and that he has escaped from confinement on his ship, moored there behind the island, by swimming.

'My father's a parson in Norfolk. Do you see me before a judge and jury on that charge?'

The young captain doesn't. He knows by immediate intuition that this isn't a case of ship's officer *versus* social offender, but of two completely self-reliant and fully human individuals, each the focus of the highest kind of moral responsibility. The irony, not a reductive but an intensifying kind, that enforces this—the fact and the recognition—is that (it comes out incidentally) they are both Conway boys.

Some knowing psychological and esoteric subtlety has been written about the double. The significance, however, is not psychological but moral. I don't mean by that to endorse the modish esoteric suggestiveness you find served up about guilt, or guilt-feelings, in the young captain (and, of course, in us). The young captain *has* no guilt-feelings: that's essential to the significance. But he *would* have had guilt-feelings if he had not recognized his supreme moral—and human—responsibility and acted on it. He sees in the double who has killed a man an *alter ego*. 'It might very well have been myself who had done it' —that is his attitude. He doesn't mean humbly that *he* might have been guilty; there's no question of guilt by the ultimate criterion that's invoked in Conrad's art. By which I don't mean that the spirit of it is *Jenseits von Gut und Böse*. On the contrary, there is an insistence on the inescapable need for individual moral judgment, and for moral conviction that is strong and courageous enough to forget codes and to defy law and codified morality and justice.

There is, in short, the very opposite of that 'simplification of

man's problems in the world', that craving for a moral security
to be found in firm sheltering convention and routine discipline,
of which he has been accused. Let me recall from a passage I have
quoted two sentences in which we come, so very soon, to see
the relevant irony:

Only as I passed the door of the forecastle I heard a deep, quiet,
trustful sigh of some sleeper inside. And suddenly I rejoiced in the great
security of the sea as compared with the unrest of the land, in my
choice of that untempted life presenting no disquieting problems,
invested with an elementary moral beauty by the absolute straightforwardness of its appeal and by the singleness of its purpose.

Faced with the quietly explanatory swimmer, the captain knows
that it is his own supreme responsibility (he doesn't argue this—
he knows it immediately) to trust his judgment about another
man in such circumstances as these when its report is so unequivocal. 'It might very well have been myself who had done that;
in a sense, it virtually is myself who has.' That is, he knows how
little the 'great security of the sea', moral security based on a
simple view of human realities, exists for the completely self-
reliant, courageous and responsible individual—which is what a
Conway boy ought to be.

The significance comes out in the young captain's implicit
attitude as the stranger who is not a stranger tells his tale—an
attitude of something like self-identification that is conveyed in
the way the young captain passes the tale on to us. We too feel
the terrible immediacy of the cruel weather and the mountainous
seas in the unending battle round the Cape—a battle for the ship
and life, always desperately threatened.

My double gave me an inkling of his thought by saying:
'My father's a parson in Norfolk. Do you see me before a judge and
jury on that charge? For myself I don't see the necessity. There are
fellows that an angel from heaven—And I'm not that. He was one of
those creatures that are just simmering with a silly sort of wickedness.
Miserable devils that have no business to live at all. He wouldn't do
his duty and wouldn't let anybody else do theirs. But what's the good
of talking! You know well enough the sort of ill-conditioned snarling
cur—'

He appealed to me as if our experiences had been as identical as our clothes. And I knew well enough the danger of such a character where there are no means of legal repression. And I knew well enough that my double then was no homicidal ruffian. I did not think of asking him for details and he told me the story roughly in brusque, disconnected sentences. I needed no more. I saw it all going on as though I were myself inside that other sleeping-suit [one of his own].

Neither the double nor the young captain questions that the skipper, in having his Chief locked in his cabin ('Mr Leggatt, you've killed a man'), and making it plain that there was no hope of any opportunity to escape handing over to the law, acted with strict correctness, but they convey unmistakably their strong sense that, in his righteousness, he is odious, mean, and contemptible. The whole ship's company share the cold condemning enmity towards the 'murderer'—he *is* that for them; with a herd-like unanimity they make him that. And in having a sense of them as odious, mean, and contemptible, our young captain and we with him are identified with the mate: the ship, society, and social justice are seen as mean enemies, to be, if possible, defeated— enemies of human worth, of human decency, of life.

Without knowing it, skipper and crew, we feel, hate the so-called 'murderer' for his rightness, his decision, and his adequacy. The young mate, the Conway boy, the one man on board equal to the emergency, has taken the instinctive, and (given a good mate) inevitable, strong measures with the shirking and mutinous brute. He has saved the ship, in fact. The young captain can hardly be said to judge; he sees himself in that situation, and *knows*, without argument or hint of doubt, that his double must be saved from the law.

The young captain, we're aware, doesn't know his officers and crew: they are strangers to him. His immediate self-identifying sympathy with the double leads to behaviour that puts him on bad terms with them. He hides the double in his cabin, which is conveniently L-shaped and has a bathroom leading off it. When the double's skipper comes on board with a search-party to inquire after the fugitive from justice, the captain soon discovers that his own men share the visitors' ill-concealed suspicions. The tone of his narrative (he being, as we've seen from *The Shadow-Line*, very close to Conrad himself) conveys his contempt and something like hatred for *them*: he loathes their righteous will that the fugitive from the law shall be caught. He's a ship's master and a Conway boy, but—or rather and—it offends against his basic ethical sensibility.

Then follows the agonizing drama of the double's hair's-breadth escapes from detection during the long days of concealment in the captain's cabin. The captain's odd behaviour as he watches and pounces and takes his measures to prevent discovery more than confirms the crew's ill opinion of him. Nerve-racked, tense, and preoccupied (in two places at once, he feels) he catches himself addressing his own Chief Mate in whispers. And he catches odd expressions in the eyes of his officers and men. This is *not* the ideal, if bewitched and bedevilled, ship of *The Shadow-Line*, where adversity gives proof of perfect relations, and reveals a crew that the captain feels (and we feel with him) to be fairly represented by Ransome, the good seaman ('the man positively had grace').

A part of the significance is of course that a good ship, symbol of the 'third realm' or human world, is created. Conditions and circumstances tell, of course, but creative action makes it, and creative action, collaborative though it must be, depends upon creative individuals and creative will.

The main emphasis, however, falls on the lengths to which the young captain, in response to his profoundest ethical sense, is prepared to go to save a Conway boy who has killed a man from 'justice'. The culmination is the close, in which he deliberately and terrifyingly—for we share the suspense of the crew—risks the ship. After discussion of the possibilities of an escape before the arrival in port, the captain and his double, knowing that the ship will pass in the dark close to the south point of the rocky island of Koh-ring, agree that it shall be there. He, the captain, will take her in as close as he reasonably can—say, within half a mile. All the arrangements are made for the double to slip out of the cabin and into the water without being observed.

When the challenge comes, the young captain answers it with an extremity of response that he himself couldn't have contemplated beforehand:

The great black mass brooding over our very mast-heads began to pivot away from the ship's side silently. And now I forgot the secret stranger ready to depart, and remembered only that I was a total stranger to the ship. I did not know her. Would she do it? How was she to be handled?

I swung the mainyard and waited helplessly. She was perhaps stopped, and her very fate hung in the balance, with the black mass of Koh-ring like the gate of the everlasting night towering over her taff-rail. What would she do now? Had she way on her yet?

It is one of those effects called 'melodramatic' by Mr Hopkinson in the *London Magazine*, but the vividness and intensity, as always in Conrad, carry and enforce the significance. The young captain, as a deliberate, calculated matter of conscience, has, with his officers and crew for appalled witnesses, pushed defiance of the rules of seamanship to an extreme and almost lost the ship. The escaper, it has been borne in on us, is impressively sane, self-possessed and realistic—a model Chief Officer—and the captain we now tell ourselves at this paradoxical moment is *his* double: the significance of the tale is given there.

It doesn't run counter to Conrad's symbolic use of the Merchant Service—of the Conway training (shall I say?). In fact, the tale conveys his sense of the immense value of such a training, but at the same time his insistence (a matter of communicated perception, not of preaching or saying) that the profit, the disciplined condition that results, is not, where what he means by training is in question, a mere matter of readiness to act by automatic reflex; a preparedness to react to all routine contingencies, exhaustively foreseen, by the code. That there *should* be a trained readiness to react appropriately he does, of course, mean. Here is a passage from *The Secret Sharer* that illustrates the deplorable effect on the young captain of the abnormal situation, the need to keep the double concealed:

It's to no commander's advantage to be suspected of ludicrous eccentricities. But I was also more seriously affected. There are to a seaman certain words, gestures, that should in given conditions come as naturally, as instinctively as the winking of a menaced eye. A certain order should spring to his lips without thinking; a certain sign should get itself made, so to speak, without reflection. But all unconscious alertness had abandoned me. I had to make an effort of will to recall myself back (from the cabin) to the conditions of the moment.

I felt that I was appearing an irresolute commander to these people who were watching me more or less critically.

And, besides, there were the scares.

Yes, the trained readiness to respond like a winking eye—that is necessary. But what Conrad's art presents—in *The Secret Sharer* and *The Shadow-Line*—as the admirable type of human excellence (for it's the type of human excellence, and not merely the good seaman, he has in mind) isn't just what that account might seem to imply. When (with Conrad's aid) one reflects, one tells oneself that readiness of that kind, decision so describable, might have subtler and higher manifestations such as one doesn't think of as bred by disciplines that one associates with a training in conventional responses. What the young captain is confronted with when he discovers the swimmer holding on to the rope ladder is something to which, he recognizes at once, a conventional response is out of place. A Conway boy, he recognizes in the fugitive—in his speech and bearing—a man of courage, fortitude, and complete moral responsibility. And in defiance of what is conventionally expected of a ship's master, he acts on his full human judgment. A man's supreme obligation is to recognize his own moral responsibility—to have the courage to recognize it and to act on it. There is no hesitation about the young captain's response to what he perceives; it is immediate and unqualified. You might say that he reacts by higher reflex.

The significance, the communication of the tale concerns the relations between training, law, society, and personal responsibility. There can be no doubt about what the attitude conveyed by the tale is, but it can't be simply stated. The communication, though, is simple compared with that of *The Shadow-Line*—the problem confronted is a limited one. In *The Shadow-Line* we have the theme intimated by the title. When you've crossed the line out of the state of being young, in which you ask no ultimate questions, what answer do you find to the questions that begin to put themselves, the question above all: 'What ultimately for?' Is a prosperous career enough to give meaning to life—to bring fulfilment? Will it have been when I shall have lived through the career? The young chief mate doubts it and throws up his happy berth. Nevertheless, when the chance of a command penetrates to his introspection-bound consciousness he jumps to seize it. Then you have the added life-dimension Captain MacWhirr can never have known, that which is given in the young captain's response to the ship's beauty: it is good to be alive in a world in which such things exist. The beautiful ship, of course, is representative and symbolic in this matter.

Have we there the answer to the question? Hardly that. The question has to be lived with: that is the communication of the novel. But the part played by the ship's beauty is an essential element in such effect of an answer as the novel gives. For there is no neat or determinate answer, though there is a potent suggestion as to the kind of complex answer a Conway boy who is also an intellectual novelist will have proposed to himself as given by the experience of life.

1966. Lecture given at the University of York.

VIII

PUDD'NHEAD WILSON[1]

PUDD'NHEAD WILSON is not faultless—no book of Mark Twain's is that—but it is all the same the masterly work of a great writer. Yet it is very little known. One cannot easily find anyone, English or American, who has read it (at least that is my experience), and it would seem never at any time to have had the beginnings of the recognition that is its due. Its reputation—if it may be said to have a reputation—would not encourage a strenuous search for a copy of the book, unless in an admirer of *Huckleberry Finn* who was curious to look over one of the author's ephemeral productions, one that also dealt in its way with life in Hannibal, Missouri, the village of Mark Twain's childhood.

The explanation, I think, is partly that *Pudd'nhead Wilson* is so very unlike *Huckleberry Finn*. But it is also, I think, that the nature of the greatness of *Huckleberry Finn* itself tends not to be fully recognized. There are, then, two reasons for hoping that *Pudd'nhead Wilson* may come to be appreciated as it deserves: it is a classic in its own right (if an unrecognized classic may be said to *be* one); and, further, for all the unlikeness, it bears a very close relation to *Huckleberry Finn*; a relation of such a kind that to appreciate the lesser work is to have a surer perception of the greatness of the greater.

Huckleberry Finn, by general agreement Mark Twain's greatest work, is supremely the American classic, and it is one of the great books of the world. The significance of such a work doesn't admit of exhaustive recognition in a simple formula, or in several. Mark Twain himself was no simple being, and the complexity of his make-up was ordinarily manifested in strains, disharmonies, and tormenting failures of integration and self-knowledge. These,

[1] Written as an Introduction to the Zodiac Press edition of *Pudd'nhead Wilson* (London: Chatto & Windus, 1955).

in his supreme masterpiece, can be seen to provide the creative drive. There is of course the aspect of return to boyhood, but the relation to complexity and strain represented by *Huckleberry Finn* is not one of escape from them—in spite of the qualities that have established the book as a classic for children (and in spite of Mark Twain's conviction, at times, that its appeal should be as such). It is true that the whole is given through Huck the embodiment of that Western vernacular, or of the style created out of that, in which the book is written. But that style, perfectly as it renders the illiterate Huck, has been created by a highly sophisticated art to serve subtle purposes, and Huck himself is of course not merely the naïve boyish consciousness he so successfully enacts; he is, by one of those triumphant sleights or equivocations which cannot be judiciously contrived, but are proof of inspired creative possession, the voice of deeply reflective maturity —of a life's experience brooded on by an earnest spirit and a fine intelligence. If Mark Twain lacked art in Arnold Bennett's sense (as Arnold Bennett pointed out), that only shows how little art in Arnold Bennett's sense matters, in comparison with art that is the answer of creative genius to the pressure of a profoundly felt and complex experience. If *Huckleberry Finn* has its examples of the unintelligence that may accompany the absence of sustained critical consciousness in an artist, even a great one, nevertheless the essential intelligence that prevails, and from the poetic depths informs the work, compels our recognition—the intelligence of the whole engaged psyche; the intelligence that represents the integrity of this, and brings to bear the wholeness.

For in his supreme creation the complex and troubled Mark Twain did achieve a wholeness; it is manifested in the nature of the creative triumph. The charged significance of *Huckleberry Finn* brings together a strength of naïveté and a strength of mature reflective wisdom. Let me quote, with immediate relevance, Mr Bernard DeVoto, most penetrating of the commentators on Mark Twain I am acquainted with:

fundamentally Huck is an expression—a magnificent expression, a unique expression—of the folk mind. The folk mind that is, in mid-America in the period of the frontier and immediately following, the folk mind shaped for use by the tremendous realities of conquering a hostile wilderness and yet shadowed by the unseen world. He is one of the highest reaches of American fiction.

But if Huck expresses the folk mind, he is also Mark Twain's surrogate, he is charged with transmitting what that dark, sensitive, and complex consciousness felt about America and the human race. . . . Mark Twain was not a systematic thinker. Customarily, like the creature of fable who was his brother Orion, he held in succession all possible opinions about every subject he tried to analyse, held none of them long, and was able to drive none very deep beneath the surface. Especially as a metaphysician he was as feeble a novice as ever ventured into that stormy sea. But in what he perceived, in what he felt, in the nerve-ends of emotion, in the mysterious ferments of art which transform experience, he was a great mind—there has been no greater in American literature. Be it said once more and ever so wearily: insufficiencies and defects prevented him from ever completely implementing the artist throughout the whole course of a book. That does not matter—in *Huckleberry Finn* we get the finest expression of a great artist, the fullest report on what life meant to him.[1]

When Mr DeVoto speaks of the 'folk mind' in *Huckleberry Finn* he is making a plainly valid observation; an observation duly offset, as the quoted passage shows, by the recognition of quite other aspects of the book. But insistence on the 'folk' element sometimes goes with an attempt to make *Huckleberry Finn* American in a sense that would make it an immeasurably lesser thing than the great work it is. Mr Van Wyck Brooks writes: 'He was the frontier story-teller, the great folk writer of the American West, and raised to a pitch unrivalled before him the art of oral story-telling and then succeeded in transferring its effects to paper.'[2] Such an account (and there is a formidable representative intention behind it) serves as a licence for insisting on the force of the reply—the obvious and unanswerable reply: Mark Twain was something very much more than a folk-writer, and the art of *Huckleberry Finn* is no mere matter of managing effects—suspense, surprise, climax, and so on. One cannot intelligently discuss the art without discussing the complex and reverse of naïve outlook it conveys. Mr Brooks, recognizing, as

[1] Bernard DeVoto, *Mark Twain at Work*, p. 99.
[2] *The Times of Melville and Whitman*. Mr Brooks says much the same in *The Ordeal of Mark Twain*.

any reader must, an insistent moral preoccupation in the theme, quotes Paine, Mark Twain's biographer: 'the author makes Huck's struggle a psychological one between conscience and the law on one side, and sympathy on the other'. But there is more to the moral theme of *Huckleberry Finn* than that suggests. What the book conveys is the drama in a mind in which conscience finds that it is not single, and that the 'law' doesn't speak with one voice, and that what Paine calls 'sympathy' itself engages a moral imperative. In fact, as I have noted elsewhere,[1] *Huckleberry Finn* has as a central theme the complexity of ethical valuation in a society with a complex tradition—a description that applies (for instance) to any 'Christian' society.

The book is a profound study of civilized man. And about its attitude towards civilization as represented by the society depicted in it there is nothing simple or simplifying, either in a 'frontier' spirit or in a spirit of reductive pessimism. It is not to the point to adduce such private utterances of Mark Twain's as: 'We have no real morals, but only artificial ones—morals created and preserved by the forced suppression of natural and healthy instinct.' 'Never trust the artist; trust the tale': Lawrence's dictum might have been addressed to Mark Twain's case. *Huckleberry Finn*, the tale, gives us a wholeness of attitude that transcends anything ordinarily attainable by the author. The liberation effected by the memories of youth and the Mississippi was, for the creative genius at his greatest, not into irresponsibility but the reverse. The imaginatively recovered vitality of youth ministered, in sum, no more to the spirit of *Pudd'nhead Wilson's Calendar* than to nostalgia or daydream, but to the attainment of a sure and profound moral maturity. That is, to call *Huckleberry Finn* a great work is not an exaggeration.

I insist in this way because of a tendency in America (and Transatlantic fashions regarding American literature tend to be taken over uncritically here) to suggest that the beginnings of the truly American in literary tradition come from the frontier and the West. According to this view Mark Twain is a more truly American writer than Hawthorne or Henry James. It is a view

[1] In the Introduction to Marius Bewley's *The Complex Fate*. [See below, p. 152.]

that, in offering to exalt him, actually denies his greatness, for it makes the attributed advantage in Americanness a matter of his being alienated from English and European tradition as Hawthorne and James are not. Such an alienation could only be an impoverishment: no serious attempt has been made to show that any sequel to disinheritance could replace the heritage lost. Mark Twain is indeed 'frontier' and Western, but in being greatly American he bears as close and essential a relation to England and Europe as that which we recognize in Hawthorne or in James (in some ways he strikes an English reader as being less foreign, less positively un-English, than either of them). The Americanness of alienation may be represented by Dreiser, Scott Fitzgerald, and Hemingway: the author of *Huckleberry Finn*, when we think of those writers, seems to belong to another world. Nor as we read the book are we prompted to reflect that he is a fellow-countryman of Walt Whitman.

It is not my business to enforce these observations in a detailed analysis of *Huckleberry Finn*, but, with them in view, to suggest how that book is related to *Pudd'nhead Wilson*, which, different as it is (it makes no show of frontier naïveté, but belongs frankly to sophisticated literary tradition), is nevertheless unmistakably by the same hand, develops the same preoccupation and expresses the same moral outlook. With the oral tradition of story-telling, the potent element of recovered boyhood that has so recommended *Huckleberry Finn* is absent too. But the Mississippi *is* there in *Pudd'nhead Wilson*, and its evoked presence occasions a significant expansion:

The hamlet's front was washed by the clear waters of the great river; its body stretched itself rearward up a gentle incline; its most rearward border fringed itself out and scattered its houses about the base-line of the hills; the hills rose high, inclosing the town in a half-moon curve, clothed with forests from foot to summit.

Steamboats passed up and down every hour or so. Those belonging to the little Cairo line and the little Memphis line always stopped; the big Orleans liners stopped for hails only, or to land passengers or freight; and this was the case also with the great flotilla of 'transients'. These latter came out of a dozen rivers—the Illinois, the Missouri, the Upper Mississippi, the Ohio, the Monongahela, the Tennessee, the

I

Red River, the White River, and so on; and were bound every whither and stocked with every imaginable comfort or necessity which the Mississippi's communities could want, from the frosty Falls of St Anthony down through nine climates to torrid New Orleans.

Here, quite plainly, speaks a proud imaginative delight in the memory of the great river; the great river as Mark Twain had known it in boyhood and in his piloting days; and in the memory, or vision, we feel the sense of freedom, beauty, and majesty that informs *Huckleberry Finn*; but there is something further too: the passage unmistakably conveys the sense, sanguine and exalted, of an expanding and ripening civilization.

Mark Twain, we are told, was brought up in a frontier society. 'Think', it has been written, 'of the squalor of those villages, their moral and material squalor, their dim and bounded horizon, their petty taboos: repression at one extreme, eruption at the other, and shiftlessness for a golden mean.' But what *Pudd'nhead Wilson* should make us recognize is that 'frontier' is an insidious term. It suggests cultural deprivation and loss—a dropping of the heritage in the battle with pioneer hardship. And no doubt it could be argued that the account just quoted fairly describes Dawson's Landing; or that so we should have agreed if we had had to live there. But as a matter of fact this is not the tone, this is not how the stress falls, in *Pudd'nhead Wilson*. After the evocation of the river we read:

The town was sleepy and comfortable and contented. It was fifty years old, and was growing slowly—very slowly, in fact, but still it was growing.

It may have been sleepy, but what Mark Twain conveys with great power is an effect quite other than one of rawness and squalor:

In 1830 it was a snug little collection of modest one- and two-storey frame dwellings whose white-washed exteriors were almost concealed from sight by climbing tangles of rose-vines, honeysuckles, and morning-glories. Each of these pretty homes had a garden in front, fenced with white palings and opulently stocked with hollyhocks, marigolds, touch-me-nots, prince's feathers and other old-fashioned flowers; while on the window-sills of the houses stood wooden boxes containing moss-rose plants and terracotta pots in which grew a breed of geraniums whose spread of intensely red blossoms accented the prevailing pink tint of the rose-clad house-front like an explosion of flame. When there was room on the ledge outside of the pots and boxes for a cat, the cat was there—in sunny weather—stretched at full length, asleep and blissful, with her furry belly to the sun and a paw curved over her nose. Then that house was complete, and its contentment and peace were made manifest to the world by this symbol, whose testimony is infallible. A home without a cat—and a well-fed, well-petted, and properly revered cat—may be a perfect home, perhaps, but how can it prove title?

All along the streets, on both sides, at the outer edge of the brick sidewalks, stood locust-trees with trunks protected by wooden boxing, and these furnished shade for summer and a sweet fragrance in spring when the clusters of buds came forth.

The comfort, well-being, and amenity evoked here have more than a material significance; they are the outward signs of an inward grace. Provincial as Dawson's Landing may be, it represents a society that has kept its full heritage of civilization. True, it *is* provincial, and Wilson's fate—the 'Pudd'nhead' and the long failure to make way against that estimate—figures for us its attitude towards originality of mind. Moreover, an English reader gets what are for him (the human world presented being so essentially unforeign) startling glimpses of mob lawlessness as an accepted social institution. Yet the effect of the opening description of Dawson's Landing remains: this is a civilized community—one qualified to have exacted a very much more favourable report than any brought back by Martin Chuzzlewit.

And further, it is not unaware of its provinciality, and is far from having lost the desire to keep in touch with the remoter centres of its civilization and with its past. This comes out notably in its reception of the twins, the presentment of which illustrates the complex poise of Mark Twain's attitude. The comedy of the reception is not satiric. Dawson's Landing displays, not merely its crudenesses and limitations, but also a touching positive humility, a will to pay homage to something other than provinciality and philistinism and the standards of everyday life. The exhibition of democratic *mœurs* at Aunt Patsy's is finely and subtly done, and quite clear in its significance. These democrats, without being in the least inclined to go back on their democracy, respond imaginatively to their traditional memories and to the sense of ideal values belonging to a richer life that is now remote from them. It is an utterly different thing from snobbery, and, as Mark Twain presents it, something that the social crudity of the occasion sets off as the reverse of trivial or crude:

None of these visitors was at ease, but, being honest people, they didn't pretend to be. None of them had ever seen a person bearing a title of nobility before, and none had been expecting to see one now, consequently the title came upon them as a kind of pile-driving surprise, and caught them unprepared. A few tried to rise to the emergency, and got out an awkward 'My lord', or 'Your lordship', or something of that sort, but the great majority were overwhelmed by the unaccustomed word and its dim and awful associations with gilded courts and stately ceremony and anointed kingship, so they only fumbled through the handshake and passed on, speechless.

Then, significantly, this homage to a glimpsed ideal superiority is followed by the homage to art:

Here a prodigious slam-banging broke out below, and everybody rushed down to see. It was the twins knocking out a classic four-handed piece on the piano in great style. Rowena was satisfied—satisfied down to the bottom of her heart.

The young strangers were kept long at the piano. The villagers were astonished and enchanted with the magnificence of their performance, and could not bear to have them stop. All the music that they had ever heard before seemed spiritless prentice-work and barren of grace or charm when compared with these intoxicating floods of melodious sound. They realised that for once in their lives they were hearing masters.

The poise is beautifully maintained; those first two sentences serve only to enforce the serious and profound significance of the last, the enclosing one of the chapter.

In its whole attitude towards distinction that appeals to standards other than the 'democratic', Dawson's Landing represents a subtler civilization than accounts of 'the pioneer community' might suggest. Consider, for instance, the special licence accorded Judge Driscoll in an environment that doesn't encourage moral independence or free play of mind. 'Judge

Driscoll', says Mark Twain, 'could be a freethinker and still hold his place in society because he was the person of most consequence in the community, and therefore could go his own way and follow out his own notions.' But York Leicester Driscoll isn't represented as having his leading place by pre-eminence in the qualities that one would have expected to tell most among pioneering democrats. We are told of him:

He was very proud of his old Virginian ancestry, and in his hospitalities and his rather formal and stately manners he kept up the tradition. He was fine and just and generous. To be a gentleman—a gentleman without stain or blemish—was his only religion, and to it he was always faithful. He was respected, esteemed, and beloved by all the community.

It is quite unequivocal: he is 'respected, esteemed and beloved' (a set of terms that defines something quite different from the attitudes towards the smart and therefore successful man) because he is a 'gentleman', representing as such an ideal that doesn't belong to the realm of material 'success' and is above the attainment of the ordinary member of the community. And we come here to that complexity of ethical background which I have spoken of as providing a central preoccupation of Mark Twain's, in *Pudd'nhead Wilson* as in *Huckleberry Finn*. I am not thinking merely of the persistence of an aristocratic tradition in a democratic society. That society has also its Christian allegiance, and, while the Judge is 'just and generous', the total concept of 'gentleman' is decidedly not Christian. When we come to Pembroke Howard, for whom to be a gentleman is *not* his only religion, the situation, with its irony, is focused in the one actor:

He was a fine, brave, majestic creature, a gentleman according to the nicest requirements of the Virginian rule, a devoted Presbyterian, an authority on the 'code', and a man always courteously ready to stand up before you in the field if any act or word of his had seemed doubtful or suspicious to you, and explain it with any weapons you might prefer from bradawls to artillery. He was very popular with the people, and was the Judge's dearest friend.

For the gentleman, 'honour stood first': the laws of honour 'required certain things of him which his religion might forbid him: then his religion must yield—the laws could not be relaxed to accommodate religion or anything else'. And the Christian and democratic community, with a complete and exalted conviction, gave its approval.

The people took more pride in the duel than in all the other events put together, perhaps. It was a glory to the town to have such a thing happen there. In their eyes, the principals had reached the summit of human honour.

There is nothing remarkable about the ability to observe such facts. What is remarkable is the subtlety of the appraising attitude that Mark Twain, in terms of impersonal art, defines towards them—as towards the whole inclusive situation presented in the book. Astringent as is the irony of *Pudd'nhead Wilson*, the attitude here has nothing of the satiric in it (the distinctively satiric plays no great part in the work as a whole). Mark Twain unmistakably admires Judge Driscoll and Pembroke Howard. And it is important to note that, if they are 'fine', the 'fineness' is not a mere matter of their being 'just and generous'. The total attitude where they are concerned is not altogether easy to describe, not because it is equivocal, but because it is not a simple one, and has called for some subtlety of dramatic means to convey it. The two most sympathetic characters in the drama give the 'code' itself their active endorsement. It is not for instance suggested that Wilson, in acting as second in the duel, does so with any self-dissociating reservations or reluctance, and he rebukes Tom for not telling his uncle about the kicking and 'letting him have a gentleman's chance': 'if I had known the circumstances', he says, 'I would have kept the case out of court until I got word to him and let him have a gentleman's chance.'

'You would?' exclaimed Tom, with lively surprise. 'And it your first case! And you know perfectly well there would never have *been* any case if he had got that chance, don't you? And you'd have finished your days a pauper nobody, instead of being an actually launched and recognised lawyer to-day. And you would really have done that, would you?'

'Certainly.'

Tom looked at him a moment or two, then shook his head sorrowfully and said:

'I believe you—upon my word I do. I don't know why I do, but
I do. Pudd'nhead Wilson, I think you're the biggest fool I ever saw.'

This reminder of the circumstances of the rebuke will serve to
enforce the point that Wilson, the poised and pre-eminently
civilized moral centre of the drama, whom we take to be very
close in point of view to Mark Twain is not, all the same, to be
identified with him. Wilson *is* an actor in a dramatic whole that
conveys its significances dramatically. The upshot of the drama
is to set a high value on the human qualities fostered by the
aristocratic code: to endorse the code even as far as Wilson does
would be quite a different matter, and no reader of the book can
suppose it to be doing that. Against the pride and the allegiance
to an ideal of conduct that make personal safety a matter of
comparative indifference, we see the ignominy and ugliness of
Tom's complete self-centredness, which is as unchecked by pride
or concern for any ideal as by imaginative sympathy. Hearing
that the Judge, fighting in *his* cause, has survived the duel, he
reflects immediately, with an exasperation untouched by shame,
how blessedly all problems would have been solved had the
Judge been killed: the duel has been wasted.

The exposure of human nature in Tom Driscoll has an essential
part in the total astringency of the book. But it will not do to
suggest that human nature, as the book presents it, reduces to
Tom. If the Wilson of *Pudd'nhead Wilson's Calendar* is not the
Wilson of the drama, neither does he represent the imagination
and the sensibility that inform this as a conceived and realized
whole. Such utterances of Mark Twain's as this marginal note
from a book, characteristic as they are, mustn't be credited with
a kind of conclusive authority they certainly haven't:

What a man sees in the human race is merely himself in the deep
and honest privacy of his own heart. Byron despised the race because
he despised himself. I feel as Byron did and for the same reason.

The exhibition of Tom's viciousness has its convincing force,
no doubt, because *we* recognize in ourselves the potentiality, as
Mark Twain did in *himself*. But it would be misleading to say
that we despise Tom; that would be to suggest an animus that we
do *not* feel when we place him, unequivocally, as contemptible;

we are not engaged and involved in that way. The irony of the work as a whole means a very secure poise, and the poise is secure because the author has achieved a mature, balanced, and impersonal view of humanity. He himself is not involved in the personal way that involves animus in condemning.

The attitude of *Pudd'nhead Wilson* is remote from cynicism or pessimism. The book conveys neither contempt for human nature nor a rejection of civilization. It is concerned with the complexities of both human nature and civilization as represented in a historical community—for Dawson's Landing, it may reasonably be said, is one that, at a given time in actual American history, Mark Twain had intimately known.

We are not, by way of dismissing the suggestion of any general contempt, confined to adducing Wilson himself and the 'fine, brave, majestic creatures' who uphold the code of the F.F.V. Most impressively, there is Roxy. It is true that her heroic maternal devotion plays against the extremity of mean heartless egotism given us in Tom. But her significance is not exhausted in that irony. We feel her dominating the book as a triumphant vindication of life. Without being in the least sentimentalized, or anything but dramatically right, she plainly bodies forth the qualities that Mark Twain, in his whole being, most values— qualities that, as Roxy bears witness, he profoundly believes in as observable in humanity, having known them in experience. Although born a slave, she is herself a 'fine, brave, majestic creature', whose vitality expresses itself in pride, high-spiritedness, and masterful generosity. Her reckless presence at the duel defines Mark Twain's attitude towards the 'code' more decisively than Wilson's participation does. When she proudly tells Tom that he is descended from the best blood of Virginia the effect, for all the irony, is not satiric. And her confident and justified reliance on the loyal comradeship, not only of her fellow-niggers, but also of the officers of the *Grand Mogul*, has its part in the appraisal of human nature conveyed by the book as a whole.

Mr DeVoto makes the point that she represents a frank and unembarrassed recognition of the actuality of sex, with its place and power in human affairs, such as cannot be found elsewhere in Mark Twain. That seems to me true and important. It is an aspect of the general fact, that she is the presence in the book of a free and generous vitality, in which the warmly and physically human manifests itself also as intelligence and spiritual strength. It is this far-reaching associative way in which, so dominating a presence, she stands for—she *is*—triumphant life that gives the book, for all its astringency and for all the chilling irony of the close, its genial quality (to be both genial and astringent is its extraordinary distinction).

How far from satiric the spirit of *Pudd'nhead Wilson* is may be seen in the presentment of the subtleties of conscience and ethical sensibility in Roxy. Consider the episode of the stolen money and the threat to sell the negro servants down the river. We are no doubt very close to the satiric note in the irony with which the chapter ends—in Percy Driscoll's self-gratulation on his magnanimity: 'that night he set the incident down in his diary, so that his son might read it in after years and be thereby moved to deeds of gentleness and humanity himself.' But we are remote from satire here:

The truth was, all were guilty but Roxana; she suspected that the others were guilty, but she did not know them to be so. She was horrified to think how near she had come to being guilty herself; she had been saved in the nick of time by a revival in the coloured Methodist Church, a fortnight before, at which time and place she had 'got religion'. The very next day after that gracious experience, while her change of style was fresh upon her and she was vain of her purified condition, her master left a couple of dollars lying unprotected on his desk, and she happened upon that temptation when she was polishing around with a dust-rag. She looked at the money awhile with a steadily rising resentment, and then she burst out with— 'Dad blame dat revival, I wisht it had 'a be'n put off till to-morrow!'

Then she covered the tempter with a book, and another member of the kitchen cabinet got it. She made this sacrifice as a matter of religious etiquette; as a thing necessary just now, but by no means to be wrested into a precedent; no, a week or two would limber up her piety, then she would be rational again, and the next two dollars that got left out in the cold would find a comforter—and she could name the comforter.

Was she bad? Was she worse than the general run of her race? No. They had an unfair show in the battle of life. . . .'

In spite of that last phrase, we know that what we have been contemplating is not just an exhibition of negro traits: 'her race' is the human race. These naïve and subtle changes and adjustments of conscience and the moral sense we can parallel from our own inner experience. But there is nothing cynically reductive in Mark Twain's study of the moral nature of man; he shows the clairvoyance of a mind that is sane and poised, and the irony that attends the illustration of subtleties and complexities throws no doubt on the reality or the dignity or the effectiveness in human affairs of ethical sensibility.

I have not yet touched on the central irony of the book, the sustained and complex irony inherent in the plot. *Pudd'nhead Wilson* should be recognized as a classic of the use of popular modes—of the sensational and the melodramatic—for the purposes of significant art. The book, I have said, is not faultless, and an obvious criticism lies against the unfulfilled promise represented by the twins—the non-significant play made with them, their history, and the sinister oriental dagger. Mark Twain, we can see, had intended to work out some interplay of the two parallel sets of complications: twins and interchanged babies. He abandoned the idea, but didn't trouble to eliminate that insistent focusing of expectation upon the twins. The fault is in a sense a large one, and yet it is not, after all, a very serious one: it doesn't affect the masterly handling of the possibilities actually developed.

The ironic subtleties that Mark Twain gets from the interchange of the babies in their cradles seem, as one ponders them, almost inexhaustible. There is the terrible difference, no more questioned by Roxy than by her master, between the nigger and the white. The conventionality of the distinction is figured by the actual whiteness of Roxy, whose one-sixteenth of negro blood tells only in her speech (with which, indeed, it has no essential relation, as is illustrated later by the inability of 'Valet de Chambers', now revealed as the pure-white heir, to shed the nigger-speech he learnt in childhood). So awful, ultimate, and unchangeable is the distinction that Roxy, as, in order to save her child from the fate hanging over the slave (to be 'sold down the river'), she changes the babies in their cradles, justifies herself by the example of God. The rendering is an irresistible manifestation

of genius, utterly convincing, and done with a delicate subtlety
of ironic significance:

She flung herself on her bed and began to think and toss, toss and
think. By-and-by she sat suddenly upright, for a comforting thought
had flown through her worried mind:

'Tain't no sin—*white* folks has done it! It ain't no sin, glory to
goodness it ain't no sin! *Dey's* done it—yes, en dey was de biggest
quality in de whole bilin', too—*kings!*'

She began to muse; she was trying to gather out of her memory
the dim particulars of some tale she had heard some time or other.
At last she said:

'Now I's got it; now I 'member. It was dat ole nigger preacher dat
tole it, de time he come over here fum Illinois en preached in de
nigger church. He said dey ain't nobody kin save his own self—can't
do it by faith, can't do it by works, can't do it no way at all. Free
grace is de *on'y* way, en dat don't come fum nobody but jis' de Lord;
en *he* kin give it to anybody he please, saint or sinner—*he* don't kyer.
He do jis' as he's a mineter. He s'lect out anybody dat suit him, en put
another one in his place, en make de fust one happy for ever en leave
t'other one to burn wid Satan.'

There is of course a glance here at the Calvinism of Mark
Twain's youth. And it is to be noted that Roxy, while usurping
the prerogative of the predestinating Deity, has shown a wholly
human compassion, and has invoked a compassionate God in
doing so:

'I's sorry for you, honey; I's sorry, God knows I is—but what *kin*
I do, what *could* I do? Yo' pappy would sell him to somebody, some
time, en den he'd go down de river, sho', and I couldn't, couldn't,
couldn't stan' it.'

In saving the child from the consequences of the awful distinction
that she assumes to be in the nature of things she demonstrates
its lack of any ground but convention; she demonstrates the
wholly common humanity of the nigger and the white. The
father himself cannot detect the fraud: he cannot tell his own
child from the other. And—one of the many ironies—it is his
cruel, but confidently righteous, severity that imposes the full
abjectness of slave mentality upon his own child, who becomes
the defenceless and rightless servant of the slave's child. On the

other hand, Roxy's success in saving Valet de Chambers (the name her proud tribute to an ideal 'white' lordliness) from the fate of the slave erects a dreadful barrier between child and mother. Treated as 'young Marse Tom', not only does he become that different order of being, the 'master'; in Roxy herself the slave attitudes that she necessarily observes towards him find themselves before long attended by the appropriate awe. When at last, outraged by the humiliating and cruel rebuffs that meet her appeal for a little kindness (she is in need) to the old 'nigger-mammy', she forgets habit and the ties of motherhood, and pants for revenge, she has to recognize that she has placed him in an impregnable position: no one will believe her tale. A further irony is that, if he has turned out bad, a portent of egocentric heartlessness, that is at least partly due to his spoiling as heir and young master, the lordly superior being.

It is a mark of the poised humanity characterizing the treatment of the themes of *Pudd'nhead Wilson* that, worthless and vicious as 'Tom' is, we feel, when he has to face the sudden revelation that he is a nigger, some compassion for him; we don't just applaud an irony of poetic justice when he is cornered into reflecting, with an echo of his mother's self-justifying recall of the Calvinistic God:

'Why were niggers and whites made? What crime did the uncreated first nigger commit that the curse of birth was decreed for him? And why is this awful difference made between black and white?'

Compassion, of course, soon vanishes as the dialectic of utter selfishness unfolds in him. The developments of his incapacity for compassion are done with a convincingness that the creator of Tito Melema would have envied. When Roxy offers to be sold back into slavery in order to save 'Tom' from being disinherited, and he, with dreadfully credible treachery, sells her 'down the river', the opposite extremes of human nature are brought together in an effect that belongs wholly to the mode of *Pudd'nhead Wilson*, and is equally removed from melodrama and from cynicism. It can hardly be said, when we close the book, that the worst in human nature has not been confronted; yet the upshot of the whole is neither to judge mankind to be contemptible nor to condemn civilization. And it is remarkable how utterly free from animus that astringency is which takes on so intense a concentration in the close:

Everybody granted that if 'Tom' were white and free it would be unquestionably right to punish him—it would be no loss to anybody; but to shut up a valuable slave for life—that was quite another matter.

As soon as the Governor understood the case, he pardoned Tom at once, and the creditors sold him down the river.

It is an irony of the tale that this, the fate to secure him against which Roxana had committed her crime, is, as an ultimate consequence of that crime, the fate he suffers.

IX

THE AMERICANNESS OF AMERICAN LITERATURE[1]

WHATEVER may be Mr Van Wyck Brooks's distinctive mark in the contemporary American literary world, the five-volume work[2] that comes to a close with *The Confident Years* seems to me to be in an essential respect very representative—representative, I mean, of a prevailing climate: while it is, to a portentous tune, inflationary in tendency, it at the same time shows an indifference to the real American achievement. The indifference must be judged to be unawareness, and if one asks how such unawareness could be preserved by a critic intent on exalting and magnifying an established American literature, the explanation is to be seen in the nature of the inflationary bent itself. An English observer, then, who (besides the impulse of protest that takes him when a major achievement in the common language is slighted—in fact, ignored) permits himself to feel a keen concern about the present and the future of American letters and has accepted an invitation to express that concern in an American journal, mustn't reflect too much that he is committed to a delicate task. (And after all, I can, by way of dismissing this worry, remind myself of the pleasure and relief I should feel if an American critic, with directness and force, would say about the English literary scene and the prospect for literature in England the things that need saying—the things that will never be said in *The Times Literary Supplement* or the *New Statesman* or a BBC talk.)

The very contemporary spirit of Mr Van Wyck Brooks's

[1] Reprinted from *Commentary*, November 1952.

[2] The five volumes of Van Wyck Brooks's *The Makers and Finders: A History of the Writer in America* are as follows: *The Flowering of New England* (1936); *New England: Indian Summer* (1940); *The World of Washington Irving* (1944); *The Times of Melville and Whitman* (1947); *The Confident Years* (1952).

survey as a whole is given in the adjective of his concluding title, *The Confident Years*. The confidence asserting itself in the years covered by the volume (1885–1915)—confidence that an American literature was emerging—has, in this subsequent period, Mr Brooks's own, been beyond question vindicated: here we have the implicit position (it is explicit enough too) from which Mr Brooks writes. But while this confidence, as he rests upon it, is so patently a convinced assumption of ample grounds, standing undeniably there (so to speak) in the public world—too undeniably, in fact, to need demonstrating—its essential character is to be wholly without definition. That is, it doesn't express itself in terms of any considered or considerable ideas of what a literature, or a significant work, might be; it is wholly unrelated to any such ideas—to anything that can properly be called a conception at all (for a positive conception must surely have an examinable content).

It was not of course a part of Mr Brooks's scheme in planning his 'history of the writer in America' (his own phrase) to maintain that kind of observance of critical standards—criteria of value and significance—which is proper in the history of a long-established literature, where (that is) we expect the field to be more or less strictly delimited in accordance with the conception of literature as a matter of memorable works. Nevertheless, it is impossible to judge that the enormous number of names of authors and titles of books appearing in Mr Brooks's pages along with some kind of descriptive commentary finds anything remotely approaching justification in light thrown on the origin and growth of a literature. It is not easy, in fact, to suggest any account he can have given himself of his justifying conception, or to divine a critical purpose that was in view—unless the quasi-creative evocation of a rich American past comes under that head.

But the inflationary bent presents itself in overt and challenging forms, forms where the critical significance is clear; as, for instance, in the treatment of W. D. Howells. Mr Brooks offers us Howells as an author of established major status; over and over again in *New England: Indian Summer* we read of Howells and Henry James, Henry James and Howells, coupled as no one *could* couple them to whom it was plain that, brought into the presence of James, a Howells just doesn't exist as a creative writer; there is nothing there for comparison. Howells, it seems to me, has even less substance than Trollope, and the classical standing of Trollope (there is the sumptuous edition that Oxford is bringing out, prepared and garnished with all the resources of scholarship) has always seemed to me one of the most betraying absurdities of British literary culture—I mean, conventional high culture.

But for Mr Brooks there is Henry James and there is W. D. Howells—magnitudes, one gathers, that are not at any rate too ridiculously assorted to be habitually brought together for comparison and contrast. Mr Brooks, in fact, prefers Howells; or at least he approves of him, and disapproves of James: Howells qualifies as positively and unequivocally American, and James doesn't. Howells was a good American: his 'scorn for all things European precluded any danger that Howells would follow the course of Henry James'. Of course Mr Brooks wouldn't accept the simple equivalence that a good American writer is a writer who is a good American, but all the same there is something that can only be called crude in his bias against James. And there is certainly something wrong about the preoccupation with Americanness that makes Howells more significantly American than James and more acclaimable as a glory of American literature.

One might at first be inclined to say that the informing idea in the preoccupation, the idea of what being American would—or could—amount to, is too simple and positive. But as one examines the idea in its working one becomes more inclined to say that it is, in itself, illusory, and, in its tendency, negative and nullifying. It is essentially not, in short, an idea that could give an account of itself, and its confidence turns out to be indistinguishable from that disability. To give an account of its tendency is to give an account of what it comes to: one has to note the significance for the American literary future of the blindness that it induces towards the great, the real, achievement of the past. What it portends, as far as it may prevail, is emptiness.

This may seem a severe account. But consider what Mr Brooks does with *The Europeans*—an American classic, and a crucial one, the astonishingly original and perfect early work of a great

American genius. In it James achieves complete command of the thematic preoccupation that appears in *Roderick Hudson* (itself a much more remarkable novel, deserving a much higher valuation, than would seem to be commonly recognized). *The Europeans* gives us a consummate example, and (one would have said) a supremely clear one, of that drama of critical interplay between America and Europe, conceived as different civilizations (the differences compelling such poignant interest because of the closeness of the kinship), which figures so largely and so significantly in the Jamesian *œuvre*. Mr Brooks in *New England: Indian Summer*, by way of clinching the observation 'All that was not European repelled and bored James', writes:

Like the baroness in *The Europeans*, after a year in America, he felt the annoyance of a swimmer 'who, nearing shore, to land, finds a smooth straight wall of rock' instead of a 'clean firm beach'. He could not scale this wall, and America was too big and vague. He felt that his only safety lay in flight.

Someone might perhaps be inclined to point out that Mr Brooks here is dealing with the later James, and suggest that he intends a special felicity of irony in casting this James for the role of Eugenia, Baroness Münster of Silberstadt-Schreckenstein, the representative in *The Europeans* of that Europe which, in the drama of mutual criticism and appraisal, is ironically 'placed' (for that the defeat of the Baroness records an unequivocal major score *against* Europe is beyond question). One can only reply that no reader of the book who has appreciated the significance of the passage that Mr Brooks recalls could have recalled it in bringing Mr Brooks's kind of criticism against James. No one who had appreciated the significance and consummateness of *The Europeans* could have had that kind of criticism to bring.

In fact, the inadequacy of Mr Brooks's idea of how a novelist may qualify as truly American is inseparable from the inadequacy of his notion of what a novel may be and do. The following, from *New England: Indian Summer*, is wholly characteristic of the author:

The influence of Hawthorne is marked in his stories, and perhaps if there had existed a great American realist to show the way for him and interpret the scene,—during his formative years,—James's whole career might have been different. As it was, he could make nothing of the country.

Howells was a 'realist' (we gather); but he presumably was either not a great enough one, or too late. With Howells, James himself is bracketed as a realist, but we gather that *he* was not a sufficiently *American* realist. 'In England', we are told, 'Defoe was a realist, and even Jane Austen.' It might be difficult to find a satisfactory definition of a term used in this way; but the negative and anaesthetizing force of the operative criterion it represents is plain enough. Hawthorne was not a realist: the remarkable good fortune that America had to produce so original a creative genius so early will not, then, be celebrated by Mr Brooks. There is no sign that he has any perception of what that genius consisted in, and it is fair to judge that he sees no reason to deplore the pressure of opinion that would have had Hawthorne turn himself into a kind of anticipatory W. D. Howells, dealing acclaimably with the contemporary surface of American life.

Mr Brooks's implicit account of Hawthorne's influence on James is necessarily of a negative order. Hawthorne was not a great American realist, and therefore couldn't help James to become an acceptable and really American glory of American literature. When I referred above to *The Europeans* as a 'crucial' classic, what I had in mind was the way in which the influence of Hawthorne appears in it. This first of James's fully achieved novels is wholly Jamesian; but it couldn't have been so but for Hawthorne. What James learned from his very different predecessor (the learning was of course a great creative feat) was how a profoundly reflective intelligence, one preoccupied with what lay beneath the surface of life and with the nature and prospects of the civilization into which it had been born, could deal with its preoccupations in prose fiction.

This creative relation was possible between these great original artists because the problem facing either was, for all the differences the problem of an *American* writer. And when *The Europeans* appeared, or at any rate ten years (say) after *The Europeans*, by which time the proofs James had given of the range and fertility of his genius should have been found irresistible, *the* American writer might have been acclaimed; the idea (one would have thought) being now sufficiently defined and charged to become a most potent kind of fact. For Hawthorne and James were more in American history than merely two individual writers; their greatness and their difference, together with the significant relation between them, established the reality of an American literature: there it was, Cooper, Hawthorne, Melville, and James, undeniably (again, one would have thought) an American central tradition, American and not provincial, carrying with it the promise of a robust continuing life.

But if only, instead of Hawthorne, 'there had existed a great American realist to show the way for him and interpret the scene ... James's whole career might have been different'. Mr Brooks avowedly wishes that James's whole career *had* been different. The achievement, of course, did not find itself at all undeniable; it is not there, so to speak, for Mr Brooks, who may take it as a justifying concession when one observes—it is a timely moment—that the promise was not fulfilled. But, instead of what James actually did for America, what, ignoring this, does Mr Brooks think he ought to have done; or—with better luck 'in his formative years'—might have done? Anticipated Dreiser or Frank Norris or Dos Passos?

'Realism' might sound a positive enough prescription; but when one examines what Mr Brooks's 'realism' amounts to, all that one can confidently report is the negation in it. It means indifference to the Americanness—and that is, to the art—of Hawthorne and James. In fact, one is compelled to judge that where Mr Brooks says 'interpret the scene', 'interpret' means nothing; it is an empty word. He has left no content for it. And if you exclude the kinds of interest and preoccupation in the working out of which Hawthorne and James, in their very different ways, became great American artists, no treatment of American life or the American scene, however complete its 'realism', can tend otherwise than to an effect of emptiness—emptiness, that is, of significance and of the substance given by that.

The negativeness of Mr Brooks's positive, the nullifying efficiency of his preoccupation with Americanness, comes out strikingly in the following passage from *The Confident Years*:

In part, through his attacks on Dickens and Thackeray [Howells] had destroyed, in America, the ascendancy of the English Victorian novel, endeavouring to sever American fiction from the tradition of England and bring it into the main stream of the fiction of the world. This cause he assisted in the critical essays on French, Spanish, Russian and Norwegian authors. . . .

In the phrase describing the aims and achievement attributed to Howells we have, unmistakably, Mr Brooks's own habit of mind. To be American is to be *not* English; in his preoccupation with the negative, he confuses, with disastrous effect, some utterly different things. There was the old 'colonial feeling', carrying with it a 'dependence on literary England' that certainly needed to be challenged. And Mr Brooks tells us that 'others besides Howells were spreading the idea that literature in the United States was by no means inevitably conditioned by English opinion'. The most effective way of spreading that idea, and banishing the colonial feeling, would have been, surely, to spread the idea that, so far as fiction was concerned, Hawthorne and James had patently made the colonial feeling ridiculous. But that line Mr Brooks himself, if, even with the advantage of the later perspective, he could be transported back in time, wouldn't be prepared to take.

He represents Howells as endeavouring to bring American fiction into the 'main stream'. But there was nothing more fitly to be called a main stream than that into which Hawthorne and James had actually brought it. The inability to see this is an inability to see their greatness as American writers. It goes with the ability not to recognize that 'literary England' is not English literature, and that, in demonstrating his independence of 'British traditions and standards',[1] an American writer might be testifying in the most significant of ways to an essential relation between American literature and (in the narrower sense) English.

---

[1] 'Meanwhile, cosmopolitan influences were pouring into the mind of New York, where others besides Howells were spreading the idea that literature in the United States was by no means inevitably conditioned by English opinion. The Columbia professor Brander Matthews, a peppery defender of American speech, was one of a number of critics who shared what he described as his wholesale distrust of British traditions and standards' (*The Confident Years*).

That 'tradition of England', that 'ascendancy of the English Victorian novel' which got (and gets—is Mr Brooks free of it?) in the way of a due recognition of the American achievement is as deplorable to the English critic as to the American—I mean, to the English critic who thinks it important that the cis-Atlantic part of the whole achievement in the common language should be duly recognized too.

I had better be quite explicit about what I have in mind. The 'tradition of England' in the matter of the Victorian novel seems to me both absurd and pernicious because, inflationary as it is, it imposes a blindness to as great a chapter as literary history has to show. In the nineteenth century the strength—the poetic strength—of the English language went into prose fiction. I might properly have paired an essay[1] I wrote on the influence of Milton in reply to Mr Eliot with one enforcing this observation. I will merely offer the proposition (sufficiently acceptable perhaps) that in Jane Austen, Dickens, Hawthorne, Melville, George Eliot, Henry James, Conrad, and D. H. Lawrence we have the successors of Shakespeare. I will add that I am not, in this proposition, to be taken as saying, with extension to other writers, the kind of thing that is said about Jane Austen when she is compared to Shakespeare because of her power of creating characters. The same kind of thing is said about Scott; and the criteria I have in mind exclude Scott—to note which is a way of intimating their nature. They point to novels that, because of their organization and their kind of significance, it is critically profitable to think of as 'dramatic poems': such novels are to be thought of, if organization and significance are to be understood, as grouping with Shakespeare's plays rather than with *Moll Flanders*, or *Tom Jones*, or *Tristram Shandy*, or the novel of manners. And in this line of fiction the actual influence of Shakespeare can, in different ways, be felt as a profound and decisive, if unmeasurable, presence.

I do not mean my list as exhaustive of the writers who might relevantly be adduced. (And, not irrelevantly, I do not like Mr Brooks's bracketing of Dickens with Thackeray.) But I confine myself to those who present themselves as the great compelling

[1] It is the first one in *The Common Pursuit*—I give the reference in order to make plain that in insisting on the relevance of that essay I am quite serious.

instances when this judgment is being advanced, the justice of which seems to me so obvious: if depth, range, and subtlety in the presentment of human experience are the criteria, prose fiction in English between Jane Austen and D. H. Lawrence has a creative achievement to show that is unsurpassed—unsurpassed by any of the famous great phases or chapters of literary history.

I am not suggesting that there is any equal of Tolstoy among the novelists of the English language; it is the richness of the whole 'chapter', the array in it of varied yet related great writers, that gives it its pre-eminence. And they *are* related, even if nothing simple that includes them all can be said about the relatedness, except that they are all of the English language. To include the great American novelists is not in the least to deny that they *are* American, or that there is an American literature to which they belong. It is (let us say) to illustrate the obvious truth that an American illustrates whenever, without feeling at all the less American, he recognizes that the language of Hawthorne and Lincoln and Mark Twain is the language of Shakespeare—and that Shakespeare belongs no less to America than to England.

I feel a little embarrassed as I look back at these rhetorical truisms. But the complex reality the truisms point to is not the less important because it is complex. And Mr Brooks, instead of studying the complexity (about which there is a great deal that a literary critic and historian might helpfully find to say), contemplates, with an optimistic and positive air, the idea of escaping from it. He judges Mencken to have gone too much to extremes in his anti-Anglo-Saxonism (see chapter 25 of *The Confident Years*), but the Americanism that he produces with a palpably endorsing sympathy is not less a matter of negation and illusion. There is that idea that the true American tradition derives from the West, and that the really American literature must come—has come and will come—from those regions which are Western enough to have escaped from the Anglicizing dominance of New England and the East. He tells us that:

> Theodore Roosevelt looked to the country beyond the Alleghenies. ... He felt that the more the West dominated the national life the better it would be 'for all of us',—a wish that was to be realized in literature within two decades.

The writers whom Mr Brooks adduces[1] as justifying this last judgment do not seem to me to justify his estimate of the achievement and the promise, and we may profitably examine this idea of the 'West'—test it for content, so to speak—by considering the really great American writer whom the West did produce, Mark Twain. He is unmistakably Western and frontier, and unquestionably very different from Hawthorne and James. But does the difference countenance in any way the spirit of that reliance on the West which Mr Brooks records, and sees, apparently, no reason to criticize?

And here I have to say that *Huckleberry Finn* as I read it is a very different kind of work from that offered us by Mr Brooks. I cannot help thinking that my *Huckleberry Finn* is the greater work, and my Mark Twain a greater artist. In *The Times of Melville and Whitman* we are told:

He was the frontier story-teller, the great folk-writer of the American West, and he raised to a pitch unrivalled before him the art of oral story-telling and then succeeded in transferring its effects to paper.

Yes, but it won't do to suggest that the art of *Huckleberry Finn* is a naïve art, or that there is anything naïve or simple about the outlook of the author. And to the question, 'Was it not the moral of *Huckleberry Finn* that all civilization is a hateful mistake?' ... one can only answer that to come away from the book with *that* would be to have simplified it into something very different from the great work of art it is.

It wasn't Huck who wrote *Huckleberry Finn*; the mind that conceived *him* was mature, subtle, and sophisticated. Mark Twain had had very wide and varied experience of men and the world, and he was not only a shrewd observer; he observed out of a ripe

[1] E.g.: 'In his highly developed artistic sense [Hemingway] was the type of a generation that cared, all but uniquely, for the art of writing. . . . He shared this sense with several of the writers through the sheer weight of whose talents alone the supremacy in American letters would have passed to the West—the poets Sandburg, Eliot and Pound, the novelists Dreiser, Anderson, Lewis, Dos Passos, Steinbeck, Farrell and Scott Fitzgerald' (*The Confident Years*). I will only comment on the irresponsible and characteristic way in which Mr Brooks makes Eliot a representative of the 'West'—Eliot, who hardly goes to strengthen any suggested idea of it.

wisdom. If he was tender-hearted, he had, when his genius was engaged, too firm a hold on reality to indulge any sentimental bent. And when Mr Brooks, in *The Confident Years*, calls *Huckleberry Finn* 'that paean to the inborn goodness of man, or the goodness of boys peculiarly as nature made them', and makes it a document that justifies the grouping of Mark Twain with Emerson and Whitman, one can only protest against a disastrous misrepresentation. There is nothing simple or simplifying about the moral outlook of *Huckleberry Finn*. The irony is sophisticated: faced with a (for him) inescapably complex situation, Mark Twain is intent on doing justice to the complexity. It might be said that the essential theme of the book, that which makes it a world classic, is the complexity of ethical valuation in any society that has a complex tradition. Mark Twain, that is, though so unmistakably and profoundly American, writes out of a full continuity with the European past.

One way of enforcing the truth of this account is to compare *Huckleberry Finn* with another book of Mark Twain's, one that I very much admire though Mr Brooks dismisses it with contempt: *Pudd'nhead Wilson*. It is 'about' murder and detection, just as *Huckleberry Finn* is 'about' boys' adventures on the Mississippi; but it is an ironical masterpiece, and the irony is essentially that of *Huckleberry Finn*; the ethical preoccupation is the same. But in *Pudd'nhead Wilson*, Mark Twain, instead of making his conventions out of the frontiersman's art of story-telling as he knew it, adopts a style and a convention of sophisticated literary tradition, and handles them with the supreme skill of a writer perfectly at home in them. And when one goes back to *Huckleberry Finn* it should be plain that to have made out of a Western vernacular the instrument that Mark Twain made, and used for such purposes, required an author of the cultural background and intellectual sophistication necessary to the writing of a *Pudd'nhead Wilson*. There is no paradox in the putting of such an instrument to such a use. The society that formed Mark Twain, and is depicted by him in *Huckleberry Finn*, might have been 'frontier', but it had kept a vigorous hold on its heritage of civilization.

The fact is, 'frontier' and 'West' in these uses tend to be

insidious words: they suggest the dropping of an outworn heritage and (it is often implied) its replacement by something more distinctively American. There is no hint of contempt for, or oblivion of, the heritage in the society depicted in *Huckleberry Finn* and *Pudd'nhead Wilson*, though it may be provincial. But as the frontier moved west there was, we know, a dropping. A testimony to the loss, and an implicit commentary on the faith that the loss entailed the promise of a positive American culture, can be seen in what Mr Brooks records of Hamlin Garland's disillusionment:'... and in time Garland's first resentment of Sinclair Lewis's *Main Street* "softened" as he said, in the light of these glaring facts.'

Closely associated with the idea of the 'West' is the idea of the 'new interracial consciousness', destined to replace the older traditional American culture. A commentary on this idea is to be found in the pages of *The Confident Years* that deal with Ole Rolvaag, 'who remained, while living in America, a Norwegian writer':

He was obsessed with the thought of the loss which every immigrant underwent when he forfeited the cultural heritage of the old country; when, without becoming a part of the culture that surrounded him, he became a stranger to his own. He clung to the energizing spiritual memories, the collective aspirations which the old-world people were discarding in their new-world setting, constantly asking himself the question, what was to follow pioneering among all these races that were losing their traditions together? ... When to compensate for all they lost their gains were material only, when the old loyalties vanished and the old traditions with them, would not this land become a spiritual wilderness, inhabited by shallow, drifting 'cultural tramps'?

These questions are put with a force that, even if in these admirable pages Mr Brooks (as so often) is mainly quoting, he must, one feels, have appreciated. But he nowhere gives any sign of having glimpsed an answer—an answer in the spirit of the questions—or of having noticed that he hasn't. Dreiser, surely, represents what 'the interracial consciousness' comes to. I will not dwell on Mr Brooks's apparent indulgence (I find it character-istic) towards the estimate of Dreiser as a great writer, comparable to 'the great Europeans'.

It is time to turn to the significance of Ezra Pound. Mr Brooks, I think, reflects a generally held view when he speaks of Pound's 'feeling for the European tradition as a whole'. To me the significance of Pound is just this: that while he sees himself, and is widely accepted, as being what Mr Brooks reports, actually he shows himself utterly unable to understand what the conditions were—what kind of things were the 'culture' and the 'tradition' —out of which European art and literature grew. 'Really one DON'T need to know a language. One NEEDS, damn well needs, to know the few hundred words in the few really good poems that any language has in it.' And, 'The Greek populace was PAID to attend the great Greek tragedies, and darn well wouldn't have gone otherwise, or if there had been a cinema.'

What goes with the ability to say and mean this kind of thing is the conception of Culture as something apart and aloof, forming a special consecrated realm, and having only external contacts with profane living. Pound's own art belongs essentially to this conception; his poetic is something cultivated apart, in that consecrated realm (which in some ways resembles a void), and it is applied externally to the interests—the didacticisms about Usury and so on—that supply him with his themes. And in the association (so characteristic) in Pound of a refinement of 'art' with a habit of thoroughly unrefined vocabulary and attitude we have, I think, a representative significance: there is, as it were, a complementary relation between the given conception of Culture (which plays an interesting part in Mr Brooks's work, and makes its most notable appearance, perhaps, in his astonishing exaltation of James Branch Cabell) on the one hand, and, on the other, the actual cultural conditions contemplated in a despondent way (despondency being of course not the only possible kind of response) by Rolvaag and the disillusioned Hamlin Garland.

I am not suggesting that all Americans who read Pound accept his view of himself (and after all, Pound is not without his cult in England). But he does, all the same, seem to me to represent something very significantly American—something in the conditions in which the American writer works. No other country could have produced a Pound; no other civilization could have produced so robust a talent that had so little sense of what a living

cultural tradition is, so little sense of the organic. It was this I
was thinking of when, on another occasion, I was moved to
observe that Mr T. S. Eliot himself, with his immensely greater
gifts and finer intelligence, was after all, a fellow-countryman of
Pound. The provocation was (though there are other grounds)
Mr Eliot's record in respect of D. H. Lawrence; not his disliking
Lawrence and judging him adversely, but the nature and manner
of the dislike, and the terms of the justification alleged; the blindness to such genius going with the ability to give *that* weight to
an Irving Babbitt.

I do not make these points with any happy complacency.
America could not have produced a Lawrence; but nor will
England be able to produce another. The representative talent
that England produced just as Lawrence died was W. H. Auden—
who is now an American poet. One can say of Auden that only
England could have produced *him*. There he is, unmistakably
English upper middle class, English Public School, and Oxford;
and yet, since the time when he 'arrived', the point to make
about him has always been that he belongs to 'this American
world'. There is no paradox about his easy exchange of allegiance
and habitat. The fact is, as the phrase just quoted recognizes, the
conditions that Pound's case brings up for contemplation in a
highly challenging way present themselves in some form—they,
or something essentially akin—pretty generally. Auden was such
a portent because of his easy and complete conquest of literary-
intellectual England. Only in a 'culture' in which the continuity
with the past had failed, a 'culture' that had in effect lost, with its
finer tradition, the sense of what maturity and creative achievement are like, could Auden have been accepted, and remained
accepted, as a major poet and an intellectual. He was claimed by
the ethos, or state, that he expressed.

We are all, then, faced with the same problem. The difference
between England and America is perhaps that in England it is
easier, as yet, to hold on to the recognition that there *is* a problem.
It seems to me in any case that *The Confident Years* should be an
occasion for recalling that America *has* had a literature, distinctively and strongly American, and promising an American development, yet in full continuity with the common past.

X

THE COMPLEX FATE[1]

I AM present in this book (having been honoured by the invitation to be so) as disagreeing with Mr Bewley over some particular judgments. But my disagreements are minor indeed compared with the major concurrence that makes me welcome his book with a wholly sincere warmth and with great relief. Here is an American critic saying, with the authority of what is unmistakably criticism of a rare intelligence and force, what has long needed saying—or so I have thought. And I am hardly the only English observer who has contemplated with distress and apprehension the lines on which, in America in our time, the conviction that America has, or ought to have, a great literature has developed.

For an Englishman to feel and to express such a concern is no impertinence. What happens to American civilization has clearly the greatest importance for Europe. But, as it is the virtue of Mr Bewley's book to make so plain, an Englishman has special reasons for taking a poignant interest in the prevailing American ideas about the present and future of American literature. In any case it is wholly proper that he should bear his testimony when a great creative achievement—and this one, belonging to the common language, may be fitly appraised by an Englishman— is slighted.

Mr Bewley, then, seems to me to be unquestionably right when he says that in the nineteenth century America 'produced a line of novelists'—he names Cooper, Hawthorne, Melville, and James—'who represent her greatest achievement in art'. It is a very impressive achievement, and an English critic cannot claim that it has had in this country the attention it deserves. More seriously, it is far from enjoying in America, as Mr Bewley points

[1] Introduction to *The Complex Fate*, by Marius Bewley (London: Chatto & Windus, 1952).

out, the honour and the influence that are its due—more seriously, because of the significance of such a default for the prospects of American literature. Of the writers whom he names as forming a tradition in the American novel Mr Bewley says:

They have no considerable successors today, and what they stood for in such varying ways among themselves has been supplanted.

And he intimates, with a directness that an Englishman judging the same might well think proper to leave to an American critic, that something has gone wrong, and that the trouble is a mistaken preoccupation with being American. It is mistaken, because it rejects something profoundly and essentially American that held the promise of a rich future, and rejects it for what is American in an excluding and impoverishing way such as holds no possibility of a great American literature:

That school of literary appreciation which claims American literature simply because it is American has been represented by a strong body of critical opinion in the United States, and it has led to an insidious magnification of the frontier colloquial tradition in American literature. This tradition is one of great importance, but it is not the tradition embodied in America's four major novelists. . . . This frontier tradition has its own high points of achievement, but it represents the extreme isolation of American literature, and it is fragmentary and misleading because it does not provide sufficient scope in itself to treat the largest problem that confronted the American artist in the nineteenth century, and which still occupies him: the nature of his separateness, and the nature of his connection with European, and particularly with English, culture.

And, adducing the 'ancient tendency to regard Henry James as a European rather than an American novelist', Mr Bewley testifies:

Yet it is of the essence of James's genius that he was an American in a fuller and finer sense than any of the American-Firsters in criticism who have found his quality beyond their comprehension.

Mr Bewley puts what seems to me an unanswerable truth with a very timely force that, backed as the statement is by the critical analyses that follow, I should like to believe final. But such propositions, I know, ask for something far more difficult to obtain than formal assent. It might, for instance, seem paradoxical that his challenge on behalf of James should be needed; for James —together with the James family—has been made into an American institution. But that, of course, is the trouble; it is of the essence of an institutional cult of that kind *not* to find itself at odds with the faith that the true American tradition—the one that ought to prevail in the American literature of the present and the future— is that which looks back to the frontier tradition for its beginnings.

And I should like to make here a point that did not lie in Mr Bewley's path, intent as he was on the theme indicated by his title. When, as against the tradition discussed by Mr Bewley, the 'frontier tradition' is made the source of a truly American literature, the idea, I think, derives an illicit respectability from the aura of Mark Twain. I need not presume to discuss what the frontier tradition amounted to, or what was Mark Twain's connexion with it. When it is exalted in that way, what we have (it is enough to note) is the spirit of which it may be said that its essential definition of Americanness is given in the collocation of Whitman, Dreiser, Scott Fitzgerald, and Hemingway. I am not offering to plot a 'tradition' with those names. But what that is more plausibly a tradition has been anywhere proposed by way of vindicating the narrowly 'American' bent? The writers I have named have all been distinguished with favour as significantly American; and the significance has to be defined in terms of an antipathetic unlikeness to Mr Bewley's line. The unlikeness, it is true, differs in kind from one to another of them: I picked on them as representative—the prevailing will to go back on the strength and the greatness of the American literary past has unavoidably to be represented in that way if we ask what, positively, it points to instead.

Returning now to Mark Twain: no one, I imagine, disputes that Mark Twain is a truly American writer. Yet if, in accordance with the spirit that asserts itself so formidably, we are to define Americanness by the collocation of Whitman, Dreiser, Scott Fitzgerald, and Hemingway, and say that the promise of a truly American literature lies *there*, that is to leave Mark Twain behind, in a too European past, along with Cooper, Hawthorne, Melville, and James, for, if we value him for what he is, there can be no question which of the two companies he belongs to.

I am thinking of the great Mark Twain, author of American classics. The English reader of *Huckleberry Finn* doesn't find himself reflecting: 'This is by a fellow-countryman of Whitman.' American as the book is, it is not American in Whitman's way, and conveys no suggestion of a world or an ethos out of which a Whitman might emerge as a characteristic voice. As for Dreiser, it is impossible to think of him as belonging to one tradition with the author of *Huckleberry Finn*, if only because he so clearly belongs to no tradition. He represents the consequences of the later influxes from Europe and the sudden polygot agglomeration of big raw cities, and may with some point be said to belong to the culturally dispossessed. It is possible, of course, to call the state of those who have lost their distinctive heritage, and acquired nothing comparable in its place, distinctively American; but the tendency to treat this state as a positive American tradition out of which a great national literature may be expected to come is depressing. Out of the conditions represented by Dreiser (who writes as if he hasn't a native language) no great literature *could* come; and nothing that can properly be called the beginnings of literature came in his case.

There would seem to be no good reason for believing that literature could any more come out of the conditions represented by Scott Fitzgerald, who shows that a writer, while using English as unquestionably a native inheritance, may yet have inherited little else with it. As the one positive alternative to the actual and very unideal kinds of relation between the sexes ordinary in the milieu he depicts, he never gets beyond the teen-age Romeo-and-Juliet notion of romantic love. Such love is what the hero is baulked of by social snobbery in *The Great Gatsby*. And it is not merely that, in Fitzgerald's world, no vestige, and no suspicion, of any standard of maturity exists. The extremity of the destitution that disqualifies him as a novelist and a creative writer (in spite of the almost classical status that has been conferred on him) is what can be seen in the accounts of his life; those accounts which, offered us so often in apparent unawareness of their implication, have the closest critical bearings on what he wrote.

The state of dispossession they illustrate—dispossession of the interests, the awarenesses, the impulsions and the moral perceptions out of which a creative rendering of human life might come—is such that he seems to have had hardly any sense of even the elementary decencies that one had thought of as making civilized intercourse possible (if he was aware of them it was to show—the relevant episodes are very striking—resentful hostility to any regard for them in others). There is nothing in his writings to contradict what we know of the life.

In Hemingway, we have, it may be granted, something positively American. But it is hard to see why, in this, he should be thought to promise well for an American literary future—in saying which one is registering the portentous distance between Hemingway and Mark Twain. The author of *Huckleberry Finn* writes out of a full cultural heritage. The life he depicts is not crude —with the case presented by Hemingway in sight, the critic would be very improvident to use that adjective in connexion with *Huckleberry Finn*. Compared with the idiom cultivated by Hemingway, Huck's language, as he speaks it, it is hardly excessive to say, is Shakespearian in its range and subtlety. Mark Twain, of course, had made of the colloquial mode he took such pride in rendering accurately a convention of art and a literary medium. But in doing so he has achieved an inevitable naturalness; the achievement, in fact, is the creation of Huck himself, about whom, I imagine, it has rarely been complained that he is unconvincing. And in Huck, the embodiment of an ungenteel Western vernacular, he has made a *persona* for the expression of a mature criticism of life—mature and subtle by the standards of the great European literatures.

I need not enlarge on the relevant significance of this fact. What I will allow myself to emphasize is the maturity and refinement of the criticism. It is not merely that Mark Twain was a generous, compassionate, and tender-hearted man, as well as a shrewd and widely-experienced observer. In the poised humanity, genial but unillusioned, conveyed by the whole work—conveyed in the quality of the life observed and presented, as well as in the attitude towards it—we cannot but recognize the presence of a mature and full heritage of civilization. In the attitude, the radical inclusive attitude of *Huckleberry Finn*, there is nothing of the wisdom of the tough or undeveloped and no bent towards a simplifying reduction of life. There is nothing sentimental or tough about the irony. It is the irony of an unusual adequacy to experience, and an unusual preoccupation with fullness of appraisal, the book having for essential theme the complexity of ethical valuation in any society that has a complex tradition.

In passing from *Huckleberry Finn* to *Pudd'nhead Wilson* one is obviously—one could tell with ease from internal evidence—passing to another work by the same master; and who would not say that the author of *Pudd'nhead Wilson* (that neglected masterpiece which no one, English or American, to whom I have mentioned it has read, so that my rhetorical question hasn't, perhaps, the point it might have had) did not belong rather, and very decidedly, with James than with Whitman or Dreiser or Fitzgerald or Hemingway?

But Mr Bewley has his focused preoccupation. He defines a tradition in the American novel that has peculiar relevance to the needs of the present, and is (he contends, with what seems to me valid reason) the significantly American tradition in literature. Of the authors he associates (and his account explains why he doesn't include Mark Twain, who isn't significantly American in this way) he says that they

dealt with the American scene, but this is not the basis of their resemblance, which lies rather in their sense of the dangers and deficiencies which they saw encircling the possibilities they believed the country possessed. The tension between their faith and their fears created the best art America has ever produced. They form a tradition, not by virtue of their relation with each other, but because, each in his own fashion, they were *seriously* concerned with the new nation in a way that European novelists are rarely or never concerned with theirs. They felt that the possibilities of creative achievement were intrinsically involved with the new patterns of life which were forming in America, and they feared with all their hearts, though not always consciously, the concomitant losses that inevitably came with the gains.

And Mr Bewley intimates[1] that an Englishman may properly feel himself to have a peculiar interest in the vindication and

---

[1] *Op. cit.* See especially pp. 73 and 74.

renewal of this tradition. There is, of course, the obvious general sense in which the American literary future will have a special importance for the other peoples speaking the common language; and in the tradition in question lies the possibility of a literature worthy to be called one. But Mr Bewley has something more pointed to say. Of the 'Hawthorne-James line' he observes that the essential, and far from ineffective preoccupation of these writers was with the possibility for the American 'cut off from his antecedents and embarrassed by the burden of his "commonplace prosperity"', of developing a 'refined consciousness' of the 'unity that underlies the divisions of the English-speaking world'. He adds:

It was a tremendously complex problem, and as the world is going, it was and is a problem of such importance that even today one hardly dare plot limits to what it may eventually mean in terms of a future English-speaking civilization.

An Englishman who agrees should make it plain how little he is merely agreeing that a problem faces 'the American'. I myself then (let me say) see Mr Bewley as pointing to a major significance that Henry James has for me, a significance bound up with my sense of his greatness. I am thinking of that drama of critical interplay between different traditions which has so large a part in his *œuvre*. It represents, as I have remarked elsewhere, a comparative inquiry, enacted in dramatic and poetic terms, into the criteria of civilization, and the possibilities. It transcends the vindication of one side against the other, or the mere setting forth of the for and against on both sides in a drama of implicit mutual criticism. The essential spirit of the drama is positive; James is feeling, creatively, towards an ideal possibility that is neither Europe nor America (for 'Europe', as James settled down to his 'complex fate', becoming a good deal of an Englishman while, like Mr Touchett, remaining an American—and being manifestly more than either—we may read 'England').

This, we know, represents the drama James actually lived; the drama the felt presence of which in his *œuvre* is not confined to those novels and tales which we first think of as answering to the description I have just given. I should like to think that this

James figures for us the Anglo-American literary—and so more than literary—future. In such a future, England would be England still, and America America; but the critical-creative interplay relating them, made possible by the difference and the unity, would be such as answered fully to the symbol, justifying and developing its suggestions.

Whatever may be thought of the idea put in this large way, there are two applications of it suggested by Mr Bewley's book that have a good chance of being recognized at once as acceptable. One is that the line of novelists judged by Mr Bewley to represent the great American achievement in art provides what should be a study of major importance on this side of the Atlantic. When I say 'of major importance' I am thinking, among other things, of the place such a study might have—should have—in an advanced 'English' course at the university. Think, for instance—if I may illustrate from my local point of view—of the eminent suitability of such a study as a Special Subject for Part II of the English Tripos. It is well-defined, compact, and manageable. The major works of the main authors who form the line (Cooper, Hawthorne, Melville, and James) are for the Englishman classics of English literature, yet he cannot but recognize them as American. And Mr Bewley hints pregnantly at ways in which that American line (for the writers forming it are, as he says, in most significant relation and constitute an American literature) offers the Englishman an incomparable approach to the study of a civilization intimately related to his own, and related in ways that make it of peculiar moment that he should understand both the affinities and the differences. As a source of suggestions as to the ways in which an intelligent literary-critical approach may develop into a study of that scope, the student now has Mr Bewley's book (a promise, one trusts, of much to come) to put with the very small group that includes Mr Yvor Winters' *Maule's Curse*.

The other 'application' I spoke of would be to constate the present urgent need for a lively play of literary criticism between the two major English-speaking countries. Formal agreement, perhaps, comes readily enough on this point. The trouble is that what we have, in practice, in this country, is an undiscriminating readiness in the quarters where our literary fashions are controlled (the literary world, metropolitan and *universitaire*—the system is a comprehensive one) to acclaim American criticism in general for its superior vigour and seriousness. What the specious generosity of recognition expresses and ministers to is the reverse of a concern for vigour and seriousness in English criticism. The tightness of the system in this tight little island remains unimpaired: 'American criticism' becomes a vague ally in the business of making things safe, and putting a face on the suppression of the *mauvais sujet* who won't play the game. What an Englishman concerned for life must count on is a real cross-Atlantic interplay that will make the confident substitution of the unanimities of British 'social' civilization for the standards of criticism more difficult: there is after all a more important society. Meanwhile he has to note with deep discouragement how easily the valuations of London, the British scene being in question, seem to get themselves accepted in New York (though the British Council writ doesn't run there), and in America generally—even when they are represented by visiting families of aristocratic geniuses.

About the ways in which an intelligent interest in the American literary scene on the part of critics here might help the function of criticism in America Mr Bewley would no doubt have something interesting to say.

I am not (I had better, in closing, be quite explicit) assuming that he agrees with everything—every particular judgment or emphasis—in what I myself have said above.

XI

POUND IN HIS LETTERS[1]

ONE would say that the volume of *Letters*, in sum, made tragic reading, if only the disaster it records weren't accompanied by so much that is brutally without dignity, and where it is comic, often odious too. The disaster, in fact, was a long degeneration, and is tragic only in that there had been something so admirable and heroic about the hero. The Pound who came to England in 1908 showed a wonderful energy of disinterested intelligence and public spirit. Never, in the literary world, has there been a more courageous single-mindedness. 'Until someone is honest we get nothing clear.' 'It is only when a few men who know get together and *disagree* that any sort of criticism is born.' 'Isn't it worth while having *one* critic who won't say a thing is *good* until he is ready to stake his whole position on the decision?' 'You offer to find a publisher ... if I abrogate my privileges, if I give way to, or saddle myself with, a damn'd contentious, probably incompetent committee. If I tacitly, tacitly to say the least of it, accept a certain number of people as my critical and creative equals, and publish the acceptance.' 'Dear H[arriet] M[onroe]: No, most emphatically I will not ask Eliot to write down to any audience whatsoever. I dare say my instinct was sound enough when I volunteered to quit the magazine quietly about a year ago. Neither will I send you Eliot's address in order that he may be insulted.'

He forced Eliot on Harriet Monroe's Chicago *Poetry*, and, with a patent absence of concern for anything but the reputation, livelihood, and development of poets and writers, did what he could to get them published and known, and to make such organs as he could start, commandeer, or get a hand in, serve his magnanimous purposes. To discover and launch Eliot—that is a historic

[1] Reprinted from *Scrutiny*, June 1951. A review of *The Letters of Ezra Pound*, ed. D. D. Paige, and *Ezra Pound: A Collection of Essays*, ed. Peter Russell.

achievement. He may claim also a large part of the credit for Joyce. Whom else did he push?—Wyndham Lewis, in recording which item we come, it seems to me, to the other side of the account, and to Pound's limitations. For these, which are very serious in a man who has been so influential, have—and especially in view of the second volume under discussion—to be insisted on, and at length.

Wyndham Lewis's reputation as a writer was established by the efforts of the Egoist group, in which Pound played so large a part. As a result, that reputation—which cannot, I believe, bear the beginnings of critical scrutiny—enjoyed the support of Eliot's rising prestige in the 1920s. Eliot remained faithful till at least the middle 'thirties (and today we are in danger of having *Tarr* and *The Childermass* revived and pressed on us as memorable works). I stress the instance of Wyndham Lewis, because he is representative; he represents a kind of toughness—a truculent inhumanity or anti-humanity ('My God, they stink!'), a mechanistic externality—an attraction to which is to be found in Eliot as well as Pound. (It is to be noted, too, that while Pound backed Mussolini, and Wyndham Lewis wrote a book in favour of Hitler, Eliot drew inspiration for such distinctive ethos as *The Criterion* had from Charles Maurras.)

If we ask what other poets Pound backed (other than Robert Frost), the answer is that it is hard to remember, because on the whole they matter so little. And here again we have Pound's limitations.

And yet it was, beyond question, a strong intelligence that influenced Eliot—and Yeats—beneficently at a crucial moment, and earned Pound an illustrious place in the history of English poetry. He encouraged Yeats in his emergence out of the incantations of the Celtic Twilight into speech-rhythms and a use of language spare, taut, and ironical. He knew what, in a post-Swinburnian climate, had to be said to the young talent if there was to be any hope of a prosperous development. 'Verse ought to be at least as well written as prose'—this was a dictum that Pound could enforce in cogent (and constructive) particular criticism.

'I think', says Mr Eliot in the essay of his reprinted in Mr

Russell's volume, 'that Pound was original in insisting that poetry was an art, an art which demands the most arduous application and study, and in seeing that in our time it has to be a highly conscious art.' In order to indicate the nature of a promising addiction to 'art', more, of course, is needed than a reference to the Provençal patterns that Pound cultivated. What more, Mr Eliot provides a couple of sentences further on:

The business of the poet is to be more conscious of his own language than other men, to be more sensitive to the feeling, more aware of the meaning of every word he uses, more aware of the history of the language and of every word he uses, than other men.

The more one ponders it the more difficult a concept does 'language' become to delimit. To be sensitive to a language is to be sensitive to a culture. You can only hope to be sensitive to a language of the past, or to a foreign language, out of your sensitiveness to your own language, your sensitiveness and consciousness in the present.

And here we come again to Pound's limitations. How can he have offered with such conviction his Guides, his *How to Reads*, his quintessential propædeutics for poets, with their prescriptions of Provençal, mediaeval Italian, Chinese, and so on? How could he discriminate so perversely and confidently in favour of so dull a set of conventions as the Provençal—conventions with so inferior a culture behind them and in them? when the Middle Ages have so much to offer that is so much more worth study, and in the past of his own language? 'Really one DON'T need to know a language. One NEEDS, damn well needs, to know the few hundred words in the few really good poems that any language has in it.' He didn't really know what a culture was at all—in spite of his noble desire 'to set the arts in their rightful place as the acknowledged guide and lamp of civilization'. Though he boasted that, 'neither Irish nor Catholic, I have had more mediaeval contact than most, through Dante and my Provençal', he knew about mediaeval civilization essentially nothing. And he knew about Europe, one is driven to say too, essentially nothing.

For the admirable American energy and disinterestedness and generosity that were his virtues carried with them certain

attendant disabilities. He glimpsed in poetry and art light and significance that should, he felt, make life worth living; and he
devoted himself with magnificent single-mindedness to the service
of what he saw. But of the nature of that, and its relation to life,
he had only the most limited understanding—barbarian, one is
inclined to say, but the barbarians had cultures in precisely the
sense that Pound remained unaware of. He could judge that he
had been born 'in a half-savage country', but the unawareness
persisted invincibly. 'It takes about 600 to make a civilization',
he says in 1928. Anyone who doubts the significance of this
should ponder the following:

The Greek populace was PAID to attend the great Greek tragedies,
and darn well wouldn't have gone otherwise, or if there had been a
cinema.

Shakespeare was 'Lord Somebody's players'; and the Elizabethan
drama, as distinct from the long defunct religious plays, was a court
affair.

As for the degeneration, that becomes apparent when Pound
takes to Social Credit (and Mussolini). 'He saw', says the editor
in his Foreword, 'Europe drifting towards a war that could have
been avoided by a simple currency reform.' About the bullying
wilfulness of conviction with which Pound, in and out of season,
asserted that things *were* as simple as that there was not only an
element of Jonsonian comedy; there was also something repellently brutal, a certain native tough and truculent insensitiveness
turning into a positive vice. And here we come to the famous
'brilliant epistolary style'.

The letters do indeed exhibit a racy vigour and a strong
directness and bite, conveying the courage and grapple of a live,
disinterested mind. But from early on there are characteristics
that, long before the end of the volume, have become a boring
exasperation. There is that facetious and utterly pointless mis-
spelling which Pound indulges in as soon as—which is very readily
(even—a piquant situation—in writing to my old headmaster)—
he feels that he has established an epistolary familiarity with a
correspondent. So far from growing out of it he grows into it,
and at the best it is the sign of a portentous established immaturity.

But it is worse than that; it goes with something that is also

immaturity *and* worse: 'The French', he says, 'have a word of
five letters and the English of four.' In the one letter I have from
Pound (and which I did not hand over to the editor—but because
of its manner of referring to a distinguished poet and critic, and
early friend of Pound) the 'brilliant epistolary style' is mainly a
matter of the repetition of the English word. That word, in the
Letters, has for abundant company a great deal of the same order,
and, in spite of some variety of a kind (e.g. 'bug-headed ape'), the
total effect is that of the maddening and depressing monotony of
Army obscenity.

It is more than a superficial foible; as we see it growing on the
letter-writer we see a certain native (or cultural) insensitiveness,
indulged and sanctioned, developing into a repellently ugly and
inhuman brutality. Pound, translating the Shelleyan exaltations
about the creative mind, writes: 'Humanity is malleable mud, and
the arts set the moulds it is later cast into.' It is significant that,
in the same letter, two sentences further on, he writes: 'Victoria
was an excrement, Curtis, Lorrimer, *all* British journalism are
excrement', etc. The significance—the relation of these habits of
expression to the bullying and overbearing absoluteness with
which Pound advanced his simple panacea—is to be seen in the
scatological Cantos. 'Inhuman brutality' too strong a description
for what the toughness, the coarseness, the lack of something,
comes to be?—Consider the attitude that Pound found himself
able to take towards the systematic, and unspeakably atrocious,
doing to death of the Jews of Europe. The spectacle of Pound's
degeneration is a terrible one, and no one ought to pretend that
it is anything but what it is.

And this painfully limited mind, which does not know what a
civilization is, and can suppose that to appreciate the best poems in
a language you need only know as much of the language as the
poems contain, is credited (see the essays in Mr Peter Russell's
collection) with having created a modern epic: 'No one ever knew
his own mind more clearly', says Mr Hugh Kenner. 'Indeed the
didactic gestures emerge naturally from the store-house of voli-
tional forms. . . .' The poet of the Cantos 'knows his own mind'
clearly in the sense that what his technique is devoted to conveying is nothing substantially more than what, at the platform level,

the didactic, conscious will dictates. And that confident domineering didactic consciousness is not the servant of any vital underlying theme, or of any rich sense of positive life. Mr Eliot said the damning thing about Pound's moral inspiration when he remarked that Pound's hells 'are for the other people'. What comes up from below is hatred and the will to reduce life to what can give excuse for hatred and contempt and disgust. (Pound, like Eliot, dislikes Lawrence and is drawn to Wyndham Lewis—who also dislikes Lawrence.) Whatever the intensity of 'art' represented by the Cantos, the effect, for all the famous skill and variety of versification, is barrenness and monotony. *Mauberley* stands alone—a great poem; the art there is creative, the expression of a young, strong, generous, and still sensitive mind.

XII

'LAWRENCE SCHOLARSHIP' AND LAWRENCE[1]

I HAVE tried, but I find it impossible to be grateful to Professor Harry T. Moore for what he has 'done for Lawrence'. The provocation, in the present volumes,[2] to an ungracious and apprehensive stiffening comes at the very outset, on the page after the title-page. We read there:

> The Editor dedicates this collection of D. H. Lawrence's letters to
> Richard Aldington
> David Garnett
> Laurence Pollinger.

The implicit pretension is ominous, and the more offensively so because of its particular terms. Who is Professor Harry T. Moore, one asks, and what standing does he suppose he has in relation to the genius of whom he has taken academic possession, that he should dedicate a collection of Lawrence's letters? Had he dedicated it to Aldous Huxley, that indeed one would have acclaimed as an appropriate and graceful gesture. Mr Huxley's volume was an act of personal judgment and self-committal, and, taking effect as it did a couple of years after Lawrence's death, at a time when it was possible for the distinguished editor of the *Criterion* to judge him not worth an obituary notice, it has an important place in the history of Lawrence's reputation. But Professor Moore takes over Lawrence as an established classic on whom he has been able to consolidate his own position as an 'authority' with immediate academic credit and munificent institutional support. And we are contemplating a familiar kind of irony when we reflect that no one at all intelligent about what

[1] Reprinted from the *Sewanee Review*, Winter 1963.
[2] *The Collected Letters of D. H. Lawrence*, edited by Harry T. Moore, 2 vols. (Heinemann, 1962).

makes Lawrence truly a classic and a writer worth devoted study could have put that dedication in front of a body of intimate Laurentian text.

Laurence Pollinger as a dedicatee one could have passed; there is no significance in a tribute to a literary agent. But the two co-present well-known writers constitute an infelicity so disconcerting that there is much significance in Professor Moore's being unaware of it—as he obviously is. David Garnett's acceptance as a distinguished contemporary writer was a phenomenon of that literary world the nature and power of which were what those who worked for the recognition of Lawrence's genius had most to contend against. Lawrence himself, in one of the letters printed by Professor Moore, mildly calls *Lady into Fox*, the book that established Garnett's fame, 'pretty piffle'. As for Richard Aldington, Professor Moore tells us under 'Who's Who in the Letters': 'His most famous novel is *Death of a Hero* (1928). . . .' In the prose of that work we find chunks of would-be D. H. Lawrence side by side with chunks of H. G. Wells. It is a familiar case that the author, a scholarly critic with a classical culture, should feel himself a sure judge of form, and be capable, in a contribution to the Nehls 'composite biography', of telling us that Lawrence 'worked too carelessly and his lack of form was sometimes an exasperation'.

The apprehensions started by the dedication are confirmed by the Introduction, where it is borne in on one how lamentably an industrious scholar, specializing in a great creative genius, may be unaware of his own limitations and misconceive his place in the scheme of things. Professor Moore's limitations are such that he should have been particularly careful not to offer anything not strictly required of him as scholar-editor of the texts he has collected and arranged. But one has no sooner said this than one has to recognize that, in the nature of the case, the discrimination is itself beyond him: he has no criterion. And, in a disabling way of which he has no suspicion, he is a complete foreigner in regard to the England to which Lawrence ('thin, red-haired Bert Lawrence'—but was Lawrence ever what 'red-haired' conveys, at any rate in cis-Atlantic English?) so essentially belonged.

We are pulled up near the beginning when we read: 'Among

these correspondents Jessie Chambers soon appears—the serious
farm girl whom Lawrence later portrayed, in his fiction, with the
artist's combination of sympathetic understanding and cruel detachment.' What jars to the point of offending is not the 'farm
girl' (Jessie Chambers was born and brought up at Haggs Farm,
but that doesn't make her a 'farm girl'—at any rate in Lawrence's
English); it is the ominous confident wisdom about 'the artist'.
'Cruel' from what point of view? It is a word that might decently
come from E. T. of *D. H. Lawrence: a Personal Record*, but not
from a literary critic. Lawrence has suffered too much from
critical naïveté, and when it gets such countenance and alimenta-
tion from an 'authority' as Professor Moore gives it, and on a
large scale, in the pages of a Lawrence classic, then there is a duty
of protest. Professor Moore's own critical naïveté is extreme.
One has reason for supposing that he was not among those who
most trenchantly condemned the offer to film a novel of Lawrence's as an outrage on a great artist. And how, it is immediately
relevant to ask him, would he, advising the director of such an
undertaking, suggest that the 'artist's combination of sympathetic
understanding and cruel detachment'—or, in the filming of any
of Lawrence's novels, the subtleties of a great writer's inner
attitude—could be reproduced? The signs are that Professor
Moore's sense of Lawrence's art is not such that he would see any
insuperable problem here.

If the reader would like some compact justifying evidence for
these adverse judgments of mine, let him look at the three suc-
cessive paragraphs beginning at the bottom of page xii.[1] 'The
relationship between Lawrence and Murry, which somewhat
parallels that of Rupert Birkin and Gerald Crich in *Women in
Love* . . .'—this might perhaps pass in a very careful critical
context, delicately prophylactic and refining, but there is no such
context to any of Professor Moore's statements. In the same paragraphs we read: 'He satirized Murry in several short stories,
including "Smile", "The Border-Line", and "Jimmy and the
Desperate Woman"—portraits somewhat similar to that of Denis
Burlap in the subsequent novel, *Point Counter Point*, by Lawrence's
friend Aldous Huxley.' Why on earth, one asks, should Professor

[1] *Op. cit.*

Moore conceive it his business as an editor to tell us this sort of thing? It is no more sound factual information than it is intelligent criticism. It merely retails that kind of casual accepted commonplace which, without Professor Moore's help, might form the substance of slack gossip in any very moderately literary company. It reveals, however, a basic habit and an ethos; for 'Lawrence scholarship', as Professor Moore conceives it, makes a major justifying function of accumulating kindred 'data' and of telling us, authoritatively, who this and that created character in Lawrence's fiction were in actual life. The real admirer of Lawrence's genius will not be grateful. He will reflect that it was 'knowledge' of the kind Professor Moore proffers us that was used recently to enforce a charge of cruelty brought against Lawrence, and that a lady qualified to speak with unanswerable authority pointed out that, while acquaintance with her childhood home and her family certainly counted for a great deal in 'England, My England', to suggest that Lawrence had 'put' them or their life or any identifiable episode or drama of the family history into that tale was very wide of the truth—so wide that the charge of cruelty had no ghost of an excuse. And such a reader, faced with the assertions of 'Lawrence scholarship', will be sufficiently justified in asserting that Lawrence *never* put people into his tales or his novels: he was a great creative writer. And the important critical observation to make when we think of *Point Counter Point* and Middleton Murry is that the equivalent of Burlap is not anywhere to be found in Lawrence's work.

If I had felt any hesitation about expressing in this insistent way a disparaging view of Professor Moore's qualifications as a critic, I could soon have settled it by considering the effect to which Professor Moore so easily and confidently pronounces on Lawrence's. '... Lawrence in addition to disliking Murry's elusiveness was not constituted to appreciate his qualities as a critic, which were high indeed.' Again, in the same paragraph: 'But Lawrence ultimately treated Murry with some injustice, and undervalued his contribution as a creative critic.' Who and what, one exclaims, is Professor Moore that he should take it on himself to pronounce on both Lawrence's treatment of Murry and his limitations as a critic in this way (neither question being one that could be settled by academic scholarship)? Professor Moore's reply, implicit in his habitual unselfconscious licence, is that he pronounces as the Lawrence authority.

I lay my main emphasis so much on this basic misconception of the editorial function because, so far as I know, other reviewers have not referred to it. Yet, as manifested in these volumes, it is a signal and peculiarly offensive instance of what, as, with the growth of industrial literary scholarship, 'authorities' multiply (in England too the industry spreads with the universities), we are likely to see more of. In any case, Professor Moore was called on only for what the scholar as such can properly attempt. Instead of occupying space in his introduction with impertinent matter, he should have told us (he doesn't) how his collection of Lawrence's letters comes to be on so large a scale incomplete, just how incomplete it is, and where the missing letters (of those known to exist) are to be found. I won't hold forth on this theme, but refer the reader to the review which appeared on the front page of the *Times Literary Supplement* for April 27, 1962. The incompleteness is recorded there with a painstaking particularity for which we owe the writer an immense gratitude. I will merely make my comment on one of Professor Moore's inclusions.

On page 206[1] we read:

To Katherine Mansfield, from Palazzo Ferraro, Capri [6 February, 1920] . . . I loathe you. You revolt me stewing in your consumption. . . . The Italians were right to have nothing to do with you. . . .

That is all we are offered as the Lawrence text, and I think that the subjoined note doesn't constitute a justification for the inclusion; far from it:

This fragment of Lawrence's letter to Katherine Mansfield, then on the Riviera, was quoted in a letter she wrote to Murry, who later said that he had destroyed the original letter after Katherine Mansfield's death. Murry wrote to Lawrence, who in the missing part of the letter had called him 'a dirty little worm', to say 'that he had committed the unforgivable crime: that I sincerely hoped we should thrash him'

It seems to me a radical misconception of the editorial business and obligation, entailing here a grave offence against Lawrence,

[1] *Op. cit.*

that permitted the inclusion of those minute conjoined snippets, selected, from a letter that Professor Moore hasn't seen, by Katherine Mansfield herself for an emotionally charged and very intimate context. Professor Moore's note aggravates the offence, for it will certainly convey to the innocent reader that Professor Moore has put him in possession of an interesting historical drama, in which (though 'these friendships did not yet end') Murry reacted with creditable violence to a cruelty of Lawrence's at Katherine Mansfield's expense; a drama of which (presented by the scholarly editor of the letters) we have here the clear document. 'Lawrence was cruel'—for the university lecturer or literary journalist touching on that theme it will be a useful illustration. Yet, with one's knowledge of Katherine Mansfield's peculiar temperament added to one's knowledge of Lawrence, one finds it easy to imagine Professor Moore's snippets as constituents of a letter that was no more to be called 'cruel' than medicine would be. Lawrence's genius manifested itself in sympathetic insight and an accompanying diagnostic intelligence, and cruelty was not in him.

These truths about Lawrence can be enforced abundantly from the letters: they enforce themselves as one reads. Unhappily one cannot for long give oneself to the text without some fresh annoyance from the misconceived and obtruded editorial authority. From the notes I have I could fill pages illustrating the waste of space (and space, one gathers, was a problem), the insult to the reader, and the outrage on Lawrence entailed in this habit of lumpishly possessive impertinence. The ethos is that of the egregious *D. H. Lawrence Newsletter*, the 'Lawrence scholarship' of which is a matter of accumulating impertinences—anti-critical identifications of *personae* and fictive episodes with actual persons and collected facts, gratuitous annotations, useless and betraying vulgarities of insensitiveness and unintelligence—to the glory (not of poor Lawrence, whose spirit and significance are thus with crass industry defied) of 'Lawrence scholarship' and of the 'authority'.

My notes compel the judgment that the editor's specialist zeal hasn't sufficiently strong counterpoise of general education. The [*sic*]s that so often jerk one's attention from Lawrence to the

Lawrence-expert are not only often unnecessary; they now and then make it plain that in Lawrence's English Professor Moore is faced unawares (though his acquaintance with English literature should have adverted him) with a foreign language. The French and German in the text present a good many errors (and there is a strikingly deformed Latin tag). It is impossible to see them all as uncorrected misprints; we know that there has been misreading and mistranscription, as when (we suspect) Lawrence, who evidently wrote '*rongé*', is made to refer[1] to Whitman as '*rougé* with unsatisfiedness'.

The only other correction I will find room for here is of another order. I can make it with authority because I myself attended meetings of the Union of Democratic Control at about that time, or a little earlier. In the following[2] addressed to Bertrand Russell in April 1915, the 'W. D. C.' should be 'U. D. C.': 'Do you still speak at the W. D. C. of the nations kissing each other, when your soul prowls the frontier all the time jealously, to defend what it has and seize what it can.'

Although Professor Moore's two volumes contain 1,200 letters against Aldous Huxley's 800 (of which more than one quarter are left out), the effect made on one thirty years ago remains much what it was. The incomparable genius manifests itself in the ways one knows so well, and the appraisal and commentary called for are much the same. There is the marvellous sympathetic responsiveness with which, while he is always unquestionably spontaneous and sincere, Lawrence's tone and manner vary with the correspondent. One might fill pages illustrating the variety and attempting to do justice to the flexibility and range. One might write an essay on the category that could be established in terms of the letters addressed to Lady Cynthia Asquith, Lady Ottoline Morrell, and Sir Edward Marsh. Eliot called Lawrence a snob, but nothing could be freer from any tendency to snobbery than Lawrence's attitude to those wealthy and socially distinguished patrons.

It isn't that he doesn't adjust his tone to them, he does. He wouldn't have that quintessential human courtesy which characterizes him if he didn't. But he is always his spontaneous self, and

---

[1] *Op. cit.*, p. 257.   [2] *Op. cit.*, p. 331.

M

the self is always, without the least assertiveness, that of a genius —quietly and selflessly sure of its perception, its judgment and its right to them. How could he have written some of his most intensely earnest letters to women—ladies of the *beau monde*— so intellectually undistinguished as, in different ways, those two were? An essay could be written on that theme: it would be central to his genius and illustrative of its strength. And how, we ask, considering some of the sustained correspondences, could he be so forbearing—or, rather, have no need to be forbearing— towards insufferable people? The answer, again and equally a challenge to analysis, is that to him they were not insufferable; his genius made them otherwise. And this genius here we see as a penetrating human intelligence, something indistinguishable from a complete and irresistibly impersonal disinterestedness that, without condescension, overbearingness, self-blinding, or indulgence on his part, enables him to be on sympathetic terms of person to person, or human life to human life, with the other. He elicits an unegotistic sincerity of response. I need not specify instances—that would be a delicate matter (I knew one of the insufferable persons); the reader will find his own readily enough.

I will refer instead to a related case, that of his relations with Sir Edward Marsh. I shall be able so both to continue my theme and to introduce a new one: Lawrence's incomparable genius as a literary critic. This is strongly manifested in the letters, and Professor Moore might, if his kind of interest had permitted it, have found there abundant evidence to make his own confident adjudication between Lawrence and Murry look silly. One of the most impressive pieces of evidence is the letter to Marsh that begins on page 235.[1] The reader should remind himself that the writer is a young ex-elementary-schoolteacher, and that the patron addressed is the prime convoker of Georgian poetry. Marsh liked deference, and Lawrence, with a perfect spontaneous naturalness, meeting sufficiently the recipient's expectation and yet without any kind of falsity, shows that he knows it. And at the same time, with simple yet unoffending directness and finality, he not only disposes of one of Marsh's great contemporary poems, but gives him some basic instruction that, for us, is proof of a rare

[1] *Op. cit.*

gift of critical insight, analysis, and expression—a critical genius
such as the author of *The Problem of Style* most certainly (*pace*
Professor Moore) had not. It is hardly possible to distinguish
between the easy personal tact of the manner (a delicately sure
impersonality) and the specific gift of the literary critic. Lawrence
had a sure valuation of Marsh; he had no illusions, but no
'superiority'. He was amused, but there was nothing in him of
the *de haut en bas* impulse, the tendency to the poised self-exalting
sneer or sub-sneer, that one knows as a characteristic of the
London literary world, even in its dealings with the recognized
great (it is to be found in books on Lawrence). Marsh for him
was another human being and another centre of life. We and
Aaron on his train journey (chapter XV) meet what is immediately identifiable as the specific type in *Aaron's Rod*, and
the same Lawrence is manifest creatively in the presentment. It
is comedy, alive with amused and placing observation, but wholly
free from malice or complacency. The absence of these and of
egocentric pettiness is basic to Lawrence's genius.

With my eye still on this theme, I want for a close to lay a
fresh emphasis: the great creative writer, the poetic master of
the English language who is above all a great *novelist*, challenges
us, in the letters, to fresh recognition. Take for instance this—
it comes in a letter[1] to Lady Ottoline Morrell:

> The death of Rupert Brooke fills me more and more with the sense
> of the fatuity of it all. He was slain by bright Phoebus' shaft—it was
> in keeping with his general sunniness—it was the real climax of his
> pose. I first heard of him as a Greek god under a Japanese sunshade
> reading poetry in his pyjamas, at Grantchester,—at Grantchester upon
> the lawns where the river goes. Bright Phoebus smote him down. It
> is all in the saga.
> O God, O God, it is all too much of a piece: it is like madness.

The passage really *belongs* in its epistolary context—it has been
thrown off with an unstudied spontaneity; but how marvellous
is the living precision with which the delicate complexity of
the reaction, the wholeness of the characteristic Laurentian response, is conveyed! And how few words he takes for it! The

[1] *Op. cit.*, p. 337.

appalled sense of tragic fatuity stated in the first sentence establishes the ground tone. Without abrogating the prepotence of
this, Lawrence can, in the next sentence, move into the irony—
which in another context would have been satiric irony—of
'He was slain by bright Phoebus' shaft'. It is satiric here only in
so far as it recalls the amused placing observation that had
registered the King's[1] Hellenism of Brooke's pre-war Cambridge.
The irony of the 'Bright Phoebus' can produce with an inevitable
ease of transition the 'sunniness'—a sympathetic tribute; the
'pose' (the diagnosis becomes fully explicit in this word) is
ridiculous, but there was never any animus in Lawrence's amusement. And he can make the development of 'pose' that follows,
the piquant comedy evocation of that culture of affected atti-
tudinizing, at the same time the expression of a poignant tragic
sense ('I first heard of him . . .'). The comedy for Lawrence—
I recall in contrast a sentence of Santayana's from a letter that is
tucked away in a drawer somewhere: 'The dons, with their bevy
of simpering prigs, I can only see as figures in a pleasant comedy'
—yields the tragic irony of 'Bright Phoebus smote him down',
the tone and feeling of which resound in the concluding protest
(for the climax of this pose is death): 'O God, O God . . . it is
like madness.'

Lawrence—there seems point in this for a final emphasis—was
not a stylist; he was a master of perfect expression, and, if 'form'
means anything worth bothering about, of form.

[1] I refer to King's College, which was Brooke's.

XIII

T. S. ELIOT AS CRITIC[1]

How can a book of criticism be at once so distinguished and so unimportant? The question is the more worth asking because the author of this volume[2] was at one time so unquestionably a major critical influence. As I ask it, I recall that I bought my copy of *The Sacred Wood* (the fly-leaf carries the evidence) in 1920. How I came to buy it so soon after the publication I can't now say. I had never heard of Eliot, and I had no more literary sophistication than I had acquired at school before the war. And though I turned the book over a good deal, and no doubt profited, I won't pretend that I absorbed rapidly what it had to give, or that it became for me, after a short acquaintance, decisively formative, or anything but a vague and minor stimulus. In those early years after the great hiatus, as in a dazed and retarded way I struggled to achieve the beginnings of the power of articulate thought about literature, it was Santayana—I picked up Logan Pearsall Smith's *Little Essays from the Writings of George Santayana* also when it came out—and Matthew Arnold who really counted. (Let me say at once that I didn't, and don't, find Santayana fundamentally congenial: indebtedness to an influence needn't mean radical sympathy or approval—the generalized observation has, perhaps, its point in a note on T. S. Eliot's place in criticism.)

The Sacred Wood, I think, had very little influence or attention before the Hogarth Press brought out *Homage to John Dryden*, the pamphlet in which the title essay was accompanied by 'The Metaphysical Poets' and 'Andrew Marvell'. It was with the publication in this form of those essays (the Hogarth Press had recently published *The Waste Land*) that Eliot became the important contemporary critic. It was the impact of this slender

[1] Reprinted from *Commentary*, November 1958.
[2] *On Poets and Poetry*, by T. S. Eliot.

new collection that sent one back to *The Sacred Wood* and confirmed with decisive practical effect one's sense of the stimulus to
be got from that rare thing, a fine intelligence in literary criticism
—the fine intelligence so certainly present in the earlier and larger
collection. And the nature of the peculiar force of the criticism—
the condition of the authority with which it claimed one's
attention—was now plain. 'Sensibility alters from generation to
generation in everybody, whether we will or no: but expression
is only altered by a man of genius.' Again, in the same essay, one
of his finest—it is in fact a model of critical writing—Eliot says
of certain 'second-rate' poets that 'They have not the sensitiveness and consciousness to perceive that they feel differently from
the preceding generation, and therefore must use words differently.' Eliot was the man of genius who, after the long post-
Swinburnian arrest, altered expression. Such an achievement was
possible only to a poet in whom the creative gift was a rare gift
of consciousness. An intense and highly conscious work of critical
intelligence necessarily preceded and accompanied the discovery
of the new uses of words, the means of expressing or creating the
new feelings and modes of thought, the new rhythms, the new
versification. This is the critical intelligence manifested in those
early essays; Eliot's best, his important, criticism has an immediate
relation to his technical problems as the poet who, at that moment
in history, was faced with 'altering expression'.

Never had criticism a more decisive influence. The poetry
would without its aid in any case have compelled recognition; it
was the poetry that won attention for the criticism, rather than
the other way round. What the criticism did was to insure that
recognition of the poetry should be accompanied by a general
decisive change, not only of taste, but of critical idea and idiom,
of critical approach to questions of 'poetic', and of the sense of
the past of English poetry, and of the relation of the past to the
present.

It was an impressive achievement. What was not at once
apparent to all those impressed was that some of the ideas, attitudes, and valuations put into currency by Eliot were arbitrary:
some of the most distinctive and influential neither followed
from his best critical insights nor drew any valid authority from

the creative successes that seemed to lend them force. The attribution of 'consciousness' to Eliot should not be allowed to mislead. The radically distinctive thing about him, in fact, is that he should have fallen so short of achieving the consciousness that one thinks of as necessary to the great creative writer. The limitation, the disability—it is a case challenging a diagnostic approach —has its ominous document in a famous early essay: 'Tradition and the Individual Talent'. It was on this essay pre-eminently that was based Eliot's reputation as a thinker, a disciplined intelligence notably capable of rigorous, penetrating, and sustained thought.

Actually the trenchancy and vigour are illusory and the essay is notable for its ambiguities, its logical inconsequences, its pseudo-precisions, its fallaciousness, and the aplomb of its equivocations and its specious cogency. Its offered compression and its technique in general for generating awed confusion help to explain why it should not have been found easy to deal with. Yet the falsity and gratuitousness of its doctrine of impersonality are surely plain enough. 'And I hinted by an analogy', says Eliot (referring to the famous platinum shred), 'that the mind of the mature poet differs from that of the immature one not precisely in any valuation of "personality", not in being necessarily more interesting, or having "more to say", but rather in being a more finely perfected medium in which special, or very varied, feelings are at liberty to enter into new combinations.' But one can be as free as D. H. Lawrence was from any romantic inclination to say that the artist's business is 'to express his personality'—one can see a truism in Lawrence's diagnostic placing of the 'personality', in relation to vital intelligence, as the associate of 'will' and 'idea' —and at the same time believe as intensely as Lawrence did that without the distinguished individual, distinguished by reason of his potency as a conduit of urgent life and by the profound and sensitive responsibility he gives proof of towards his living experience, there is no art that matters.

Eliot's doctrine of 'impersonality' is insidiously designed to eliminate this conception of the artist; he gives the possibility no recognition. The word 'experience' recurs in his argument and he speaks of 'passions'; the mind of the poet (the 'shred of platinum'), he tells us, 'may partly or exclusively operate upon the experience of the man himself; but the more perfect the artist, the more completely separate in him will be the man who suffers and the mind which creates'. This, plausible or discussible as it might for a moment seem, is a wholly arbitrary dictum, any appearance to the contrary being a matter of the complexity, the ambiguities, and the specious and tendentious inconsequence, of the total context. The analogy of the catalyst gives it no support (all it does is to make the underlying intention plain). When we ask how a platinum shred can 'digest and transmute the passions which are its materials', we note that it has become also a 'more finely perfected medium in which special, or very varied, feelings are at liberty to enter into new combinations'. How we get from a 'liberty to enter into new combinations' to 'the mind which creates' Eliot does nothing at all to explain; it is surely a long way —it is in fact a yawning gap in his theory or diagram. A little further on the 'medium' becomes something even more flatly inert: 'The poet's mind is in fact a receptacle for seizing and storing up numberless feelings, phrases, images, which remain there until all the particles which can unite to form a new compound are present together.'

Nothing is done to supply the absent something answering to the verb 'create' ('the mind which creates') by the reference, a couple of sentences later, to the 'intensity of the artistic process, the pressure, so to speak, under which the fusion takes place', for Eliot does nothing to explain or suggest what the process is, or where the pressure could come from. Instead, he offers us, with the air of the most cogent quintessential relevance, such inconsequent propositions as the 'ode by Keats contains a number of feelings which have nothing to do with the nightingale, but which the nightingale, partly because of its attractive name, and partly because of its reputation, served to bring together'. As if there were not something else, more important, to be said about the relation of the ode to the life, the living from which it derived the creative impulsion; derived something without full recognition of which there can be no intelligent appreciation of the 'artistic process' or the art.

It is not then a coherent conception of art that is figured in

Eliot's 'artist'. It *is*, however, a familiar ethos or case. 'The more perfect the artist, the more completely separate in him will be the man who suffers and the mind which creates': the perfection of this artist is something different from what we admire in *Anna Karenina*. No one with Tolstoy in mind as the type of the great creative writer could have advanced that proposition: 'separate', for such a use is not a possible word, whether one thinks of Tolstoy or Lawrence (the perfection of many of whose tales will, I hope, be granted) or Shakespeare—or George Eliot or Mark Twain. But when we recognize that the artist implicitly proposed is Flaubert, then the proposition becomes intelligible, if not acceptable. And that it should be so gives us Eliot's own case.

In contemplating the work of one of the great creative powers we don't find ourselves impelled to think of the pressure of the artistic process as something apart from the pressure of the living —the living life and the lived experience—out of which the work has issued; for that the work *has* so issued, deriving thence its sustenance and the creative impulsion, we don't question. An intensity of art devoted to expressing disgust at *la platitude bourgeoise*—Flaubert's opposing art to life as something apart from and superior to it—entails a self-contradiction; it portends an inner thwarting disorder, a profound vital disharmony that has defeated intelligence in the artist and made any but a strained and starved creativity impossible.

It clearly is a most significant defeat of intelligence that presents itself to us in Eliot's essay. What pressure, what need, we ask, explains this earnestness of intellectual subtlety devoted in so strenuous a play of trenchancy, confusion, and inconsequence, to absolving the artist from the need to have lived—the need to be a fully living individual wholly committed to life, in whom the impulsion of the lived experience and the courage of responsibility towards it appear as the 'intensity of the artistic process'? We can't help seeing the answer in the co-presence in *The Sacred Wood* of the essay on *Hamlet*, which in so odd, confident, and arbitrary a way reduces that tragedy to a matter of an inexpressible emotional state, one of disgust, occasioned in Hamlet by his mother. It isn't that the play doesn't face us with problems. But to assert with so little argument so drastically simplifying an account of it, while relying as for support that makes even the show of first-hand analysis unnecessary on J. M. Robertson, the ironclad Scottish rationalist, and Professor E. E. Stoll—is this, we ask, a manifestation of critically poised and disinterested intelligence? It isn't that there aren't grounds for calling *Hamlet* the 'Mona Lisa of literature'. But what, we ask, are the grounds for such a pronouncement as this: '*Coriolanus* may not be as "interesting" as *Hamlet*, but it is, with *Antony and Cleopatra*, Shakespeare's most assured artistic success.' It is a significantly odd preoccupation with the criteria of 'assured artistic success' that betrays Eliot into such an emphasis at the expense of (say) *Macbeth*; and I personally find enough artistic success in *Measure for Measure*, which in the same paragraph Eliot seems to associate with *Hamlet* as another (also 'profoundly interesting') artistic failure dealing with 'intractable' material (Eliot's adjective), to compel my placing it among Shakespeare's very greatest things. Why does Eliot call its material 'intractable'? That behind the important part played by 'disgust' in *Hamlet* there is material that is in some sense 'intractable' may be plausibly argued; but where is the 'disgust' or the comparable 'intractability' in *Measure for Measure*? What I find is a wonderfully sure, direct, profound, and delicate treatment of sex, and I suspect that it is this which for Eliot constitutes the 'intractability'—I suspect that for him it assimilates to the 'disgust' of *Hamlet*—so that in respect of that very different work too he is an untrustworthy reporter. And as for his exaltation of *Coriolanus* and *Antony and Cleopatra*, it is significant that in neither of those plays do we feel Shakespeare to be as wholly or profoundly engaged as in the other great tragedies; if we were bent on exposing the absurdity of the dictum, 'the more perfect the artist, the more completely separate in him will be the man who suffers and the mind which creates', it is precisely *not* to *them* that we should go.

Our sense that Eliot's essay tells us more about Eliot than about Shakespeare's *Hamlet* finds a striking, if hardly necessary, confirmation in Eliot's own *Family Reunion*. It is remarkable how much of his account of the artistic problem facing Shakespeare seems to describe his own problem (as we divine it) in writing that play.

'Hamlet (the man) [Harry] is dominated by an emotion which is inexpressible because it is in excess of the facts as they appear.' The account of that feeling which Eliot describes as baffling Hamlet (and Shakespeare)—doesn't it strike us as being, in the emphasis it lays on the peculiar baffling and 'inexpressible' quality, an account of the feeling we associate with Eliot's play? 'It is thus a feeling which he cannot understand; he cannot objectify it, and it therefore remains to poison life and obstruct action.' And our sense of Eliot's personal engagement in Harry, an engagement that he is largely unaware of, representing as it does a complexity of profound feeling in himself that he doesn't understand, is such as to cause some embarrassment, especially when the play is acted.

There is in Eliot's criticism abundant evidence of negative attitudes towards life, attitudes of disgust and fear and rejection, that play a part of which he is not properly conscious; entailing as they do the Flaubertian kind of self-contradiction, they portend a radical failure of wholeness and coherence in him, and consequently a defeat of intelligence. 'To reduce one's disorderly and mostly silly personality to the gravity of a *jeu de quilles* would be an excellent thing: yet for this a great poet, Landor, has been condemned to obloquy.' In the conception of poetry as a '*jeu de quilles*', and the corresponding absurdity of our being offered Landor as a great poet, we have, one might say, what Eliot's theory of 'impersonality' logically points to—if it were a coherent theory, and could be said to point logically to anything. The significance of this elevation of Landor appears plainly enough in another of Eliot's references to him. Landor, we are told, is a test of whether we go to poetry because we are interested in poetry, or merely in order to have our own feeble lusts and desires flattered. The startling gratuitousness of this alleged alternative as part of a proposition about the merits of Landor's *jeu de quilles* reveals the nature and strength of the pressure behind the strained intellection with which Eliot offers to establish 'impersonality'. The violence of 'lusts and desires' is a violence of repudiation, and it is enhanced by that conveyed in 'feeble' and 'flattered'; and one can say with confidence that, if he had been conscious of the effect to which the whole proposition would be significant for the critical reader, he could not have let it stand. But no vigilance or caution ('This classiosity is bunkum, but still more cowardice', said Lawrence) will preserve a critic who carries in him so disturbing a pressure of disordered inner life, of emotion that he fears and distrusts and cannot understand ('it therefore remains to poison life and obstruct action'), from such failures of intelligence.

As a poet, of course, Eliot himself, even at the time of his early criticism, was not a platinum shred, or a 'medium' in which feelings, phrases, and images were merely at liberty to enter into new combinations. He didn't need to be critically conscious about the 'intensity of the artistic process' or the nature of the 'pressure under which the fusion took place', but—or rather, for—the pressure was there. His artist's intelligence manifested itself in the judgment that determined him to the creative undertakings his powers were fitted for; he didn't attempt a *Hamlet* (though he was, much later, to commit himself to a *Family Reunion*) or anything requiring the insight into human emotions, and the intelligence about life, of a major novelist. It was as the poet who, intent at that moment of history on 'altering expression', was conscious that he 'felt differently, and therefore must use words differently', that he applied a focused critical intelligence most consciously and effectively. The resulting criticism, that which—with him—we recognize as his best ('it is a by-product', he says in the present volume, 'of my private poetry workshop, or a prolongation of the thinking that went into the formation of my own verse'), doesn't commit him to the testing kinds of value-judgment.

His work in general as critic has its value in spite of the fact that what one is apt to think of as an essential function of an important critic either hardly comes into the question, or is performed in a way that is far from exemplifying the critic's strength. There is, of course, value-judgment (though not an *appraisal* of, say, Donne or Marvell or Dryden) entailed in the very effectively directed critical observations by which he established a general taste for the Metaphysicals and a general understanding of its relevance to the appreciation of his own creative achievement. But the force and justice of the limiting suggestions

I am making become very plain when we consider his critical dealings with the dramatists. He made some stimulating observations about dramatic verse and the conventions of poetic drama, but no radically intelligent—no truly critical—appraisal of any of the Elizabethans or Jacobeans; he has done, in fact, nothing to disturb at all seriously, where Elizabethan-Jacobean drama is in question, the institutional valuation coming down from Lamb and Swinburne; rather, he has confirmed its inflationary habit.

Eliot's standing as a distinguished critic, then, depends as little on his penetration and sureness in the more important kinds of value-judgment as on his powers of sustained coherent and trenchant thought. His performance as a judge of his contemporaries has been consistently disastrous. It is represented at its most respectable by his backing Joyce—the significance of which election, all the same, is given in his dismissal of Lawrence. The author of *The Waste Land* (the notes to which, or some of them, have an essential supporting function—even a constructive one— for all the light cynicism of Eliot's amused and superior self-dissociation from them in the present volume) did naturally prefer to the great creative writer of his time, fertile in works that have an irresistible living wholeness, the writer whose ingenuities and pedantries of constructive will are signals of the default of organic life, betraying the failure of imaginative creativity. And I don't doubt, though this seems to me a severe thing to have to say, that his lifelong backing of Wyndham Lewis has represented a genuine taste. Yet I can't believe that he could have committed himself to such extravagant appraisal of this last as a creative writer and a thinker if he hadn't known him personally (one tries to give Eliot credit for a kind of loyalty that isn't at all a virtue in a critic as such), and belonged to a dominant literary-social milieu in which such appraisals were current. What in fact I have come to is the radical conventionality of judgment that contradicts Eliot's distinction as a critic and so disconcertingly qualifies his intelligence.

Thus when in the present volume one reads of Spenser's *The Faerie Queene* as a 'long poem in the first rank' one can't think of the conventionality as merely superficial, or anything but representative and significant; there is too much supporting evidence. For instance, the limiting 'but' doesn't at all take from the significance of this: 'Yet one cannot but feel that a play like Congreve's *Way of the World* is in some way more mature than any play of Shakespeare's: but only in this respect, that it reflects a greater maturity of *manners*.' What is significant here is the completeness of Eliot's surrender to the consecrated and current nonsense about supreme wit, consummate prose, and perfection of lightness in *The Way of the World*; for that is what we must invoke to explain the irresponsible way in which he abuses and cheapens so essential a term as 'maturity' (he is writing on 'What Is a Classic?'). '*Maturity* of manners': what can it mean where manners are isolated in this way—what can maturity of manners be if not something to be discussed in terms of the relation between manners and more radical things (moral values, shall we say?) lying behind them? The conventional acceptance of *The Way of the World* as a summit of civilization and literary refinement goes with an inability to see a consummateness of wit and humour and a delicate living mastery of tone, manifestations of a supreme vitality of intelligence, in D. H. Lawrence—where they are.

Then, if one had really judged for oneself that there was something at all great about Shelley's orgy of such very embarrassingly Shelleyan Shakespearizing, could one have written that, of the verse plays by nineteenth-century poets, the 'greatest is probably *The Cenci*?' In the same essay, 'The Music of Poetry', I see, as I turn over the pages, a solemn reference to the nonsense verse of Edward Lear: 'We enjoy the music which is of a high order, and we enjoy the feeling of irresponsibility towards the sense.' That kind of inert and banal conventionality suggests the simple conclusion that the weakness under consideration may be summed up as just the natural accompaniment of the specialized and limited kind of interest in poetry, the lack of concern with radical value-judgment, characterizing, as we have noted, Eliot's early and decisive criticism. The judicial reference to Dryden's *The Hind and the Panther* as a 'great poem' could fairly be adduced in confirmation: for the Eliot of the best early criticism there was no strong reason for resisting the impulse to describe the brilliance of Dryden's characteristic and so un-Swinburnian poem, that triumph of polemical and expository wit, as greatness.[1]

Yet the case has another aspect and a very important one for the student of English literary history of the last forty years. We come on it when we read, not for the first time in Eliot, of W. P. Ker as a scholar who was also a notable critic—as pre-eminently the type of the truly valuable scholar-critic. Well, I have myself in the past gone again and again to Ker's books for help in the fields in which he offers it and never found anything but dis-appointment. Nor have I met anyone else (whose opinion matters to me—on Eliot himself I have never had the opportunity to press my questions) who has also tried and reports otherwise. My explanation of the uncritical appraisal so confidently offered is that Ker, a metropolitan professor, belonged in the 1920s to a select social-literary world, and Eliot met him in the right places and the right company. I am the less troubled by any sense of taking an impertinent hazard in coming out with this, because of the great deal in Eliot's critical record that admits of no other explanation.

Consider, for instance, the early appreciation of Charles Whibley that he has gone on reprinting: how, one asks, can Eliot have supposed that the too-familiar kind of accomplished 'personal' and literary prose of which he offers us samples could impress us as justifying his estimate of Whibley? How can he have supposed that he could get such an estimate taken seriously by an intelligent public? The answer can only be that, forty years ago, Charles Whibley was a well-known figure, a current social literary value (a matter of accepted convention—I remember quarrelling in a minor way with Sir Arthur Quiller-Couch, who wanted me to be impressed by Whibley's essay on Swift), in an English social world of the 'best people'.

The importance for my theme of this aspect of what I have called Eliot's conventionality can be illustrated from his magazine, the *Criterion*. How, one asks, looking at the opening instalment of Hugh Walpole's *The Old Ladies* in the issue for February 1926,

[1] Eliot says that he considers Dryden one of the three greatest critics of poetry in English literature, the other two being Samuel Johnson and Coleridge—a judgment that seems to me a portent of conventionality.

can Eliot ever have thought anything written by that industrious, utterly untalented, manufacturer of Book Society 'classics' worth printing in a review with such a title and the accordant pretensions? The answer (apart from the fact that Eliot has never shown any intelligence about prose fiction) can only be that Walpole at that time was embarked on his campaign to get admitted to membership of inner 'Bloomsbury'. ('Hugh is so humble', one was told a little later by slightly embarrassed minor members, when one pressed them to explain the signal evidence of his success: that is, he made no effort to conceal his admiration, his unqualified, his satisfyingly adequate admiration, for Virginia Woolf as a creative genius.) That the first book-publication of *The Waste Land* was by the Hogarth Press one knew. What I myself was slow, I confess, to realize was that Eliot was as completely *of* that Bloomsbury world—in acceptance and (the necessary condition) loyalty or docility—as the memoirs and autobiographical matter by members and associated writers and Etonians that have come out subsequently have shown him to have been.

Yet the evidence provided by himself as critic and editor was plentiful enough. The absurd (and orthodox) over-estimate of Virginia Woolf implied in his references to her might seem to be a natural and spontaneous aberration, closely correlated with his unquestionably and profoundly personal prepossession against D. H. Lawrence (*'non seulement est elle civilisée, elle préfère la civilisation à la barbarie'*, 'not only is she civilized, she prefers civilization to barbarism', he wrote in a 'Letter' to *La Nouvelle Revue Française*). Yet, contemplating the strikingly unguarded and uncharacteristic rashness with which he indulges the prepossession in emphatic, righteous, and indefensible pronouncements of overtly damning intention at Lawrence's expense, we have to remind ourselves that in this prepossession too he had Bloomsbury with him; he was expressing in his boldness of ungrounded conviction the confident orthodoxy of that consciously dominant élite—which in this matter had with it the large ox-eyed world of Philistinism and moral conventionality it loved to think of itself as despising and shocking. And that same 'Letter' in *La Nouvelle Revue Française* from which I have just quoted shows us the critic who so exalts Virginia Woolf offering the French intellectual public David Garnett as a significant writer, a master of English prose. Garnett of course was at that time established currency as such in the best circles in England, and that this should have been possible illustrates notably both the power and the proclivity of Bloomsbury.

It is impossible to think of Garnett as a spontaneous taste of Eliot's; it is impossible that Eliot could have made the 'pretty piffle' (Lawrence's kind enough dismissing phrase) of those pseudo-moral *contes* into significant art except as the hardly altogether unconscious—and the critically annulled—transmitter of the orthodoxy that had made Garnett a contemporary classic. Hardly unconscious—certainly not unconscious; but how conscious of being, as I have put it, critically annulled and a mere transmitter? It is perhaps (a distinguished mind being in question) the most disquieting aspect of the conventionality we are contemplating that we should be left unable to say. The impulse it represents is so radical that the surrender, the connivance, need not be fully conscious. Yet, reading the British Academy lecture on Milton (reprinted in this volume with, I see when I compare it with the reply that I—not, of course, challenged there by any actual mention of my name—made to the original, some unsignalled and very substantial omissions),[1] who can believe that the writer and lecturer could have been unaware of the felicity of touch, the tactics, the strategy, the phrasing, the whole thing, for the reassurance and ingratiation of a British Academy public?

And yet (again!) can one believe the critic unaware of the self-stultifying feebleness of this criticism as criticism, and of the way in which, for the reader who gives it the attention due to the thought of a distinguished poet-critic (thought about a matter of central relevance to the critic's achievement as a poet), it implicitly, in its equivocal kind of noble and sophisticated innocence, concedes all that one needs for putting the case against Milton that is ostensibly suffering refutation—to the confusion (the reviewers gleefully commented) of Eliot's too early admirers?

[1] 'Each item is substantially the same as on the date of its delivery or first publication.'—T. S. Eliot, Preface. This one isn't.

N

Of course, neither the reviewers nor the British Academy audience noticed this effect of the lecture, any more than they noticed the related effect of a hardly disguised lack of interest in Milton and the argument on the part of the lecturer. And, to come to a further observation that has to be recorded when Eliot's 'conventionality' is being appraised, one suspects that if as a critically articulate admirer of his achievement one pointed out this state of affairs to him, he might meet one's demonstration with something—oh! of a very refined and subtle equivocalness, of course—in the nature of a wink.

It is unpleasant to have to entertain this kind of suspicion, but there is no escaping it. Consider, for instance, that solemn, that hardly credible, discussion of Kipling's verse which is reprinted in the volume under review.[1] It emanates, one told oneself (when it first came out) from the British Subject who used to write those letters to *The Times* about Stilton cheese and the ordination of Bishops—which was not to say that he didn't suppose himself to be taking it seriously: such astonishing miscalculation couldn't be *mere* calculation. And yet, for a genuine admirer of Eliot, is it possible to believe that he expected such admirers to take this performance seriously? And if he didn't expect them to—and how, when reprinting it after all the disabusing commentaries he must have heard and read since 1941, *could* he?—what kind of look are they to divine in the critic's eye as meant for *them*? They will recall such things as the obituary on Robert Bridges that appeared in the *Criterion* or the ambiguous piece of correctness about A. E. Housman (the occasion being *The Name and Nature of Poetry*) that can be found there too.

I have perhaps gone some way towards answering the question with which I opened: how is it possible for a book of criticism to be at once so distinguished and so unimportant? At any rate, I have done something to bring out the significance of that question as the form taken by one's summary comment on the book. One feels that one ought to be able to expect a book of Eliot's criticism to be important, to make a difference. And there is, as a matter of fact, a great deal of distinction in this book of a kind that, represented in quotation, suggests an impressive context. There are

[1] *Op. cit.*

what one may take as authoritative formulations of important issues:

It is, moreover, through the living authors that the dead remain alive.

If we have no living literature we shall become more and more alienated from the literature of the past; unless we keep up continuity, our literature of the past will become more and more remote from us until it is as strange to us as the literature of a foreign people. For our language goes on changing, our way of life changes, under the pressure of material changes in our environment, in all sorts of ways, and unless we have those few men who combine an exceptional sensibility with an exceptional power over words, our own ability, not merely to express, but even to feel any but the crudest emotions, will degenerate.

The essay from which these extracts come, 'The Social Function of Poetry', is one of the more interesting in the book. If one asks oneself why one should feel that the promise they suggest of a disinterested play of strong and responsible critical thought, the duly influential expression of a mind courageously alive in the present, is not borne out, is notably not fulfilled either in the book as a whole or anywhere in it, one finds the answer in the reflexions aroused by this sentence from the same essay, or by the paragraph in which it comes:

I would even press my first point and say that if a poet gets a large audience very quickly, that is a rather suspicious circumstance: for it leads us to fear that he is not really doing anything new. . . .

Yes, one thinks, Auden—that was the major relevant case in Eliot's time. Auden's newness was of a kind that could be appreciated at once by a large public of British Academicians, acclaimers of Bridges's *The Testament of Beauty*, classical dons—poetry-lovers in general, who had confidently rejected Eliot himself. Auden became almost overnight an accepted major poet, and for twenty years British schoolboys of literary bent were exceptional in intelligence or negativism or luck if they didn't believe that the great contemporary poets were Eliot, Auden, and Yeats.

But the importance of *not* confusing the glib modish novelty of the Audens with creative originality, and so stultifying one's 'appreciation' of the Yeatses and the Eliots—that is an inescapable moral of Eliot's essay. To postulate, as the essay does, the effective existence of an élite capable of making, and insisting on, the distinction is to postulate the need for a strongly functioning contemporary criticism. And one remembers the *Criterion*—the great critical quarterly that is now an established legend—and that Eliot was its Editor. The legend (it is perhaps in bad taste, but it is certainly necessary, to say) bears no relation to the actuality. The actuality is fairly represented by the *Criterion*'s performance of the function of criticism in respect of Auden and the Poetical Renascence of the early 1930s. Anyone who investigates the back files will see that, from the outset steadily onwards, the review pages of that Classicist, Anglo-Catholic, and Royalist organ were as unmistakably as those of the *New Statesman* (Socialist and egalitarian) at the disposal of the 'gang' for its own purposes, which, in the nature of the case, were essentially anti-critical, so that Spender's status as a very distinguished poet, discussible as such along with Eliot and Yeats, was no more to be questioned there than Auden's. Speaking as one of the very small minority that was concerned in those days to insist, in published criticism, on the essential differences—those between real creative originality and what was represented by Auden and Spender (and in those days Day Lewis was a Modern Poet too), I can testify that to be known for such a bent was to have earned one's reward—there is no need to specify the modes of retributive treatment—in the *Criterion* as surely as in the *New Stateman* and the Sunday papers.

So far, then, was the *Criterion* from resisting the final triumph of coterie over the function of criticism. Its surrender, in fact, marks the end in our time of the possibility that an élite such as Eliot postulates might establish itself as a force in the British literary world and, a constant effective reminder of standards, be able to make itself felt and respected as something quite other than a coterie. The spirit of coterie is the enemy of the spirit of élite. Bloomsbury, of course, presented itself as an élite while actually promoting the spirit of coterie with a success that constitutes a major fact for the historian of literature and culture in Great Britain in the twentieth century.

The success presented the 'gang' (their own term—see Spender's autobiography) of the Poetical Renascence with the conditions of their astonishingly rapid arrival, their capture of the literary scene. The capture, in fact, was a succession, recognized and promoted by the veterans of the old Bloomsbury—the Bloomsbury of Keynes and the Woolfs; that is what we are actually told in the course of his naïve autobiographical impartings by Spender, friend and protégé of Virginia Woolf, and launched in that milieu as a distinguished talent. How then could Eliot (known—see Spender and the others—by his abbreviated Christian name in that world) *not* play the part confidently expected of him? How should he insist—how can we with any conviction assume that it even occurred to him that he ought to insist—that, the *Criterion* being dedicated to the service of an important function, the Editor had a responsibility, one the discharge of which would inevitably entail an astringent play of criticism upon the Poetical Renascence, grievous offence to the pretensions of the 'gang', and the implicit rallying of a disinterested and intelligent public, an élite, the indispensable 'small audience', against the triumphant encroachments of the spirit of coterie?

He writes (here again) as if he believed that the *Criterion* stood for a serious attempt to maintain the critical function. If he believes, or thinks he believes, that, one can see why his references in the present volume[1] to criticism and its importance should not convince us that they engage the context of strong thinking they ought, and why his handling of his themes, for all its distinction, should seem in general to lack some essential energy. An intelligent interest in criticism cannot be merely theoretical; it begins and ends in engagement, in actual discrimination and judgment, and cannot be for long very far away from them. Eliot as critic has in general been a not profoundly or wholly enough engaged one (a judgment that has its bearings on his creative achievement).

I have been enforcing the criticism: conventionality—a criticism that, I have incidentally shown, is made, as one brings it against him, with a variety of forces; all related so essentially as to give point to the one term. And we can say that a critic more wholly *engaged* couldn't have been so prone to conventionality,

[1] *Op. cit.*

in various senses, as we have seen Eliot to have been. There is a sense in which he is too much of an intellectual. To say this may sound like a very different criticism; yet I am pointing to a very closely related trait of the same man—pointing, in fact, to what may perhaps be judged to be one of the more radical manifestations of the habit, the characteristic, that appears in the conventionality. What is meant by saying that Eliot is too much of an intellectual should be plain to anyone who looks through two or three volumes of the *Criterion* and, considering the impressive weightiness of the constituent numbers, asks what the typical make-up actually amounts to, and what relation it bears, or bore, to any sense of the real problem, the problem of asserting and vindicating the function of criticism—that problem as it must have appear ed toan engaged and realizing mind, livingly aware of the state of things in England, and intent on a serious response to the challenge. It seems to me that there was nothing more adequate behind the *Criterion* than the general idea of a great European review; the idea as it might have been formed in (say) Irving Babbitt's lecture room. What Eliot learnt from Ezra Pound or Wyndham Lewis or the social-literary world in which he formed his notion of England didn't help him to anything better.

When in the present volume[1] he refers to the responsibilities of reviewing and the importance of having literary reviews, or explicitly discusses the characteristics and limitations of contemporary criticism, he gives no sign of recognizing our actual plight: the impossibility of maintaining an intelligent critical journal; the absence of an educated public (the 'small audience') coherent and influential enough to be able to insist on the maintenance of serious standards in the places where the function of criticism is supposed to be nowadays mainly performed—the weeklies and the middle-class Sunday papers. It is hardly conceivable that the criticism of a mind that, for all its distinction, is capable of such a default should have the strength and importance that the distinction at best seems to promise. It will tend to be of such a kind as to cause the pupils of Desmond MacCarthy, and the Sunday reviewers in general, no disturbance or uneasiness. And actually

[1] *Op. cit.*

they receive Eliot's criticism with acclaim, if sometimes with a suggestion of patronage; they pay tribute to a recognized distinction, while giving no sign of recognizing anything notably rarer or more to be prized or feared than what it is orthodoxy to think of as the talent of Desmond MacCarthy. That they can receive his criticism in that way is eloquent testimony to the lack of something that ought to have been there.

I must not, however, be taken to suggest that the defect is no more than a matter of what most directly and obviously relates to his 'conventionality'. We have it, as a characteristic weakness of critical thought, here, where he is writing about 'Johnson as Critic and Poet'.

In our own day, the influence of psychology and sociology upon literary criticism has been very noticeable. On the one hand, these influences of social discipline have enlarged the field of the critic and have affirmed, in a world which otherwise is inclined to depreciate the importance of literature, the relations of literature to life. But from another point of view this enrichment has also been an impoverishment, for the purely literary values, the appreciation of good writing for its own sake, have become submerged when literature is judged in the light of other considerations.

What are 'purely literary values'? I myself am firmly convinced that literature must be judged 'as literature and not as another thing'. Only when it is so judged can sociology and psychology learn from it what they have to learn. But to believe this is not, so far as I can see, to believe in 'purely literary values'. And the 'appreciation of good writing for its own sake' seems to me, for all its plausibility, a phrase that covers a failure of thought: it reminds me of Desmond MacCarthy's pronouncing about *East Coker* in the *Sunday Times* that 'Mr Eliot has never *written* better' (written italicized by way of insisting that it *means* something), and Eliot's own judgment that '*Garnett l'emporte sur tous les prosateurs contemporains pour l'habileté technique de l'écriture*' ('In the technical skill of the writing Garnett surpasses all contemporary prose-writers')—and his statement that he is not interested in what, in the *Cantos*, Pound says, but only in the way he says it. The quoted passage, in fact, reminds us that the critic is he who wrote 'Tradition and the Individual Talent', with its astonishingly untenable account of the importance of literature and the relations of literature to life. That is, it is the critic whom some radical inner condition makes peculiarly weak in value-judgment.

The manifestation of that weakness in his critical thinking is especially apparent when, in this volume,[1] he discusses his own plays. He says a good deal about the faults of *Family Reunion* and *The Cocktail Party*, but gives no sign at all that he is aware of the profounder, the essential, criticisms these works invite—the criticisms that express one's sharpened sense of the importance of literature, and therefore of the relation of literature to life. The discussion of drama in general suffers from the same weakness; the examination of the possibility and the practical problem of poetic drama comes from a mind in which the thinking about matters of form and technique hasn't the life, grapple, and force that critical thought cannot have apart from the habit of full engagement—the habit that manifests itself in the kind of pre-occupation with value, significance, and responsibility to life that makes it impossible to talk about 'purely literary values'.

In fact, one cannot escape the sense that Eliot's discussion of his themes is at bottom an insidious way of not really facing the essential responsibility of a critic. And perhaps enough has now been said about the effect of such characteristic things as 'What Is a Classic?': the curious sense one has of a strenuous *academic* quality; the sense of an intensity of intellectual energy, devoted by the critic and exacted of the reader, incommensurate with any upshot of defined, organized, and profitable thought.

[1] *Op. cit.*

XIV

JOHNSONAS CRITIC[1]

JOHNSON'S critical writings are living literature as Dryden's (for instance) are not: they compel, and they repay, a real and disinterested reading, that full attention of the judging mind which is so different an affair from the familiar kind of homage— from that routine endorsement of certified values and significances with which the good student, intent on examination-success, honours his set texts. Dryden too, it may be protested, deserves something better. No doubt; but to read Dryden critically can only serve to bring out, in the comparison with Johnson, the difference between classical documents and classical literature. Johnson's criticism, most of it, belongs with the living classics: it can be read afresh every year with unaffected pleasure and new stimulus. It is alive and life-giving.

One can say so much with confidence, and yet not be ready to say off-hand just what it is that gives Johnson's criticism its value. What do we read it for? Not for enlightenment about the authors with whom it deals (though it may impart some), and not for direct instruction in critical thinking. We might perhaps say that we read it for the vigour and weight that it shares with all Johnson's writings—the vigour that comes from a powerful mind and a profoundly serious nature, and the weight that seems to be a matter of bringing to bear at every point the ordered experience of a lifetime. This, however, is too general an answer to be satisfying: Johnson's critical writings exhibit very notably the characteristic wisdom, force, and human centrality of the great moralist, but they have also a value that is peculiarly of and for literary criticism—their specific interest is in and of that field. Johnson is always a great moralist, but in criticism he is a classic *qua* critic.

When we read him we know, beyond question, that we have

[1] Reprinted from *Scrutiny*, Summer 1944.

here a powerful and distinguished mind operating at first hand
upon literature. This, we can say with emphatic conviction (the
emphasis registering the rarity), really *is* criticism. The critic
knows what he means and says it with unescapable directness and
force ('deliberately, not dogmatically'), and what he says is
clearly the expression of intense and relevant interest. This in itself,
we can see, is enough to give Johnson's critical writings a distinctive value in the field of criticism, however difficult it may be to
define and assess the profit to be got by frequenting them. They
offer us that rare thing, the criticism of a qualified critic, for
Johnson is decidedly and impressively that, whatever the limits
of his qualifications.

And here, at this last prompting, we move towards a sharper
definition of his peculiar interest and significance: they are conditioned by the very fact of his being limited—limited, as he is,
so decidedly and specifically. The limitations are commonly both
misunderstood and overstressed. He had defects of sensibility, we
gather, analogous to his well-known myopia. This myopia, in fact,
has been adduced as partly explaining and excusing his deplorable lack of sympathy with the more poetical developments in
eighteenth-century poetry: he couldn't be interested in Nature
since he couldn't see her beauties. Now that fashions in taste have
changed, this particular physical incapacity is less likely to be
invoked, but the 'defective ear' with which he is credited seems
commonly to be thought of as an analogous incapacity afflicting
this other organ: the ear has its defect as the eye its myopia. The
analogy, of course, won't survive a moment's thought. Nevertheless, many who will recognize it at once to be absurd—disclaim-
ing, perhaps, having ever entertained it—will not have thought
of rejecting the implication (conveyed in the phrase) that Johnson's
'defective ear' is a matter of mere privation.

What is most striking about Johnson's 'ear', as about his other
characteristics, is something positive. That 'ear' is the product of
a training—a training in a positive taste. 'Taste' is a not altogether
happy word, since it suggests something in the nature of a connoisseur's palate. The taste that matters is the operative sensibility,
the discriminating 'touch', through which, in exploration and
critical response, a fine and inclusive organization engages.

Johnson's 'ear' is of that order. His training has been in a great positive tradition; a tradition so congenial to him, massively idiosyncratic as he is, that it takes on in him a highly personal quality. We see it as a literary tradition when we talk of 'taste' and 'ear', but its positiveness is a matter of its being so much more than literary: the very decided conventions of idiom and form engage comprehensive unanimities regarding morals, society, and civilization. At no other period of English history have literary interests been governed by a literary tradition so positive. Johnson, an indubitably real critic, first-hand and forceful, writes from within it, and here we have the peculiar interest of his case.

The nature of the 'defect' of his 'ear' comes out plainly enough in his comments on Milton's blank verse:

The musick of the English heroick line strikes the ear so faintly that it is easily lost, unless all the syllables of every line co-operate together: this co-operation can be only obtained by the preservation of every verse unmingled with another, as a distinct system of sound; and this distinctness is obtained and preserved by the artifice of rhyme. The variety of pauses, so much boasted by lovers of blank verse, changes the measures of an English poet to the periods of a declaimer; and there are only a few skilful and happy readers of Milton, who enable their audience to perceive where the lines end or begin. *Blank verse*, said an ingenious critick, *seems to be verse only to the eye.*

Poetry may subsist without rhyme, but English poetry will not often please . . . Blank verse . . . has neither the easiness of prose, nor the melody of numbers, and therefore tires by long continuance . . . what reason could urge in its defence, has been confuted by the ear.

This seems final enough: blank verse, in theory and in practice, is deplorable. But—

But, whatever be the advantage of rhyme, I cannot prevail on myself to wish that Milton had been a rhymer; for I cannot wish his work to be other than it is . . .

Milton, that is, is powerful enough to prevail over the critic's training. The critic reports the resistance and the favourable judgment together, giving more space to the resistance, by way of bringing out the power of Milton's genius. Johnson's very positive training (for that is what the taste, or 'ear', of so disciplined a critic represents) impels him to ask for something that

Milton doesn't offer, and he feels the impulsion even while acclaiming what Milton gives. We see the same thing in his remarks on Milton's diction:

This novelty has been, by those who can find nothing wrong in Milton, imputed to his laborious endeavours after words suitable to the grandeur of his ideas. *Our language*, said Addison, *sunk under him*. But the truth is, that, both in prose and verse, he had formed his style by a perverse and pedantick principle. He was desirous to use English words with a foreign idiom. This in all his prose is discovered and condemned; for there the judgment operates freely, neither softened by the beauty, nor awed by the dignity of his thoughts; but such is the power of his poetry, that his call is obeyed without resistance, the reader feels himself in captivity to a higher and nobler mind, and criticism sinks in admiration.

In this case the tension between acceptance and questioning criticism is likely to seem to most readers wholly respectable and unquaint. Johnson's strong Augustan training hasn't tended to disqualify him here, or to make just appreciation more difficult for him than it is for us. And, reverting to the question of blank verse, it is perhaps worth insisting on the force of that 'strong': Johnson represents the Augustan strength of eighteenth-century tradition. The author of *The Vanity of Human Wishes* has, as critic, no weakness—this will perhaps be generally recognized nowadays as a fair way of putting it—for the Miltonizing habit of his age: his taste is that of Goldsmith, who refers to 'the disgusting solemnity of blank verse'. But, faced with *Paradise Lost*, Johnson can tell the difference between Milton and eighteenth-century Miltonics, his distaste for which will hardly be urged against him as a disability: the passage quoted above in which he 'cannot prevail upon himself to wish that Milton had been a rhymer' concludes:

yet, like other heroes, he is to be admired rather than imitated. He that thinks himself capable of astonishing, may write blank verse; but those that hope only to please, must condescend to rhyme.

It is when we come to his treatment of *Lycidas* that we have something we can bluntly call disability, and the nature of it deserves to be precisely noted. His judgment is unhesitating and downright:

the diction is harsh, the rhymes uncertain, and the numbers unpleasing. What beauty there is, we must therefore seek in the sentiments and images. It is not to be considered as the effusion of real passion; for passion runs not after remote allusions and obscure opinions. . . . Where there is leisure for fiction there is little grief.

In this poem there is no nature, for there is no truth; there is no art, for there is nothing new. Its form is that of a pastoral, easy, vulgar, and therefore disgusting: whatever images it can supply are long ago exhausted; and its inherent improbability forces dissatisfaction on the mind.

—The 'diction is harsh . . . the numbers unpleasing'; that looks like 'stark insensibility'. Whatever it is, it is not a mere lapse, provoked (say) by the content of the poem. Of the songs in *Comus*, a work of which Johnson approves, he says: 'they are harsh in their diction, if not very musical in their numbers'. Those surprising judgments, imputing 'harshness' and lack of 'music', are to be explained by reference to the cultivated pre-dilection, the positive 'ear', with which they are correlated. It is the 'ear' critically formulated in Johnson's appraisal of the place in poetic history of Denham and Waller. The 'smoothness' and 'softness' of numbers ascribed to them are inseparably bound up with 'elegance' and 'propriety': 'it cannot be denied that he (Waller) added something to our elegance of diction, and something to our propriety of thought'. In the *Life* of Dryden Johnson tells us:

The new versification, as it was called, may be considered as owing its establishment to Dryden; from whose time it is apparent that English poetry has had no tendency to relapse to its former savageness.

A little earlier in the same *Life* we have had the predicate 'harsh' elucidated:

There was therefore before the time of Dryden no poetical diction, no system of words at once refined from the grossness of domestick use, and free from the harshness of terms appropriated to particular arts. Words, too familiar, or too remote, defeat the purpose of a poet. From those sounds which we hear on small or on coarse occasions we do not easily receive strong impressions, or delightful images; and words to which we are nearly strangers, whenever they occur, draw that attention on themselves which they should transmit to things.

—The 'ear', then, that judges *Lycidas* and the songs in *Comus* to be harsh in diction and unmusical is an organ that engages and brings to bear the whole complex of Augustan criteria. 'Elegance' and 'propriety' involve 'politeness'. Johnson's sense of 'music' carries with it inseparably a demand for the social movement and tone so characteristic of Augustan verse, and the demand for these is an implicit introduction of the associated norms, rational and moral.

Poetical expression includes sound as well as meaning: *Musick*, says Dryden, *is inarticulate poetry;* among the excellences of Pope, therefore, must be mentioned the melody of his metre.   (*Life* of Pope.)

But Johnson has no use for 'music' apart from meaning:

From poetry the reader justly expects, and from good poetry always obtains, the enlargement of his comprehension and elevation of his fancy. . . .   (*Life* of Waller.)

There is always to be a substance of statement in verse, and it is fair to say that the music Johnson demands is a music of meaning as much as of sound. On this passage of Denham's—

> O could I flow like thee, and make thy stream
> My great example, as it is my theme!
> Though deep, yet clear; though gentle, yet not dull;
> Strong without rage, without o'erflowing full

—a passage of which he tells us that it has been a model of versification 'for a century past', he says:

So much meaning is comprised in so few words; the particulars of resemblance are so perspicaciously collected, and every mode of excellence separated from its adjacent fault by so nice a line of limitation; the different parts of the sentence are so accurately adjusted; and the flow of the last couplet is so smooth and sweet; that the passage, however celebrated, has not been praised above its merits.
                                          (*Life* of Denham.)

On the other hand, in the *Life* of Pope we find this significant note:

I have been told that the couplet by which he declared his own ear to be most gratified, was this:
> Lo, where Maeotis sleeps, and hardly flows
> The freezing Tanais through a waste of snows.
But the reason of this preference I cannot discover.

—Johnson, that is, has no leaning towards the taste, so decidedly alive in the eighteenth century, for Spenserian-Tennysonian melodizing, the incantatory play of mellifluousness in which sense is subordinated.

When he comes to *Lycidas* he has no need to stop his ears against the music; the incantation, so acceptable to most of us, doesn't work for him—'the diction is harsh, the rhymes uncertain, and the numbers unpleasing'. The trained hearkening for another music has immunized him. He attends undistracted to the sense—attends critically, and we can't imagine him doing otherwise; which may be a limitation in him, but is certainly of the essence of his strength. The burden of *Paradise Lost* is such as to overcome all prepossessions against the kind of versification; the 'music' can overcome the trained 'ear'. Of *Comus* he can say:

it exhibits . . . his power of description and his vigour of sentiment, employed in the praise and defence of virtue. A work more truly poetical is rarely found.

But what does *Lycidas* yield if, as the duly responding reader does not, but Johnson must, we insist on reading it for its paraphrasable substance?

We know that they never drove a field and that they had no flocks to batten; and though it be allowed that the representation may be allegorical, the true meaning is so uncertain and remote, that it is never sought because it cannot be known when it is found.

This poem has yet a grosser fault. With these trifling fictions are mingled the most awful and sacred truths such as ought never to be polluted with such irreverent combinations.

It is difficult to see how, granted the approach, Johnson's essential criticism can be disposed of. The answer, of course, is that the approach is inappropriate and the poem a different kind of thing from any appreciable by Johnsonian criticism. One may perhaps add, in fairness to Johnson whose approach does at any rate promote this recognition, that it is a lesser thing than post-Johnsonian taste has tended to make it.

When we come to his treatment of Shakespeare, Johnson's limitations appear both more seriously disabling and more interesting, for his training gets more radically in the way of appreciation than where Milton is concerned. The critic for whom the Augustan use of language is the undisputed norm cannot come to terms with the Shakespearian use. He understands and he doesn't understand. He describes the Shakespearian use with characteristic strength and vivacity:

> It is incident to him to be now and then entangled with an unwieldy sentiment, which he cannot well express, and will not reject; he struggles with it a while, and if it continues stubborn, comprises it in words such as occur, and leaves it to be disentangled and evolved by those who have more leisure to bestow upon it.
> Shakespeare regarded more the series of ideas, than of words.[1]
> (*Preface*)

That such descriptions carry with them in Johnson's mind a severely adverse judgment we know well enough; the evidence abounds: 'the offspring of his throes is tumour, meanness, tedious-ness and obscurity': 'he has corrupted language by every mode of depravation'—it is easy to accumulate passages and tags of like import. Yet again and again the description itself, in its lively aptness, implies a measure of appreciation. This is most notably so in the well-known place in *The Rambler* where Johnson passes his strictures on lowness in *Macbeth*:

> Words which convey ideas of dignity in one age, are banished from elegant writing or conversation in another, because they are in time debased by vulgar mouths, and can be no longer heard without the involuntary recollection of unpleasing images.
> When Macbeth [the speaker is really Lady Macbeth] is confirming himself in the horrid purpose of stabbing his king, he breaks out amidst his emotions into a wish natural for a murderer:
> —Come, thick night!
> And pall thee in the dunnest smoke of hell,
> That my keen knife see not the wound it makes,
> Nor Heaven peep through the blanket of the dark,
> To cry, Hold, hold!

---

[1] *Cf.* '... that fulness of idea, which might sometimes load his words with more sentiment than they could conveniently convey, and that rapidity of imagination ...' (*Proposals*.)

In this passage is exerted all the force of poetry; that force which calls new powers into being, which embodies sentiment, and animates matter; yet, perhaps, scarce any man now peruses it without some disturbance of his attention from the counteraction of the words to the ideas.

Johnson, of course, enforcing that 'counteraction' with particularized commentary, goes on to stigmatize the lowness of 'dun' ('an epithet now seldom heard but in the stable'), of 'knife' ('an instrument used by butchers and cooks in the meanest employments'), and of 'peeping through a blanket'. Yet when he concludes that 'in this passage is exerted all the force of poetry' he is not, for the sake of paradox, indulging in rhetorical licence. It is not his habit to use words lightly, and how much he means what he says comes out in what follows: 'that force which calls new powers into being, which embodies sentiment, and animates matter'. The felicity of these phrases is not accidental, and can we say that the critic who finds them when trying to express his sense of the peculiar exploratory creativeness and metaphorical concreteness of Shakespare's poetry doesn't appreciate the Shakespearian use of language?

The potency of the training, the strong positiveness of the criteria, by virtue of which appreciation stultifies itself in an accompanying perversity of rejection appears the more strikingly. Nothing could be more unlike the Shakespearian use of English than that in which Johnson's mind and sensibility have been formed. For him, in this the type Augustan, expression in poetry as in prose is a matter of stating—of stating with point, elegance, and propriety. It is significant that, asked for a definition of the 'wit' that is common to Pope (who of course has more than one kind and is more than an Augustan poet), Johnson, Goldsmith, and Crabbe, together with the Gray of the *Impromptu* and the *Elegy* and the Cowper of *The Castaway*, one naturally replies in some such formula as this: 'a neatness and precision of *statement*, tending towards epigram'. When Johnson says that 'Shakespeare regarded more the series of ideas, than of words' he is thinking of the problems, grammatical and logical, with which Shakespeare in his mature styles confronts the analyst. What D. W. Harding says of Rosenberg's handling of language (see *Scrutiny*, Vol. III,

No. 4) applies to Shakespeare's—it is, in fact, the essentially poetic use:

> He—like many poets in some degree, one supposes—brought language to bear on the incipient thought at an earlier stage of its development. Instead of the emerging idea being racked slightly so as to fit a more familiar approximation of itself, and words found for *that*, Rosenberg let it manipulate words almost from the beginning, often without the controls of logic and intelligibility.

Shakespeare's 'thoughts', concretely realized moments in the development of the dramatic poem (itself a marvellously concrete and complex whole), are apt to be highly specific and, so, highly complex—which is to say, compressed and licentious in expression: hence the occasions for Johnson's vigours and rigours of censure. The Augustan cannot conceive the need for such a use of language. The ideas he wants to express are adequately provided for—and this is true of poetry as of prose—in the common currency of terms, put together according to the conventions of grammar and logic. He doesn't feel that the current concepts of ordinary discourse muffle or misrepresent anything he has to convey. His business is, while observing the ordinary rules in arranging them, to achieve further a formal pattern of meaning-structure and versification. He can express himself congenially in modes that are in such a sense, and at such a level, social that this pattern (like Augustan idiom itself) suggests formal conventions of social manners and public deportment. It is an age in which everyone of any cultivation knows so well what Reason, Truth, and Nature, the presiding trinity, are that no one feels any pressing need of definitions (and here we have an essential mark of a strong positive culture). It is not an age in which the poet feels called on to explore further below the public surface than conventional expression takes cognizance of, or to push in any way beyond the frontiers of the charted. He has no impulse to indulge in licentious linguistic creation, nor does it occur to him that such indulgence may ever with any propriety be countenanced.

And what, in such a convention, makes the poet's compositions poetry? The pattern, primarily—the extremely formal pattern which, involving metre, rhyme, and sense-organization, involves so much and asserts itself so dominatingly. It virtually involves the decorum that might have been listed as a separate head; the decorum that Johnson vindicates in his commentary on the passage of *Macbeth*. Given movement, tone, and idiom so essentially suggestive of formal deportment and company manners it is not surprising that the obligatory decorum should be so delicate and intolerant, and the 'low' it cannot abide be stigmatized so arbitrarily (it must seem to us).

There is, where Johnsonian Augustanism is concerned, a third head to be added, that of generality—the peculiar kind of generality prescribed in the well-known passage of *Rasselas*:

'The business of a poet', said Imlac, 'is to examine, not the individual, but the species; to remark general properties and large appearances. He does not number the streaks of the tulip or describe the different shades in the verdure of the forest; he is to exhibit in his portraits of nature, such striking and prominent features, as recall the original to every mind; and must neglect the minuter discriminations, which one may have remarked, and another have neglected, for those characteristics which are alike obvious to vigilance and to carelessness.'

Pope, of course, can be particular enough, but there is only one Pope, and, although *the* great Augustan, he transcends Augustanism too much to be the type Augustan, and it is fairly plain as the eighteenth century wears on that Augustanism tends inherently towards this generality, the relation of which to decorum comes out clearly in Johnson's censure of 'dun', 'knife', and 'blanket'. The relation appears again in this significantly phrased stricture on Cowley:

The fault of Cowley, and perhaps of all the writers of the metaphysical race, is that of pursuing his thoughts to their last ramification, by which he loses the grandeur of generality; for of the greatest things the parts are little; what is little can be but pretty, and by claiming dignity becomes ridiculous.

More radically, a thoroughgoing rejection of the Shakespearian use of language, and, consequently, of all concrete specificity in the rendering of experience, would seem very much to imply the quest of a compensating poetic generality. Johnson remarks (again in the *Life* of Cowley):

Great thoughts are always general, and consist in positions not limited by exceptions, and in descriptions not descending to minuteness. . . . Those writers who lay on the watch for novelty could have little hope of greatness; for great things cannot have escaped former observation.

—They should have known that the poet can only aim at achieving, in the 'grandeur of generality', *What oft was thought, but ne'er so well express'd.*

Remembering *The Vanity of Human Wishes* one hesitates to say that this use of language is essentially unpoetic—though the essentially poetic is certainly the Shakespearian, its antithesis. What one can, however, say is that the use Johnson favours and practises—the only use he really understands—is essentially undramatic. And here we have his radical limitation as a critic of the drama, and his radical incapacity as a dramatist (he being in both respects representative of his age). We may see the *literary* bias expressed in his characteristic formula, 'A dramatick exhibition is a book recited with concomitants that increase or diminish the effect', as, in an age in which elevated drama (by Shakespeare or by Home) is an opportunity for Garrick, and declamatory histrionic virtuosity the best the theatre has to offer, wholly respectable. The assumption that a work of art in words is to be judged as literature has in any case much to be said for it, whatever complications unrecognized by Johnson may attend on the qualifying 'dramatic'. Yet, as I have remarked before in these pages, when one re-reads *Irene*—so patently conceived as a book to be recited, and leaving so wholly to the concomitants the hopeless task of making it a theatre-piece—one realizes that, nevertheless, 'literary bias' misses what is most interesting in Johnson's case. That he has no sense of the theatre, and worse, that he cannot present or conceive his themes dramatically—these criticisms one doesn't need to urge. The point one finds oneself making is that his essential bent is undramatic in a sense that goes far deeper than the normal interest of the 'dramatic critic'. The weakness of *Irene* sends one back to consider the nature of the strength of his best verse.

The Vanity of Human Wishes is great poetry; but it is in a mode
that, above, just escaped being called essentially unpoetic: it is
certainly as undramatic as good poetry can be. Johnson—and in
this he is representative of his age—has neither the gift nor the
aim of catching in words and presenting to speak for themselves
significant particularities of sensation, perception, and feeling, the
significance coming out in complex total effects, which also are
left to speak for themselves; he starts with general ideas and general propositions, and develops them by discussion, comment, and
illustration. The failure in dramatic conception so patent in *Irene*
is correlated with the essential qualities of *The Vanity of Human
Wishes*. When he attempts drama, the conditions that enable
Johnson in his characteristic poetry of statement, exposition, and
reflexion to give his moral declamation the weight of lived
experience and to charge his eighteenth-century generalities with
that extraordinary and characteristic kind of concreteness—

> Unnumber'd suppliants crowd Preferment's gate,
> Athirst for wealth, and burning to be great;
> Delusive Fortune hears th' incessant call,
> They mount, they shine, evaporate, and fall

—these conditions fail him. In blank verse the wit and the pat-
terned social movement are absent, and with them the Johnsonian
weight. His characters declaim eloquent commonplaces—he cannot make them do anything else, but the dramatic aim has robbed
them of the familiar strength and substance; the great moralist,
reduced to making a show of speaking through his *personae*, is
less than himself.

The point I am making is that Johnson's limitations as a critic
have positive correlatives. But they are not the less limitations, and
seriously disabling ones. With his radically undramatic habit we
may reasonably associate his bondage to moralistic fallacy—his
censure of Shakespeare's indifference to poetic justice and Shakespeare's general carelessness about the duty to instruct:

His first defect is that to which may be imputed most of the evil in
books or in man. He sacrifices virtue to convenience, and is so much
more careful to please than to instruct, that he seems to write without
any moral purpose. From his writings indeed a system of social duty

may be selected, for he that thinks reasonably must think morally; but his precepts and axioms drop casually from him; he makes no just distribution of good or evil, nor is always careful to shew in the virtuous a disapprobation of the wicked; he carries his persons indifferently through right and wrong, and at the close dismisses them without further care, and leaves their examples to operate by chance. This fault the barbarity of his age cannot extenuate; for it is always a writer's duty to make the world better, and justice is a virtue independent on time and place.

—Not really appreciating the poetry he cannot appreciate the dramatic organization; more generally, he cannot appreciate the ways in which not only Shakespeare's drama but all works of art *act* their moral judgments. For Johnson a thing is stated, or it isn't there.

It is as well, perhaps, to insist on the inability to appreciate Shakespearian poetry—for in spite of the stress laid above on the paradoxical kind of appreciation Johnson shows in describing, inability is what, in sum, we have to recognize. Corroboration, if it were needed, is to be seen in the taste for declamatory eloquence exemplified in his starring of the passage from *The Mourning Bride* (in the *Life* of Congreve): 'If I were required to select from the whole mass of English poetry the most poetical paragraph, I know not what I could prefer ...' The paragraph is eighteenth-century eloquence of a kind that Johnson's own account suggests well enough:

He who reads these lines enjoys for a moment the powers of a poet; he feels what he remembers to have felt before, but he feels it with great increase of sensibility; he recognizes a familiar image, but he meets it again amplified and expanded, embellished with beauty, and enlarged with majesty.

This incapacity of Johnson's involves, in the criticism of Shakespearian drama, limitations more disabling than his moralism. He ranks Shakespeare's genius supremely high, of course, but it is interesting to note where he lays the stress:

Shakespeare is above all writers, at least above all modern writers, the poet of nature; the poet that holds up to his readers a faithful mirrour of manners and of life.

This therefore is the praise of Shakespeare, that his drama is the mirrour of life; that he who has mazed his imagination in following the phantoms which other writers raise up before him, may here be cured of his delirious extasies, by reading human sentiments in human language, by scenes from which a hermit may estimate the transactions of the world, and a confessor predict the progress of the passions.

(Preface)

—What Johnson acclaims in Shakespeare, it might be said, is a great novelist who writes in dramatic form (and this, if we add an accompanying stress on the bard who provides opportunities for histrionic declamation, is the eighteenth-century attitude in general). To use the time-honoured phrase, he values Shakespeare —and extols him in admirably characteristic terms—for his 'knowledge of the human heart'; and the *Preface to Shakespeare* should be a *locus classicus* for the insufficiency of an appreciation of Shakespeare's 'knowledge of the human heart' that is not at the same time an appreciation of the poetry. That Johnson's mode of exhibiting such insufficiency is 'period' doesn't make the illustrative and monitory value of the relation to Bradley's less, but the reverse; and now that Bradley's itself begins to look 'period' to Professor Dover Wilson[1] there are more recent modes that can be brought into the critical series.[2]

Johnson's case is clear enough: the radical insufficiency correlated with his abstraction of the 'drama' from the 'poetry'— with his failure to see the dramatic genius as a poetic and linguistic genius—appears when he exalts the comedies above the tragedies:

He therefore indulged his natural disposition, and his disposition, as Rhymer has remarked, led him to comedy. In tragedy he often writes,

[1] See *The Fortunes of Falstaff* (1943). Professor Dover Wilson exposes here for an awe-struck public of scholars and academics, the ineptitude of the Bradleyan approach. So the work of the past fifteen years, if it still goes unrecognized, has not been without its effect even in the inner strongholds. It is fair to add that the book gives an intelligent, if rather redundant, account of the two plays involved.

[2] In the last decade recent critical advances were recognized at Cambridge in this formulation of a subject for a prize-essay: *The Use of Poetry in Shakespeare's Plays*. Professor Wilson Knight, the followers of Caroline Spurgeon, the investigators of archetypal patterns, and the promoters of the mediaeval Shakespeare, all need to be reminded of the bearings that Johnson's case has for them.

with great appearance of toil and study, what is written at last with little felicity; but in his comick scenes, he seems to produce without labour, what no labour can improve. In tragedy he is always struggling after some occasion to be comick; but in comedy he seems to repose, or to luxuriate, as in a mode of thinking congenial to his nature. In his tragick scenes there is always something wanting, but his comedy often surpasses expectation or desire. His comedy pleases by the thoughts and the language, and his tragedy for the greater part by incident and action. His tragedy seems to be skill, his comedy to be instinct.

It is quite unequivocal. A couple of pages further on in the *Preface* he reverts to the theme; there is no need to quote again. The appreciation of Shakespeare's dramatic genius—of his 'knowledge of the human heart' and his depth and range in rendering life—that exalts the comedies above the tragedies is a calamitously defective appreciation.

The gross obviousness of the defect goes with the very strength of Johnson's criticism. What he says of Shakespeare might be adapted to himself as critic:

Shakespeare, whether life or nature be his subject, shews plainly, that he has seen with his own eyes; he gives the image which he receives, not weakened or distorted by the intervention of any other mind;[1] the ignorant feel his representations to be just, and the learned see that they are compleat.

Johnson is not invariably just or complete; but the judgment—and he never fails to judge—is always stated with classical force and point, and based beyond question on strong first-hand impressions. He addresses himself deliberately and disinterestedly to what is in front of him; he consults his experience with unequivocal directness and always has the courage of it. Concerned as he is for principle, he refers with characteristic contempt to 'the cant of those who judge by principles rather than perception' (*Life* of Pope). There is always, he says, 'an appeal open from criticism to nature (*Preface*) and:

[1] Contrast this, on Milton: 'But his images and descriptions of the scenes or operations of Nature do not seem to be always copied from original form, nor to have the freshness, raciness, and energy of immediate observation. He saw Nature, as Dryden expresses it, *through the spectacles of books*; and on most occasions calls learning to his assistance.'

It ought to be the first endeavour of a writer to distinguish nature from custom; or that which is established because it is right, from that which is right only because it is established.

It is significant that for 'nature' he tends to substitute the term 'experience'. For instance, in the number of *The Rambler* (156) from which the last extract comes, having adduced the orthodox objection to 'tragi-comedy', he asks:

But will not experience show this objection to be rather subtile than just? It is not certain that the tragick and comick affections have been moved alternately with equal force; and that no plays have oftener filled the eye with tears, and the breast with palpitation, than those which are variegated with interludes of mirth?

—The 'mingled drama' has succeeded in practice, and that would seem to dispose of the rules. It is true that Johnson then draws back:

I do not however think it safe to judge of works of genius merely by the event.

He is not prepared to say that success is necessarily self-justifying: there is always principle to be considered. And he goes on to suggest that 'perhaps the effects even of Shakespeare's poetry might have been yet greater, had he not counteracted himself', but kept the rules. This is pretty obviously a formal conservative scruple rationalizing itself. Yet there is nothing timid about Johnson's appeal to experience, and the relation in his criticism between experience and authority (predisposed as he is to the idea of authority) has nothing in common with that reconciliation between Nature and the Rules which Pope, representative here of last-phase Neo-classicism, effects with such elegant ease in his *Essay*. In fact, Johnson's recourse to experience is so constant and uncompromising and so subversive of Neo-classic authority that it is misleading to bring him under the Neo-classic head.

The strength and the limitations together, in criticism, of Johnsonian 'experience' come out best of all, perhaps, in his treatment of the Unities. Here the terms are downright and the dismissal blunt (*Preface*):

Such is the triumphant language with which a critick exults over the misery of an irregular poet, and exults commonly without resistance or reply. It is time therefore to tell him by the authority of Shakespeare, that he assumes, as an unquestionable principle, a position which, while his breath is forming it into words, his understanding pronounces to be false. It is false, that any representation is mistaken for reality; that any dramatick fable in its materiality was ever credible, or, for a single moment, was ever credited.

The truth is, that the spectators are always in their senses, and know, from the first act to the last, that the stage is only a stage, and that the players are only players. They came to hear a certain number of lines recited with just gesture and elegant modulation. The lines relate to some action, and an action must be in some place; but the different actions that compleat a story may be in places very remote from each other; and where is the absurdity of allowing that space to represent first Athens, and then Sicily, which was always known to be neither Sicily nor Athens, but a modern theatre?

This kind of commonsense, being commonsense and a real resort to experience, is adequate to the dismissal of so unreal a structure as the doctrine of the Unities. But of course, for a satisfactory account of the experience of the theatre more is needed: 'that the spectators are always in their senses' is an incomplete truth, and misleading in its incompleteness. And even if Johnson had found the theatre more congenial than he does we shouldn't have looked to him for anything of adequate subtlety—anything of the order of 'that willing suspension of disbelief which constitutes poetic faith'. The subtlety of analysis that Coleridge, with his psychological inwardness, is to bring into criticism is not at Johnson's command. But it can be said that Johnson, with his rational vigour and the directness of his appeal to experience, represents the best that criticism can do before Coleridge.

The deficient analysis has an obvious manifestation in his moralism. It leads also to his appearing sometimes to be exhibiting his moralistic disability where the appearance is deceptive, being imposed by the idiom he cannot escape.

The end of writing is to instruct; the end of poetry is to instruct by pleasing. (*Preface*)

—This way (not invented by Johnson) of resolving the dilemma represented by the traditional question, 'Is it the business of art to please or instruct?', doesn't bring emancipation from the false

analysis that the question involves. He knows, as his critical practice unfailingly exemplifies, that his business when faced with a set
of verses is to judge whether they are good poetry or not, and that
this is a different matter from judging whether they are salutary as
instruction: he knows that something more is involved. But,
admirably preoccupied as he is with technical examinations and
judgments of sensibility, he can't, when asked what this something
more is, rise above—or go deeper than—an answer in terms of
'please'. Pleasure added to instruction: that, though his perception
transcends it, is the analysis to which the critical idiom he inevitably
uses is tied. When he has occasion to insist on the serious function
of poetry, the vocabulary of 'instruction' is his inevitable resort.

In the *Life* of Gray, for instance, we read:

To select a singular event, and swell it to a giant's bulk by fabulous
appendages of spectres and predictions, has little difficulty, for he that
forsakes the probable may always find the marvellous. And it has little
use: we are affected only as we believe; we are improved only as we
find something to be imitated or declined. I do not see that *The Bard*
promotes any truth, moral or political.

This might be taken for a clear instance of the most indefensible
didacticism. Yet the context—indeed, the tone of the passage itself
—makes it plain enough that what we have here is Johnson's way
of saying that for a mature, accomplished, and cultivated mind
such as Gray's to be playing this kind of game and exhibiting itself
in these postures is ridiculous. It will be noted that his criticism
proceeds by way of commonsense analysis [1] to a final dismissing
judgment of sensibility:

These Odes are marked by glittering accumulations of ungraceful
ornaments; they strike, rather than please; the images are magnified
by affectation; the language is laboured into harshness. The mind of the

[1] E.g.: 'The *weaving* of the *winding* sheet he borrowed, as he owns, from the
northern Bards; but the texture, however, was very properly the work of
female powers, as the art of spinning the thread of life in another mythology.
Theft is always dangerous; Gray has made weavers of slaughtered bards, by a
fiction outrageous and incongruous. They are then called upon to *Weave the
warp*, and *weave the woof*, perhaps, with no great propriety; for it is by crossing
the *woof* with the *warp* that men *weave* the *web* or piece; and the first line was
dearly bought by the admission of its wretched correspondent, *Give ample
room and verge enough*. He has, however, no other line as bad.'

writer seems to work with unnatural violence. *Double, double, toil and trouble.* He has a kind of strutting dignity, and is tall by walking on tiptoe. His art and his struggle are too visible, and there is too little appearance of ease and nature.

The judgment is surely unanswerable. Johnson is a better critic of eighteenth-century poetry than Matthew Arnold. In dealing with that, at any rate, he has an advantage in his training. To be trained in so positive a tradition is to have formed strong anticipations as to the kind of discrimination one will have to make, and within the field to which the anticipations are relevant they favour quickness of perception and sureness of judgment. (An analogy: the 'native' tracker owes his skill not to a natural endowment of marvellously good sight, but to analogous anticipations: knowing the kind of thing to look for he is quick to perceive, and being habituated to the significances of the various signs, he is quick to appraise and interpret.) Johnson's disapproval of Gray's Pindarick sublimities goes with his disapproval of Miltonics. For him—and who today will disagree?—Miltonics represent the weakness of taste in this age. Now that we no longer search the eighteenth century for what is congenial to Victorian-romantic taste—for poetry from the 'soul'—we can see that the Pindarick ambition consorts with the same weakness. Drawing inspiration from the Miltonic side of Dryden, it applies resonant externalities of declamation to conventional ideas of the exalted. What Johnson singles out for praise is Gray's Augustan classic—for the *Elegy* is Augustan in its strength: it has Augustan movement, and the accompanying Augustan virtues of neat, compact, and dignified statement. The terms in which he extols it are significant:

The *Churchyard* abounds with images which find a mirrour in every mind, and with sentiments to which every bosom returns an echo. The four stanzas beginning *Yet even these bones,* are to me original: I have never seen the notions in any other place; yet he that reads them here, persuades himself that he has always felt them. Had Gray written often thus, it had been vain to blame and useless to praise him.

—These stanzas, Johnson judges, have the virtues of *What oft was thought, but ne'er so well express'd*: that is, he extols the *Elegy* as classical statement—as giving moving and inevitable form to the human commonplaces.

His treatment of Gray, who has not even yet fully emerged from the Arnoldian transfiguration, has counted for much in the traditional notion of the arbitrary Great Cham of criticism, narrow, dogmatic and intolerant. Actually, it illustrates his excellence as a critic of eighteenth-century verse.

In stressing Johnson's sureness and penetration within the limits of the field to which his training properly applies, it will not do to suggest that his distinction as a critic is confined within those limits. The truth is far otherwise. How notably he transcends them in discussing Shakespeare has already been suggested, and admirers of the *Preface* (not the only relevant document) know that there is much more to adduce. Perhaps the most striking demonstration of his uninhibited versatility of critical response is to be found in his *Life* of Cowley. That he should pick on Cowley as the best of the Metaphysicals—'Cowley adapted it [the 'metaphysick style'], and excelled his predecessors, having as much sentiment, and more musick'—is, of course, an instance of Augustan limitation: Cowley is nearer than the others, and, in his transitional quality, which relates him more closely to Dryden and Rochester than to Donne, more accessible to Augustan sympathy. But on the other hand it has to be recognized that, as a Metaphysical, he deserves no more than Johnson concedes; so far as he is concerned, the estimate is just:

Yet great labour, directed by great abilities, is never wholly lost: if they frequently threw away their wit upon false conceits, they likewise sometimes struck out unexpected truth: if their conceits were far-fetched, they were often worth the carriage. To write on their plan, it was at least necessary to read and think. No man could be born a metaphysical poet, nor assume the dignity of a writer, by descriptions copied from descriptions, by imitations borrowed from imitations, by traditional imagery, and hereditary similes, by readiness of rhyme, and volubility of syllables.

—It is not for 'period' disabilities that the eighteenth-century critic who writes this seems most remarkable. And the free and powerful intelligence compels recognition in the whole immediately accompanying discussion of Metaphysical characteristics. So powerful an intelligence, associated with so intense an interest both in letters and in human nature, could no more be narrow than shallow. Here is a concluding example of Johnson's quality:

To his domesticks [Swift] was naturally rough; and a man of rigorous temper, with that vigilance of minute attention which his works discover, must have been a master that few could bear.

In spite of what was said in the opening of this essay, such a passage might very well be pondered for the illumination it throws on the 'works'. The implications constitute a very salutary corrective for the still current sentimentalization of Swift.

XV

TOWARDS STANDARDS OF CRITICISM[1]

THE CALENDAR OF MODERN LETTERS was founded in 1925, and died two and a half years later, having been first a monthly and then a quarterly. How good it was while it lasted the following election of criticism from its pages will show—evidence the more impressive when it is remembered that they had already yielded, among other things,[2] a volume of critical essays (*Scrutinies I*, edited by Edgell Rickword). *The Calendar* commanded the services of half a dozen really distinguished critics, each one better than any that finds frequent employment in existing periodicals, and was able to count on good work from a number of others. It was lively as well as intelligent. And yet it couldn't live. No one will suggest (it would at any rate be a misleading way of putting it) that it was killed by competition, or that the band of critics who served it disappeared from current criticism because, the function being over-provided-for, their talents were superfluous. They dispersed, and did in effect disappear; and admiration for their work and concern to get it recognized and, if possible, bring them back into criticism, would have been incentive enough to this selection, even if such admiration and concern had not necessarily involved a preoccupation with the general significance of their enterprise and fate, with the general plight that the history of *The Calendar* illustrates.

The force of the illustration depends, of course, upon the intrinsic value of the work represented. This value, it may be well to repeat, is such that, for the most part, no further significance

[1] This essay formed the Introduction to *Towards Standards of Criticism*, Wishart & Co., 1933.

[2] E.g., *A Pamphlet against Anthologies*, by Laura Riding and Robert Graves, which appeared in its first form in *The Calendar; Anonymity*, by E. M. Forster; and some of the contents of *Transition* by Edwin Muir.

was necessary to justify the reprinting. Indeed, it had better be confessed at once (certain of the critics represented will probably not like the idea) that the undertaking was not altogether free from a pedagogic incentive: the bound volumes of *The Calendar* have been serving a certain educational purpose incomparably well, and further sets are unobtainable. Good criticism and intelligent discussion of literature are not common; *The Calendar* abounds with them in great variety—so far, in fact, as to be unique; and an introduction to it might make all the difference between a creditable 'Arts' course product and the development of a mature intelligence. It will be gathered, then, that the intrinsic value is very high.

But, at the moment, it is the general significance that takes the stress—the decay in a modern civilized community of the function so admirably served by *The Calendar*. For if *The Calendar* could not find enough support, what hope (in default of generous patrons) can there be for any serious critical journal? And, as a matter of fact, in ways that everyone can instance—degeneration and decease—the signs have become decidedly worse since the last issue of *The Calendar*: there is no need to particularize.

But perhaps 'function', three sentences above, takes too much for granted; inquiry may start by considering how its own function appeared to *The Calendar*. The preliminary statement [1] is cautious, but with a caution that derives not from vagueness, timidity, or lack of conviction, but from a subtle appreciation of the problem in view:

A preconceived idea is, as the artist knows, a tyrant dangerous to the proper organization of the impulse, definable in no other terms than those of the finished work, which compels him to his strange exertion. The same reticence is necessary even in the humble creation of a Review, in which activity, since it is to some extent an æsthetic one, there is virtue not in intentions but in achievement only. We lay down no programme as to *The Calendar's* performance nor prophecy as to its character, since these things cannot interest our readers till they have a tangible existence, and then we shall be ready to join our own criticism with theirs. A conviction of the value of spontaneous growth (or of growth which looks spontaneous to the watching mind), and

[1] *Op. cit.*, p. 27.

of unpoliced expression, is as near as we can come to any public challenge or editorial doctrine.

Nevertheless, something more had to be there from the outset since, as *The Calendar* says later in reviewing *The New Criterion*, 'not even the bulkiest review can be boundlessly eclectic, and as soon as the element of choice is introduced the question of a principle or a programme becomes paramount'; and about its own 'principle' *The Calendar* is, at the outset, explicit:

In reviewing we shall base our statements on the standards of criticism, since it is only then that one can speak plainly without offence, or give praise with meaning.

These 'standards of criticism' are assumed; nothing more is said about them. Nothing more needed to be said; for if we can appreciate—which is not necessarily to agree with—the reviewing in *The Calendar*, we know what they are, and if we cannot, then no amount of explaining or arguing will make much difference. (What is said of the reviewing bears, of course, on the choice of creative work.)

But the assumption of 'standards of criticism' qualifies the previous account, briefly suggested, of the modern disintegration: 'To-day there is only the race, the biological-economic environment, and the individual.' Where the recognition of standards of criticism can be counted on, then there is more than the individual; there is also some remnant of tradition, the common mind, the something more-than-individual that *The Calendar* refers to in its *Valediction*:

The value of a review must be judged by its attitude to the living literature of the time (which includes such works of the past as can be absorbed by the contemporary sensibility). . . .

Where there is a 'living literature of the time' there is also a 'contemporary sensibility', and it is always the business of criticism (whatever it may appear to be doing immediately) to define—that is, help to form—and organize this, and to make conscious the 'standards' implicit in it. (This 'contemporary', of course, as the passage just quoted indicates, includes the past or as much of it as there is any access to.)

P

When disintegration, social and cultural, has set in, the business of criticism becomes very difficult of performance. In what senses there has been disintegration, and with what embarrassing consequences for the critic, the following extract[1] from a review of Mrs Woolf's *The Common Reader* suggests:

The Victorians . . . took advantage of the lull before the storm and produced the last examples of the literature which retains its expressive value along the whole range of group-sensibilities. Since then, the reading-public has split. We have the small body of educated sharp-witted readers from whom a small spark of intelligence sometimes flickers, but being passionate, if at all, only about values and not experience, ultimately uncreative; and themselves so frequently practitioners as to be unsatisfactory even as audience. Beyond lies the vast reading-public which is led by the nose by the high-class literary-journalist-poet type and its tail tweaked by the paragraphist with pretensions not rising above personal gossip.

—Disintegration, it is plain, involves more than 'splitting', and where it has gone so far that the 'contemporary sensibility' depends on a negligible few—negligible, that is, in influence on the contemporary world—then the assertion of 'standards', now indeed a matter of assertion, becomes 'dogmatism': intellectuals by way of discrediting a study of cultural decline, will remark that in it 'there are assumed certain standards of taste, which if properly understood and applied by a sensitive person, make it possible to estimate the value of any piece of literary work, and to *place* it in relation to any other literary work, whatever'. What such characteristic phrasing makes one hopeless of getting properly understood is the nature of 'standards', the 'standards' invoked in literary criticism—how, if they are not certified weights and measures lying ready to be picked up and applied from the outside, it should not then necessarily follow that they must be merely 'immobilized personal preferences'.[2]

Explanation is impotent where the 'contemporary sensibility', the traditional 'mind', with its memory (living—really living, and so changing—always in the present or not at all) and its sense of relative value, is not there to appeal to: discussion of values in

---

[1] *Op. cit.*, p. 142.
[2] '. . . *des préférences personnelles immobilisées.*' Jules Lemaître.

the abstract, engaging nowhere, remains a barren academic exercise. When the 'contemporary sensibility' is active, then the general doubt, of the form exemplified above, does not arise to be dealt with. Nor does the abstract possibility of estimating the value of any piece of literary work, and 'placing' it in 'relation to any other literary work whatever', propose itself for consideration or need to be considered. There may be a good deal of room for difference about particular valuations, but there is enough common understanding of what value is to make differences discussible, and enough agreement to make the question whether there has been a cultural decline in the past two centuries, say, a real and urgent one, and to make the effort towards standards fruitful in further and more conscious agreement.

In the conditions of disintegration contemplated above, the function (the corresponding importance of which was at the same time implicitly brought out) of defining the organizing and contemporary sensibility must be at best extremely arduous. 'The reader we have in mind, the ideal reader', though (*The Calendar* adds) he may not be 'one with whom we share any particular set of admirations and beliefs', is the Common Reader, representing the 'standards of criticism'; but a Common Reader who has to be created rather than addressed, though *The Calendar* put the undertaking modestly:

... the readers of a paper have their share in the formation of its individuality, though it may be designed in the first place with some imagined kind of reader in the foreground. As this hypothesis is corrected by the reality, the balance of sympathies and antipathies is adjusted into an unpredictable harmony.

—At any rate, enough of the literary tradition survives to make the crystallization of a Common Reader a reasonable calculation.

The fact that the other traditional continuities have, as the introductory statement of *The Calendar* points out, so completely disintegrated, makes the literary tradition correspondingly more important, since the continuity of consciousness, the conservation of the collective experience, is the more dependent on it: if the literary tradition is allowed to lapse, the gap is complete. But what gives the literary tradition its unique importance also makes it

desperately precarious. Can it last, we ask, in isolation, unsupported by extra-literary sanctions, and not merely in isolation,
but in a hostile environment?

The question was, in a sense, raised in the brush that *The Calendar* had with *The Criterion*.[1] For the 'intellectualist reaction' and
the 'neo-classicism' animadverted upon represent a preoccupation
with the pre-conditions of literature, with extra-literary traditions
and sanctions. This is not the place to discuss the profitableness
of the preoccupation in that particular instance, or the justice or
otherwise of *The Calendar's* animadversions. But it is in place, and
fair, to remark the superior liveliness of *The Calendar*, and its
great critical superiority: there would at any rate seem to be little
profit in a concern for tradition and for sanctions that is not
associated with the 'standards of criticism'. Literary criticism
provides the test for life and concreteness; where it degenerates,
the instruments of thought degenerate too, and thinking, released
from the testing and energizing contact with the full living consciousness, is debilitated, and betrayed to the academic, the
abstract, and the verbal. It is of little use to discuss values if the
sense for value in the concrete—the experience and perception of
value—is absent.

One can have little respect for the periodical which flaunts a pretension to philosophic righteousness and yet makes as many blunders with
regard to the actual works of poetry or literature before it as the most
unenlightened of its Georgian predecessors.

It is the praise of *The Calendar* that it had a right, in pronouncing
its valediction, to say this.

At any rate, the sententious consolation may perhaps be permitted that there are worse things than death; for *The Calendar*
it was that died. But it is a poor consolation if it leaves us to
conclude that no intelligent review can support itself in the present
age. The conclusion cannot be easily evaded; it is what the history
of *The Calendar* seems to prove, and the subsequent history of
critical journalism to corroborate. Anyway, it is certain, not
merely that no good critic can now hope to make anything like a
living by the exercise of his talents, but that he will be lucky if

[1] *Op. cit.*, p. 154.

he is allowed to employ them, in public, at all. The situation is in that respect, as everyone qualified to report will agree, very much worse than it was before the episode of *The Calendar*.

And yet the Editors, in their *Valediction* (*A Valediction Forbidding Mourning*),[1] a finely poised piece of work, admirable in tone and phrasing, do not suggest hopelessness:

> We have decided to scuttle the ship, rather than have the leaks periodically stopped by a generous patron, because the present literary situation requires to be met by a different organization, which we are not now in a position to form. Could such an organization be formed, we should find means to bring it into play.

It would be interesting to know what kind of organization they have in mind. Beyond insisting that the standards of literary criticism—'the freedom to exercise an independent judgment on contemporary work'—must not be compromised, they give no hint.

The insistence shows, at least, that they have not surrendered to the Marxist conclusion—or (it becomes convenient to change the tense) had not in 1927. Some readers, perhaps, have been waiting for the force of that conclusion to be recognized here. Tacit recognition might appear to have been conceded already in the picture of disintegration drawn above. When things have, by avowal, gone so far, does not worry about a moribund literary tradition condemn itself as patently futile? Can the intelligent and courageous justify to themselves any but a concern, a direct concern, with fundamentals, with the task of social regeneration? —social regeneration, which means, in the first place, revolution, economic and political? The case looks strong. And it is unlikely that anyone who has been interested enough to read the present disquisition as far as this does not hold economic and political action to be urgent. But some may feel that 'fundamentals', above, covers a dangerous simplification.

There can be no pretence of dealing fairly with the Marxist position here. A different position must merely be asserted—that of those who think that the inevitability (and desirability) of drastic social changes makes an active concern for cultural

[1] *Op. cit.*, p. 194.

continuity the more essential, and that the conditions of clear thinking, and of wisdom with regard to human values and ends, do not need the less attention because we are, inevitably, to suffer more confusion and disorientation.

Nevertheless, the episode of *The Calendar* has a certain finality. There would be no point in repeating the experiment. It will be a radically 'different organization' that offers any hope. A review, to have any chance of surviving, must enlist a far more active support than can be won for any merely literary review, however lively and intelligent. No one doubts (is it safe to say?) that there are in the English-speaking world some thousands of potential readers of such a review as *The Calendar*: that is implied in the possibility of referring to the 'contemporary sensibility'. But if, amid the distractions of the modern scene, they are to be marshalled in sufficient numbers, it must be by finding some way of enlisting a very active conviction that the 'contemporary sensibility' matters very much to the contemporary world: the function and the conviction cannot now be taken for granted as they might in other days.

Indeed, one cannot think of success merely in terms of a review. 'Organization' would involve a 'movement' of some kind, a more general reaction, provoked by the extremity of the plight; for one must count on such a reaction as natural, and be ready to exploit it, if one finds hope worth entertaining and the cause important.

This attempt to enlarge on *The Calendar's* hint of 'a different organization' hardly gets closer to particularity: its negative effect, emphasizing the desperateness of the case, will for most readers be the predominant. This is inevitable, for, as *The Calendar*, in its *Valediction*, says: 'such a combination as we envisage is dependent on the happy meeting of many contingencies'. It must be a matter of quickness to take advantage of opportunities, and if one sees them, the only effective account of them will be the actual enterprise.

This much more may be ventured by way of suggesting possibilities—a kind of earnest of seriousness, a hostage; for, in face of the situation recognized above, only the kind of seriousness that drives directly at practice, and invites that test, has the right to persist in hope: if a campaign for standards in literary criticism, together with the relevant attention to contemporary civilization in general, could be effectively associated with a movement in the educational field—. It is, perhaps, best to leave it at the *aposiopesis*, though this will not be found, by many, exhilarating, for 'academic' and 'scholastic' are discouraging words. Yet if corporate spirit (this is not to entertain illusions about the average quality of the profession in any branch—'average' says little) can be anywhere effectively mobilized for disinterested ends it is in education. A fantastic hope?—'such a combination . . . is dependent on the happy meeting of many contingencies.'

It is now time to turn to the contents of the present volume. These are all critical. It must be said in passing that in the creative work it published *The Calendar* maintained the 'standards of criticism' as seriously as in its essays and reviews, although, inevitably, the level of actual, achieved intrinsic quality is not so consistent. It printed, among others of distinction, D. H. Lawrence (it printed some of his best criticism too) and T. F. Powys. The generosity with which it supported contemporary literature would count for much in the 'leaks' that led to the 'scuttling' of the ship. But the review that cannot attempt a similar generosity is gravely limiting its function.

The main difficulty, other than economic, is to be sufficiently encouraging to experimental and young work without any serious damage to standards. Of reviewing too the Editors say, in their introductory statement: 'It is difficult to keep those standards in a little space and still to be just to contemporary work which is perhaps immature.' In the ways in which it tackled this difficulty *The Calendar* can fairly be held up as a model for a critical journal. The illustrations in this selection are of critical method—procedure in actual reviewing. There is no need to specify examples of the analysis that is more interesting than the book reviewed: of the pretentious book disposed of with judicial quietness as a type-case; of the serious, but unachieved, intention that is, as undiscouragingly as possible, 'placed' and made the opportunity for generalizations. The variety of procedure, of profitable critical practice, illustrated, is not even suggested in these remarks; but, in any case, it hardly needs insisting on.

The point is that all this is possible where there are real critics and an intelligent conception of criticism. Where there is a grasp of principle on the one hand and an intelligent interest in the contemporary situation on the other, some sense of its outlines, structure, and points of tension, then the ordinary year's publishing offers enough opportunities for profitable criticism to keep a serious review going. But to ask for these qualifications is to ask a great deal. For instance, where is a critic to find help with 'principles' in criticizing fiction, the head under which the bulk of the output demanding attention will come? With little more than a few hints from Henry James—from the prefaces and *Notes on Novelists*—he will have to do everything for himself.

Or rather, would if there were not *The Calendar* to hand. For *The Calendar* contains—this selection from it contains—as good an introduction to the criticism of the novel as one can reasonably ask for, as much help as a potential critic needs. Not only is its critical practice good; it offers an examination and statement of principle that should have become a *locus classicus*. If anyone is still wondering why it is that Mr Percy Lubbock's *Craft of Fiction*, for all its scholarly nicety, seems to make no difference, let him read *A Note on Fiction*, by C. H. Rickword.[1] The answer is given at the outset, in the axiom from which the *Note* starts: 'the problem of language, the use of the medium in all its aspects, is the basic problem of any work of literature'. All preoccupation with 'form', 'structure', 'method', 'technique', that is not controlled by this axiom must be more or less barren.

A novel, like a poem, is made of words; there is nothing else one can point to. We talk of a novelist as 'creating characters', but the process of 'creation' is one of putting words together. We discuss the quality of his 'vision', but the only critical judgments we can attach directly to observable parts of his work concern particular arrangements of words—the quality of the response they evoke. Criticism, that is, must be in the first place (and never cease being) a matter of sensibility, of responding sensitively and with precise discrimination to the words on the page. But it must, of course, go on to deal with the larger effects,

[1] *Op. cit.*, p. 29.

with the organization of the total response to the book. The 'total response', what is it? We speak of 'form':

... the form of a novel only exists as a balance of response on the part of the reader. Hence schematic plot is a construction of the reader's that corresponds to an aspect of that response and stands in merely diagrammatic relation to the source. Only as precipitate from the memory are plot or character tangible; yet only in solution have either any emotive valency. The composition of this fluid is a technical matter. The technique of the novel is just as symphonic as the technique of the drama and as dependent, up to a point, on the dynamic devices of articulation and control of narrative tempo. But, though dependent, it is dependent as legs are on muscles, for the *how* but not the *why* of movement; and, interesting as functional technique may be to the mechanical minded and to workers in the same medium on the look-out for tips, the organic is the province of criticism.

Here we have, in more explicit form, the comment on such studies as *The Craft of Fiction*. Few reviewers will be grateful for it; it hardly makes the business of criticism any easier. And the remark that ' "character" is merely the term by which the reader alludes to the pseudo-objective image he composes of his responses to the author's verbal arrangements' will not deter the ordinary critic or conversationalist from wondering why it is that D. H. Lawrence, though not interested in character, appears to matter, or from assuming that to note the 'unreality' of T. F. Powys's characters is to make an adverse criticism on *Mr Weston's Good Wine*.

But for those who are concerned to develop for themselves a critical technique for the novel there is more here than a warning against the usual divagations and irrelevances. The positive approach is suggested, and its general nature made unmistakably plain. No one can be fitted with critical sensibility, but, having that, one can be helped to apply it. The problem is to go beyond the words on the page without losing touch with them; to develop a technique for keeping the sensibility always in control in one's inevitable dealings with abstractions and 'precipitates from the memory'. When the problem is so envisaged, it becomes plain that one can no more be given a detailed technique than one can be given a sensibility. Such help as C. H. Rickword offers must remain, in the nature of the case, fairly general. But that is not to go back on the judgment that he offers a great deal— as much, essentially, as can be taken. The generality of the follow- ing, for instance, will be rich in particular profit for those capable of taking anything. He is considering Professor Gaselee's pro- nouncement that, 'Brought up on good novels, we are bored with their rude predecessors of antiquity', since, in these last, 'Of psychology there is barely a trace ... any attempt indeed at character-drawing is faint and rough.'

If we offered him Homer, even Homer in an English prose transla- tion, we should hear, instead of these wails of hunger, the happy noises of prolonged mastication. Now, it cannot be contended that the add- ition of a little psychology and character-drawing to a chain of events makes all the difference between æsthetic starvation and satisfaction, but some quality inherent in those events. And it is this quality that is common to all great works of literature, in no matter what genre. It is a unity among the events, a progressive rhythm that includes and reconciles each separate rhythm. As manifested in the novel, it resolves, when analysed, chiefly into character and plot in a secondary, schematic sense—qualities that are purely fictitious.

This bringing together of fiction and poetry is the more richly suggestive because of the further assimilation it instigates. The differences between a lyric, a Shakespeare play, and a novel, for some purposes essential, are in no danger of being forgotten; what needs insisting on is the community. And this for the sake not merely of critical principle, but of immediate profit in critical tech- nique (principle that does not bear on technique is of little interest).

'Rhythm', as the term is used in the passage just quoted, and as explicated by Dr I. A. Richards in *The Principles of Literary Criticism*, is comparatively easy to understand and to illustrate in a lyric. *Macbeth* is extremely more complex, yet the same ap- proach and essentially the same method apply; the development is continuous, as suggested in the elaborated account of 'rhythm' (*The Principles of Literary Criticism*, p. 137):

Grammatical regularities, the necessity for completing the thought, the reader's state of conjecture as to what is being said, his apprehension in dramatic literature of the action, of the intention, situation, state of mind generally, of the speaker, all these and many other things intervene. . . . This texture of expectations, satisfactions, disappointments, surprisals, which the *sequence of syllables* brings about, is rhythm.

One may feel that 'rhythm' in this development becomes a very elusive concept, but the formulation is full of sound suggestion for approach and critical method, and has the virtue of constantly referring one back to 'the sequence of syllables' (italicized above for the present purpose)—to the words on the page. It suggests what the critical analysis of a Shakespeare play would be. If one adds that it suggests what would be the critical analysis of a novel, no one will now suppose that novel and play are thus assimilated because they both contain characters.

It is in the opposite direction that the argument points, and the room it has taken will have been justified if this proposition is now seen to have some force: that if one is not intelligent about poetry one is unlikely to be intelligent about fiction, and the connoisseur of fiction who disclaims an interest in poetry is probably not interested in literature. And the proposition holds as essentially of novels where the staple medium appears to be much like that of the essayist or the historian as of those which C. H. Rickword, anticipating a recent observation of Mr T. S. Eliot, has in mind here: 'the main thing to be noted about the new "subjective" novelists is their increasing tendency to rely for their effects not on set pieces of character-drawing, but directly on the poetic properties of words'.

To the reader who complains that he has still been brought no nearer to a working technique of criticism it must be repeated that nothing more can be done for him—unless, perhaps, by the example of good practice. Of this last there is abundance in *The Calendar*. Monthly reviewing, of course, gives little opportunities for elaborate exhibitions of critical method, and the ordinary year's publishing little occasion. But, working within the inevitable limitations, *The Calendar's* critics performed their function exemplarily.

A Note on Fiction, then, together with the varied reviews assembled with it in a section of the present book, constitutes an incomparable aid to the intelligent criticism of novels. This section alone would make the book important.

If the section relating to poetry has not the same kind of

importance, that is not because it is less remarkable, interesting, and intelligent, but because the need here is less acute: criticism of poetry is rather less desperately backward than that of fiction. Nevertheless, to do justice to the achievement of *The Calendar*, one should remind oneself of a few comparative dates. *The Calendar* was, for instance in time to review *The Principles of Literary Criticism*.[1] By the time the *Poems* of Mr Eliot appeared for review, it had, in reviews and essays, laid down the grounds of criticism upon which Mr Eliot was to be duly appraised, so that the recognition of his significance came as a matter of course. This is easily said, and may not sound impressive. But let the reader compare *The Calendar's* criticism of poetry with that of any other critical journal over those three years, and *The Calendar* will be found to stand alone. It *assumed* that re-education which was necessary before the contemporary re-orientation of English poetry could be recognized and appreciated. But where at that time, apart from Mr Eliot's essays, were the incitements and aids to such a re-education to be found?

The Calendar provided these, for its 'assuming' was a very active matter. Thus we find Mr Edgell Rickword noting, in 1925, in a discussion of *The Use of the Negative Emotions*:[2]

The modern poet is to his audience an author, not a man. It is interested in his more generalized emotions, not in his relations with the life and people round him. Yet to himself the poet should be in the first place a man, not an author. He should not be conscious of the distinction between the sensations he gets from his immediate contact with things and the sensations he uses as the material of his art. At present he is inhibited from using a set of emotions (those we call negative emotions) because of a prejudice against them . . .

At about the same date, Mr Douglas Garman, glancing over contemporary criticism,[3] is forced to conclude:

The inference, that poetry is looked upon as being unconnected with a radically intelligent activity is only too well supported by the facts. . . .

In the two essays from which these quotations come the re-orientation of the last decade is defined, and the critical basis

---

[1] *Op. cit.*, p. 139.   [2] *Op. cit.*, p. 71.   [3] *Op. cit.*, p. 78.

established for appreciating Mr Eliot, Mr Pound, and their successors.

From this brief account it must be plain that the intrinsic quality of the section *Poetry* is high. It contains some admirable treatment of general questions, some very fine examples of 'practical criticism', and a number of patterns for reviewers—illustrations, among other things, of the critical profit that intrinsically uninteresting work can be made to yield (see, e.g., the notices of Mr Noyes and Mr Binyon).[1]

Some indication has now been given of the arrangement adopted in this book. After *Fiction* and *Poetry* comes the classification, *General Criticism*. Under this head are included, with some unavoidable arbitrariness, items of various kinds, dealing with the theory and method of criticism and with general questions—essays, articles, and reviews of critical works.

The last head, *Miscellaneous*, needs no comment.

It may be well, before ending, to anticipate some criticism. The characteristic fault of *The Calendar's* critical writing may be described as corrugation—excessive difficulty. In determining, with severe effort, what the author meant, one may find, rather too often, clearer ways of saying it. But explanations enough of the fault suggest themselves at once: to have to start so much from the beginning and do everything for oneself does not conduce to smoothness of exposition. And that the difficulty is worth wrestling with is usually obvious at once.

Again, some readers may object to the tone of certain reviews as being unnecessarily inurbane and unkind. All that need be said here is that not everything chosen was chosen for its judicial poise, and that a critical organ that cannot on occasion take the kind of liberty represented is in danger of something worse than inurbanity and injustice. And what one of the Editors writes, discussing the 'Audience', would cover far more than all that might be found to need excusing in *The Calendar*:

There is no longer a body of opinion so solid as that represented by *The Quarterly*, *The Edinburgh* and *Blackwood's*. The fact that they pronounced a vigorous æsthetic creed, and were, therefore, of the greatest benefit to a lively interest in poetry, is forgotten, because they

[1] *Op. cit.*, p. 89.

were sometimes ungentlemanly, and their place has been taken, but not filled, by the torrential journalistic criticism which is poured out daily, weekly and monthly, and is so enlightened and refined that the fulfilment of its obvious function is overlooked in its efforts to be open-minded and polite. There has never been such a rubbishy flow of poetry as that which is vomited by contemporary publishers, yet the reading public has never expressed its opinion through such mealy-mouthed critics. Smut alone has moved their costive sensibilities to a definite opinion, and then their violence was only equalled by their obtuseness. For the most part their opinions are diluted with the oils of snobbism or social decorum.

It has, then, been answered—the inevitable question: Why reprint the reviewing of an obscure periodical that died half a dozen years ago? If the answer is not found convincing the fault is with the answerer, for the case intrinsically is as strong as one could ask for. But the following pages,[1] if read, will answer for themselves.

[1] *Op. cit.*

XVI

THE ORTHODOXY OF
ENLIGHTENMENT[1]

To make sure, in commenting briefly on the court proceedings over *Lady Chatterley's Lover,* that the note one hits on won't lead to one's being misunderstood isn't altogether easy. If one says that the Prosecution failed because it was as inept as the Defence was ludicrous, one might be supposed to be wishing it had been less inept. And who could have hailed the success of the Prosecution as a good thing—a proof and promise of health and creative vitality in our civilization? Yet I have to point out that the Prosecution was defeated, not by the presentment of any sound or compelling case, but by its realization that it was confronted by a new and confident orthodoxy of enlightenment— that the world had changed since the virginal pure policemen came and hid their faces for very shame. And one has to recognize that, if there had to be, as the upshot of a court trial, a definitive registration of this change in society, the thing could hardly have occurred in any essentially different way from that which has its record in the new Penguin Special.[2] I mean, in any way less disturbing to the literary critic and admirer of Lawrence.

I express here, of course, my conviction that the outcome of the trial cannot at best be seen as pure gain from the point of view I have just indicated. A fair appraisal of the probable consequences would be a delicate matter. But this is certain: a real advance, in the sense represented by Lawrence, depends upon the existence of a body of genuinely enlightened opinion, ensuring that the nature of Lawrence's genius and achievement shall be widely understood, so that these may have their proper force. *Lady Chatterley's Lover,* then—it is important that this obvious enough

[1] First printed in *The Spectator,* February 1961, under the title 'The New Orthodoxy'.
[2] *The Trial of Lady Chatterley,* edited by C. H. Rolph.

truth should be recognized—is a bad novel. Moreover, to assert, as was done again and again during the trial, and made a major point in the final speech for the Defence, that without having read it one cannot truly appreciate Lawrence's other works, and so cannot have received what the great and salutary creative writer of our time has to give, is to betray and further an alarming misconception of his genius and what he actually achieved. It is to misrepresent this disastrously. For the experts did not mean by their testimony that *Lady Chatterley's Lover*, in giving us something that violates Lawrence's own essential canons as an artist, serves as a foil to his successful and great art, and in that way may be used as an aid to its critical appreciation. The book should be current as an unquestioned literary classic—this was essential to the case for the Defence.

One of the witnesses, testifying to Lawrence's earnest and wholly conscious intentness on his purpose in writing the book, speaks of his 'integrity'. Well, no one would suggest that Lawrence was deceiving himself in his conviction that his hatred of pornography was complete. But the integrity we demand of an artist is a rarer thing than that which we testify to (perhaps) in a politician. Lawrence himself, in postulating it as the essential aim in both life and art, insisted on the most exacting conception and criteria. He is insisting on them in his caveats against 'will' and 'idea' (terms, in his use of them, intimately related).

'Will' and 'idea' certainly play a part in *Lady Chatterley's Lover* that the normal creative and critical Lawrence would have diagnosed and condemned. He is *not* the normal Lawrence in this novel—a point unwittingly made by one of the experts in the trial when, exalting Lawrence's 'integrity' of purpose, he says that the book might almost be called a tract (though there is a consensus among the witnesses that it is something else). Lawrence, of course, meant it to have the integrity of a creative work. But at this moment of his life he was too possessed by his passionate didactic purposes to be capable of achieving *that*, or of recognizing his failure (he was ill—in fact, for all his incredible vitality, slowly dying—and inflamed with rage and disgust at the thought of the 'virginal pure policemen'). That this was his state, this the essential case, should be manifest to the reader in the business of the 'four-letter words'. The intense earnestness of the hygienic aim can't be doubted, and I needn't discuss whether or not we can reasonably think of it as justified by probable success: it *is* a hygienic purpose, that is the unanswerable point I have to make. We have here, in obviously questionable relation to creative integrity, the assertive presence of 'will' and 'idea'.

But equally we have this presence, on a large scale, and in no less—or so it seems to me—questionable relation to creative wholeness in the artist, in the insistent renderings of sexual experience (sensations, emotions, and all the physical details). How these are essential to Lawrence's enterprise has been explained in the pages of the *Spectator* as well as by the body of testifying experts. They represent a hygienic purpose and they certainly engage the creative art of the creative writer. To me, I must report, a great deal in them has always been strongly distasteful, and has not become less so now that, yet again, I re-read them thirty years after I read them first. The expert may perhaps comment that *that* only shows how little I have yet been able to submit myself to the beneficent potency of which I am still in need.

That might seem to be a difficult retort to answer. Yet I remain convinced that my distaste is something that the normal Lawrence, the creative Lawrence, would have shared and justified; that (whether in his abnormal state he was aware of it or not) the will to write those passages had had a resistance to overcome, and the price of the overcoming was the artist's integrity in the profounder sense: the wholeness was violated. Lawrence would have had a resistance to overcome in himself uttering the 'four-letter words' with the ease and freedom with which the gamekeeper and Tommy Dukes use them. In the way of those frequent and insistent offers to evoke sexual experience in pondered, dwelling immediacy there was a deep-seated *pudeur*, going back to a finely civilized upbringing in a Victorian working-class home. This *pudeur* became in the developed and mature Lawrence the exquisitely sensitive human delicacy of the great artist—something so patently manifested in his novels and tales that we don't need the extraneous evidence we have that he didn't like 'emancipation'.

Q

Still, if readers—experts and others—insist that they feel no distaste, and that they confidently judge these passages, and kindred things in the book, to be justified by success, and to be thoroughly *of* the tenderness (a word made almost unusable in relation to Lawrence by the witnesses), the life and the beauty of the creative whole, we shall hardly get further here by argument: we are faced by a conflict of reports. Nevertheless, that the passionate drive of willed purpose in *Lady Chatterley's Lover* is attended by evidences of a disrupted integration in the artist, by a failure of unified wholeness in his imaginative engagement, such a failure as makes the novel a bad one from any defensible point of view, is, I think, indisputable: there are manifestations to point to, the clear significance of which, once the attention rests on them, can hardly be questioned. It has, of course, been suggested that Sir Clifford's paralysis, so usefully symbolic to exegetes and experts, is not altogether a felicity. Lawrence himself agreed that this might be so, but defended himself by saying that so the tale 'came' to him and continued to 'come', and that he had to keep it so, by the law of creative integrity.

But even a Laurentian genius in Lawrence's state cannot (the penalty of indulging the quasi-creative intervention of passionate will, didactic, corrective, and reforming) trust what 'comes' to him: his unity is broken, he cannot be engaged as a whole, his touch is no longer sure. And the questionableness of Mellors is still more destructive of the claim that *Lady Chatterley's Lover* is a good novel, or a decent work of art, or a convincing piece of reinforced didacticism, than the questionableness of Sir Clifford. Why does Lawrence make the lover working-class? The answer (not given by any of the experts) is that Lawrence doesn't. The gamekeeper is not only educated, he is an intellectual—we are told of the impressive array of books he has on his shelf. Moreover, having (we learn from Sir Clifford) held a commission, he is irretrievably and securely a 'gentleman': he has obviously the manners, the poise, the right distinction of appearance when properly dressed, and Connie reflects that he 'can go anywhere'. Why, then, does Lawrence make him drop into the dialect—drop so much and on those occasions?

A simple and (I imagine) generally acceptable answer is that

Mellors's use of the dialect is a way of putting over the 'four-letter words'—of trying to make the idea of their being re-deemed for non-obscene and undefiant, or 'normal', use look less desperate. When used by Tommy Dukes in the intellectual talk that takes place among Sir Clifford's cronies, one can't be certain how much distaste Lawrence means them to evoke, but they certainly evoke distaste (it has its part in the general un-pleasant effect produced by Tommy Dukes's emancipation). It is significant that, when she first takes note of the keeper, Connie reflects that he 'reminds her curiously of Tommy Dukes'. But Mellors can turn on the dialect. And when he does there is a 'curious' effect (I find it hateful—and it seems to me a paradigm of much that I find hateful in the book) of its being Lawrence who turns it on. Along with the dialect go, not only those words, but all those brutally insistent inflictions on Connie (and us) of 'un-inhibited' talk in keeping with the words.

If I find these performances on Mellors's part insufferable, I am sure that it isn't merely because of my still unvanquished *pudeur*. There is something hateful conveyed in the intention (here) of the dialect itself—something hateful conveyed in the turning-on. Connie perceives it and on occasion protests. We are told that she 'never knew how to take him when he used the dialect'. But Sir Clifford, in the hostile exchanges with the keeper, knows.

It is in place here to note that the outburst of bitterly ugly impassioned contempt for the 'middle-classes' that Mellors at-tributes to his Colonel ('who loved him') is relayed to Connie in the dialect. It comes, we feel, from Lawrence himself, direct. Not, I must add at once, from the whole Lawrence—from the great clairvoyant artist who said that he wrote 'out of a deep moral sense—for the race, as it were'. It is the lack of that im-personality which makes so much of *Lady Chatterley's Lover* repellent.

Those who suggest (see the Penguin under review) that Mellors's working-class status—what he has of it—must be taken as conveying something positive and basic in relation to Law-rence's otherwise despairing critique of modern civilization insult Lawrence—his character and intelligence. He had no illusion about the working classes. He was in general without class-feeling, and nothing could be more ridiculous than the one-time orthodoxy that called him a snob. Nevertheless, his history had left somewhere in him a dormant exasperation, contemptuous and resentful—it betrays itself in his calling Jane Austen a 'narrow-gutted spinster'. It is this Lawrence we have, unmistakably, in the Colonel's—or the keeper's or Lawrence's—tirade. If only we could confine him there the constatation need not have been critically very damaging. But the obtrusive presence is only the clear sign of something generally and radically wrong—the failure of wholeness of engagement, of insight and self-knowledge, of intelligence, in the creative Lawrence. It is not easy to say with any precision just how Mellors's treatment of Connie (Lawrence's treatment of the relations between Mellors and Connie) is involved, but, Mellors being the equivocal figure he is, uneasinesses and suspicions and distastes cannot be banished.

As for the treatment of Sir Clifford, the significantly manifest scandal of that can hardly be denied. Professor D. W. Harding, with some irony of understatement, has remarked in the *Spectator* that the burden of symbolic responsibilities laid on Sir Clifford grows unquestionably large. What most disturbs me is the animus Lawrence has developed towards him by the close. It is embarrassing, not because one sympathizes with Sir Clifford, but because of the evidence that something has gone radically wrong with Lawrence.

Of course, Mellors helps to give plausibility to the suggestion that the treatment of the personal theme gives us at the same time a diagnosis of industrial civilization. Actually, the evoked Midland *décor* remains merely *décor*. Industrial civilization doesn't really enter into a just appraisal of Connie's behaviour. Nor can Lawrence's presentment of that be shown to be a vindication of marriage, or an incitement to realizing the difficulty and importance of achieving a permanent relation, by quoting, as was done for the Defence, *Apropos of Lady Chatterley's Lover*. What that truly Laurentian classic betrays is the misgiving Lawrence himself had about the novel, of which it constitutes, in its essential incongruity, an admonitory criticism.

But Lawrence is henceforward 'the author of *Lady Chatterley*'. That is what the new orthodoxy of enlightenment reduces him to.

'Orthodoxy' is a fair word. When our great Liberal daily had an editorial rebuking the Archbishop of Canterbury for *his* rebuke to the Bishop of Woolwich, I wrote a critical letter to the Editor. It was quite brief, but the Editor (who, I see from this Penguin, was one of the experts who gave evidence for the Defence) declined to print it. I wrote, as I said in my letter, because, reading the testimonies now printed in this Penguin Special, I couldn't help feeling that I had a heavy responsibility. It gave me a sense of guilt when I saw those formulations, which were so familiar to me, applied to *Lady Chatterley's Lover*, to which I (explicitly) did *not* apply them, and to which they do not apply. And I will say now that, even if it could be argued that it is a good thing for children and teenagers to be able to buy and read it (as they do, figuring largely among the million purchasers), the suggestion that the book tends to promote respect for the idea of marriage is fantastically and perversely false. Lawrence, when he wrote it, had forgotten what marriage (as opposed to a *liaison*) was. The significance of this Penguin would seem to be that in the world of the enlightened—among the intellectuals of the universities and the literary world, and even the Church—it has been forgotten too. If the whole demonstration for the Defence, and the subsequent *réclame*, had not been, in this way, so terribly depressing, one would have called it Gilbertian.

INDEX

AARON'S ROD (D. H. Lawrence), 175

Abinger Harvest (E. M. Forster), 96

Adam Bede (George Eliot), 49-58

Addison, Joseph, 200

Aeschylus, 53, 54

Aldington, Richard, 167, 168

Almayer's Folly (Joseph Conrad), 93

Anderson, Sherwood, 147 n.

Anna Karenina (Leo Tolstoy), 9-32, 181

Antony and Cleopatra, 182

Apropos of Lady Chatterley's Lover (D. H. Lawrence), 23, 240

Arnold, Matthew, 10, 13, 14, 15, 16-18, 46, 177, 216

Asquith, Lady Cynthia, 173-74

Auden, W. H., 151, 191-92

Austen, Jane, 10, 74, 142, 145, 146, 240

BABBITT, IRVING, 151, 194

Bennett, Arnold, 122

Bewley, Marius, 75-80, 83, 85-86, 88-91, 152-60

Bible, the, 41

Bradley, A. C., 211

Bridges, Robert, 190, 191

Brooke, Rupert, 175-76

Brooks, Van Wyck, 123-24, 138-51

Bulwer-Lytton, Edward George Lytton, 1st Baron, 51

Bunyan, John, 33-48

CABELL, JAMES BRANCH, 150

Calendar of Modern Letters, The, 219-234

Cantos, The (Ezra Pound), 165-66, 195

Carlyle, Thomas, 50

Cenci, The (Percy Bysshe Shelley), 186

Chambers, Jessie, 169

Chance (Joseph Conrad), 95

Charles II, 39

Childermass, The (Wyndham Lewis), 162

Cocktail Party, The (T. S. Eliot), 196

Coleridge, Samuel Taylor, 187 n., 214

Collected Letters of D. H. Lawrence, The (ed. Harry T. Moore), 167-76

Common Pursuit, The (F. R. Leavis), 41 n., 145 n.

Common Reader, The (Virginia Woolf), 96, 222

Complex Fate, The (Marius Bewley), 75 n., 124 n., 152-60

Comus, 201-203

Confident Years, The (Van Wyck Brooks), 138-39, 144, 146, 147 n., 148, 149, 151

Congreve, William, 186, 210

Conrad, Joseph, 92-110, 111-20, 145

Cooper, James Fenimore, 143, 152, 154, 159

Coriolanus, 182

Cowley, Abraham, 207-208, 217

Cowper, William, 205

Crabbe, George, 205

Craft of Fiction, The (Percy Lubbock), 228, 229

Criterion, The, 162, 167, 187-88, 190, 192-94, 224

Cromwell, Oliver, 35, 38

D. H. LAWRENCE: A PERSONAL RECORD (E. T.), 169

D. H. Lawrence Newsletter, 172

Daniel Deronda (George Eliot), 51, 53, 57

David Copperfield (Charles Dickens), 80, 81-82

Death of a Hero (Richard Aldington), 168

Defoe, Daniel, 45-46, 47-48, 142, 145

Denham, Sir John, 201

DeVoto, Bernard, 122-23, 132

Dickens, Charles, 10, 38, 46, 50, 59, 71, 80, 81, 83, 88, 127, 144, 145

Donne, John, 184, 217

Dos Passos, John, 143, 147 n.

Dostoevsky, Fyodor Mikhailovich, 9-10

Dreiser, Theodore, 125, 143, 147 n., 149, 154, 155, 157

Dryden, John, 184, 186-87, 197, 201-202, 212 n., 216, 217

EAST COKER (T. S. Eliot), 195

Elegy Written in a Country Churchyard (Thomas Gray), 216

Eliot, George, 10, 49-58, 110, 145, 181

Eliot, T. S., 145, 147 n., 151, 161, 162-163, 166, 167, 173, 177-96, 231, 232, 233

Emma (Jane Austen), 74

Essay on Criticism (Alexander Pope), 213

Europeans, The (Henry James), 59-74, 140-42

Evans, Oliver, 78

Ezra Pound: A Collection of Essays (ed. Peter Russell), 161 n., 162-63, 164, 165

FAERIE QUEENE, THE, 185-86

Family Reunion, The (T. S. Eliot), 182-83, 184, 196

Farrell, James T., 147 n.

Felix Holt (George Eliot), 53, 57

Fielding, Henry, 145

Fitzgerald, F. Scott, 125, 147 n., 154, 155-56, 157

Flaubert, Gustave, 10, 49, 181, 183

Forster, E. M., 95-97, 219 n.

Fortunes of Falstaff, The (J. Dover Wilson), 211 n.

Frost, Robert, 162

Froude, James Anthony, 40

GARLAND, HAMLIN, 149, 150

Garman, Douglas, 232

Garnett, David, 167, 168, 189, 195

Gaselee, Sir Stephen, 230

Gifford, John, 39

Goldsmith, Oliver, 200, 205

Grace Abounding to the Chief of Sinners (John Bunyan), 40

Graves, Robert, 219 n.

Gray, Thomas, 205, 215-17

Great Expectations (Charles Dickens), 10

Great Gatsby, The (F. Scott Fitzgerald), 155

Great Tradition, The (F. R. Leavis), 52 n.

Green, John Richard, 48

HAMLET, 181-82, 183, 184

Hard Times (Charles Dickens), 59

Harding, D. W., 205-206, 240

Hardy, Thomas, 49

Hawthorne, Nathaniel, 34, 46, 52, 124-25, 141-42, 143-44, 145, 146, 147, 152, 154, 158, 159

Heart of Midlothian, The (Sir Walter Scott), 51

Hemingway, Ernest, 125, 147 n., 154, 156, 157

Hind and the Panther, The (John Dryden), 186-87

Hobbes, Thomas, 99

Homage to John Dryden (T. S. Eliot), 177

Home, John, 208

Hopkinson, Tom, 98-99, 113, 118

Housman, A. E., 190

How to Read (Ezra Pound), 163

Howells, William Dean, 139-40, 142, 144

Huckleberry Finn (Mark Twain), 121-124, 125, 126, 129, 147-49, 155, 156-57

Huxley, Aldous, 167, 169, 170, 173

IRENE (Samuel Johnson), 208-209

JAMES, HENRY, 9-10, 11, 12, 15, 49, 52, 59-74, 75-91, 95, 124-25, 139-144, 145, 147, 152, 153-54, 155, 157, 158-59, 228

James, William, 59

John Bunyan, Mechanick Preacher (William York Tindall), 33-35, 36, 39, 42-43

Johnson, Samuel, 36-37, 53, 187 n., 195, 197-218

Joyce, James, 162, 185

KENNER, HUGH, 165

Ker, W. P., 187

Keynes, John Maynard, 193

Kipling, Rudyard, 190

Knight, G. Wilson, 211 n.

LADY CHATTERLEY'S LOVER (D. H. Lawrence), 23, 24, 235-41

Lady into Fox (David Garnett), 168

Lamb, Charles, 185

Landor, Walter Savage, 183

Lawrence, D. H., 10-11, 12, 15, 16, 17, 18, 19, 20-25, 27, 41, 45, 47, 49, 94, 124, 145, 146, 151, 166, 167-76, 179, 181, 184, 185, 186, 188, 189, 227, 229, 235-41

Lawrence, Frieda, 21-23

Lear, Edward, 186

Letters of Ezra Pound 1907-1941 (ed. D. D. Paige), 161-66

Lewis, C. Day, 192

Lewis, Sinclair, 147 n., 149

Lewis, Wyndham, 162, 166, 185, 194

Life and Death of Mr Badman, The (John Bunyan), 45

Lincoln, Abraham, 146

Literature and Pulpit in Mediaeval England (G. R. Owst), 40-41

Little Dorrit (Charles Dickens), 10, 38, 46

Lives of the Poets, The (Samuel Johnson), 201-203, 208, 212, 215, 217

London Life, A (Henry James), 80-81, 82, 83

London Magazine, The (symposium on Joseph Conrad), 92, 98, 107, 118

Look! We have Come Through (D. H. Lawrence), 22

Lord Jim (Joseph Conrad), 96

Lubbock, Percy, 228, 229

Lycidas, 200-203

MACBETH, 182, 204-205, 207, 230

Maccarthy, Desmond, 194-95

Madame Bovary (Gustave Flaubert), 10, 49

Main Street (Sinclair Lewis), 149

Mansfield, Katherine, 171-72

Marsh, Sir Edward, 173, 174-75

Martin Chuzzlewit (Charles Dickens), 71, 127

Marvell, Andrew, 184

Matthews, Brander, 144

Mauberley (Ezra Pound), 166

Maude, Aylmer, 9

Maule's Curse (Yvor Winters), 159

Maurras, Charles, 162

Measure for Measure, 15, 182

Melville, Herman, 143, 145, 152, 154, 159

Mencken, H. L., 146

Middlemarch (George Eliot), 10, 51, 57

Mill on the Floss, The (George Eliot), 58

Milton, John, 145, 189-90, 199-203, 204, 212 n.

Molière, 73

Moll Flanders (Daniel Defoe), 145

Monroe, Harriet, 161
Moore, Harry T., 167-76
Morrell, Lady Ottoline, 173-74, 175
Mourning Bride, The (William Congreve), 210
Mr Weston's Good Wine (T. F. Powys), 229
Muir, Edwin, 219 n.
Murry, J. Middleton, 169-70, 171-72, 174-75

NAME AND NATURE OF POETRY, THE (A. E. Housman), 190
New England: Indian Summer (Van Wyck Brooks), 139, 141-42
New Statesman, The, 192
Nigger of the Narcissus, The (Joseph Conrad), 96
Norris, Frank, 143
Nostromo (Joseph Conrad), 95, 101, 104-105
Notes on Novelists (Henry James), 228

OLD LADIES, THE (Hugh Walpole), 187
On Poets and Poetry (T. S. Eliot), 177, 185-96
Ordeal of Mark Twain, The (Van Wyck Brooks), 123 n.
Oresteia, the, 53
Owst, G. R., 40-41
Oxford Book of English Prose, The (ed. A. Quiller-Couch), 97

PAIGE, D. D., 161 n.
Paine, Albert Bigelow, 124
Paradise Lost, 200, 203
Personal Record, A (Joseph Conrad), 93
Persuasion (Jane Austen), 74
Pilgrim's Progress, The, 33-48
Poe, Edgar Allan, 75
Poetry: A Magazine of Verse, 161
Point Counter Point (Aldous Huxley), 169, 170

Pollinger, Laurence, 167, 168
Pope, Alexander, 202, 205, 207, 213
Portrait of a Lady, The (Henry James), 52, 158
Pound, Ezra, 147 n., 150-51, 161-66, 194, 195, 233
Powys, T. F., 227, 229
Preaching in Mediaeval England (G. R. Owst), 40-41
Preface to Shakespeare (Samuel Johnson), 204, 211-12, 213-14, 217
Principles of Literary Criticism, The (I. A. Richards), 230, 232
Problem of Style, The (J. Middleton Murry), 175
Pudd'nhead Wilson (Mark Twain), 121-37, 148-49, 157
Pupil, The (Henry James), 81, 82, 83

QUILLER-COUCH, SIR ARTHUR, 97, 187

RAINBOW, THE (D. H. Lawrence), 44
Rambler, The, 204, 213
Rasselas (Samuel Johnson), 53, 207
Richards, I. A., 230, 232
Rickword, C. H., 228-30, 231
Rickword, Edgell, 219, 232
Riding, Laura, 219 n.
Robertson, J. M., 182
Robinson Crusoe (Daniel Defoe), 46
Rochester, John Wilmot, Earl of, 217
Roderick Hudson (Henry James), 73, 141
Rolph, C. H., 235 n.
Rolvaag, Ole, 149, 150
Romola (George Eliot), 51
Rosenberg, Isaac, 205-206
Russell, Bertrand, 173
Russell, Peter, 161 n., 162-63, 164, 165

SACRED WOOD, THE (T. S. Eliot), 177, 178-82

St. Mawr (D. H. Lawrence), 24

Sandburg, Carl, 147 n.

Santayana, George, 176, 177

Scarlet Letter, The (Nathaniel Hawthorne), 34, 46, 52

Scenes of Clerical Life (George Eliot), 49

Scott, Sir Walter, 50-51, 52, 145

Secret Agent, The (Joseph Conrad), 95

Secret Sharer, The (Joseph Conrad), 107, 111-20

Shadow-Line, The (Joseph Conrad), 94, 95, 99-110, 111-13, 116, 117, 119-20

Shakespeare, William, 15, 41, 53-54, 57, 73, 93, 145, 146, 156, 181-82, 183, 186, 203-207, 208, 209-214, 217, 230, 231

Shelley, Percy Bysshe, 186

Silas Marner (George Eliot), 57, 110

Smith, Logan Pearsall, 177

Snow, Sir Charles, 47

Spender, Stephen, 192, 193

Spenser, Edmund, 185

Spurgeon, Caroline, 211 n.

Steinbeck, John, 147 n.

Sterne, Laurence, 145

Stoll, E. E., 182

Swift, Jonathan, 218

Swinburne, Algernon Charles, 185

TALON, HENRI A., 38

Tarr (Wyndham Lewis), 162

Testament of Beauty, The (Robert Bridges), 191

Thackeray, William Makepeace, 50, 144, 145

Times Literary Supplement, The, 171

Times of Melville and Whitman, The (Van Wyck Brooks), 123 n., 147

Tindall, William York, 33-35, 36, 39, 42-43

Tolstoy, Count Leo Nikolayevich, 9-32, 146, 181

Tom Jones (Henry Fielding), 145

Trial of Lady Chatterley, The (ed. C. H. Rolph), 235, 241

Tristram Shandy (Laurence Sterne), 145

Trollope, Anthony, 140

Turn of the Screw, The (Henry James), 75-80, 83, 85, 86, 89

Twain, Mark, 72, 121-37, 146, 147-149, 154-57, 181

'Twixt Land and Sea (Joseph Conrad), 111

Two Cultures? The Significance of C. P. Snow (F. R. Leavis), 47 n.

Typhoon (Joseph Conrad), 95, 96, 97-99, 100, 111, 120

UNDER WESTERN EYES (Joseph Conrad), 95

VANITY OF HUMAN WISHES, THE (Samuel Johnson), 200, 208, 209

Victory (Joseph Conrad), 95

WAIN, JOHN, 93, 94

Waldock, A. J. A., 78

Waller, Edmund, 201, 202

Walpole, Hugh, 9, 93, 187-88

Waste Land, The (T. S. Eliot), 177, 185, 188

Way of the World, The (William Congreve), 186

Wells, H. G., 168

What Maisie Knew (Henry James), 75, 79-91

What then must we do? (Leo Tolstoy), 13

Whibley, Charles, 187

White, William Hale, 36-37

Whitman, Walt, 125, 154, 155, 157, 173

Wilson, Edmund, 78-79

Wilson, J. Dover, 211

Winters, Yvor, 159

Women in Love (D. H. Lawrence), 169

Woolf, Leonard, 193

Woolf, Virginia, 95-97, 188, 189, 193, 222

Wordsworth, William, 54, 57

YEATS, W. B., 162, 191, 192

Youth (Joseph Conrad), 96, 97